Other Books/CDs by Luis J. Rodríguez

FICTION

The Republic of East Los Angeles: Stories

Music of the Mill: A Novel

POETRY

Poems Across the Pavement

The Concrete River

Trochemoche

Seven

Two Women/Dos Mujeres

Making Medicine

Perhaps

My Nature Is Hunger: New and Selected Poems

NONFICTION

Always Running: La Vida Loca; Gang Days in L.A.

Hearts and Hands: Creating Community in Violent Times

CHILDREN'S LITERATURE

America Is Her Name/La Llamen America

It Doesn't Have to Be This Way: A Barrio Story

¡Sí, Se Puede! Yes, We Can! (by Diana Cohn, Francisco Delgado, and Luis J. Rodríguez)

ANTHOLOGIES

Honor Comes Hard: Writings from the California Prison System's Honor Yard (edited by Luis J. Rodríguez and Lucinda Thomas)

Power Lines: A Decade of Poetry from Chicago's Guild Complex (edited by Julie Parson-Nesbitt, Luis J. Rodríguez, and Michael Warr)

With the Wind at My Back and Ink in My Blood: A Collection of Poems by Chicago's Homeless (edited by Luis J. Rodríguez)

CD

My Name's Not Rodríguez (Poetry by Luis J. Rodríguez, music by Ernie Perez and the band Seven Rabbit)

It Calls You Back

AN ODYSSEY THROUGH LOVE, ADDICTION, REVOLUTIONS, AND HEALING

Luis J. Rodríguez

A TOUCHSTONE BOOK
Published by Simon & Schuster
New York   London   Toronto   Sydney   New Delhi

Touchstone
A Division of Simon & Schuster, Inc.
1230 Avenue of the Americas
New York, NY 10020

First Touchstone hardcover edition October 2011

TOUCHSTONE and colophon are registered trademarks of
Simon & Schuster, Inc.

For information about special discounts for bulk purchases,
please contact Simon & Schuster Special Sales at 1-866-506-1949 or
business@simonandschuster.com.

The Simon & Schuster Speakers Bureau can bring authors to your live event.
For more information or to book an event contact the Simon & Schuster Speakers
Bureau at 1-866-248-3049 or visit our website at www.simonspeakers.com.

Designed by Joy O'Meara

Manufactured in the United States of America

1   3   5   7   9   10   8   6   4   2

Library of Congress Cataloging-in-Publication Data
Rodríguez, Luis J.
It calls you back : an odyssey through love, addiction, revolutions, and
healing / Luis J. Rodríguez.
p. cm.
"A Touchstone book."
1. Rodríguez, Luis J., 1954–   2. Authors, American—20th century—
Biography.   3. Hispanic Americans—Biography.   I. Title.
PS3568.O34879Z46 2011
818'.5409—dc22
[B]

ISBN 978-1-4165-8416-2
ISBN 978-1-4391-0059-2 (ebook)

Acknowledgments

Some of this writing has appeared, at times in other forms, in the following publications: *Sonora Review, The Progressive, Bello, San Bernardino Sun, Eastside Sun, L.A. Weekly, The Nation, Los Angeles Times, U.S. News & World Report, Chicago Tribune, The New York Times, Philadelphia Inquirer Magazine, Grand Street, Poets and Writers, People's Tribune/Tribuno del Pueblo*, as well as various textbooks and anthologies.

A few passages were derived from my poetry collections and fiction books. Although rewritten, there are overlaps of incidents here with material in the nonfiction books *Hearts and Hands: Creating Community in Violent Times* and *Always Running: La Vida Loca; Gang Days in L.A.*

None of the people or incidents in this book was made up. However, to protect the identities of key persons some names were changed, a number of faces and places were reimagined, and a few characters are composites of more than one person. Although efforts were made to be as accurate as possible, most of this material depended on the emotional value of the incidents, scenes, and recollections. This book was not meant as an exhaustive study of anyone or anything. It was not meant to disparage or malign anyone.

Special thanks to my wife, Trini, my daughter Andrea, my sons Ramiro, Rubén, and Luis, as well as Camila Thompson, for helping with edits, focus, and chronology of events, but mostly for patience and support. To the rest of the Rodríguez family who has triumphed against great odds—I've had to open up to some painful truths in this book, but it all comes from a place of love and respect. Also apologies to all the homies, community members, family, and friends I had to avoid or cut short during this period, although I justify *not* writing for ceremonies, distress calls, suicide emergencies, interventions, or to just enjoy a quiet nonworking, peace-filled respite. And thanks to my agent, Susan Bergholz, and my editor, Sulay Hernandez, for believing in this work.

Chapter One

Y ou'll be back."

These were the last words I heard as I walked away from the clanging locks and gates, the incessant yells and howls, of the downtown Los Angeles County Jail. A sheriff's deputy taunted me with these words after I bailed out from being held on "resisting arrest and assaulting police officers" charges. If convicted, I'd do a minimum of six years in the state penitentiary.

The year was 1973.

The charges stemmed from the police beating of a handcuffed young Mexican woman lying on her stomach on the parking lot of an after-hours club in Norwalk. Several deputies were striking and kicking her as she screamed for help. The few drunkards around sauntered away. I was high—on heroin, alcohol, pills; I used to like combining those damn things. I turned to walk away as well, but something in me wouldn't let me.

At eighteen years of age I felt tired, lost, after having been forced to move away from my neighborhood and a garage where I had lived in a small room with a piss bucket and bunk, and where I got high with street girls I called "squeezes."

I did something no true gangster would do—I tried to stop the beating. In the process the deputies jumped me. I wanted to fight back but I got laid out fast, flat onto the ground, Maced and handcuffed. Before being taken to the Norwalk sheriff's substation, while immobilized I was driven around a few blocks as two deputies punched me. I yelled, "*Pinche chota*, fuck you . . . you'll never break me, man."

Or I thought I did. Maybe most of this was in my head. Either way, my words failed to break through.

At the time I was part of Las Lomas, a barrio gang in the San Gabriel Valley, in one of the poorest neighborhoods in L.A. County. In Las Lomas I had been a part of various cliques since age eleven. Although most of the time I spent with them involved hanging out, bored stiff, with nothing to do, I made myself available for drive-bys, armed robberies, hijackings.

I also did various mind-and-mood-altering drugs. As a preteen I first huffed on aerosol paint and clear-plastic spray, and then latched on to marijuana, downers, uppers, PCP, LSD, mescaline, and heroin, often chased with alcohol. I was an equal-opportunity drug user until heroin forced me to become more discriminating.

And yet, I managed to attend political meetings among Chicano activists in East L.A. and then a mixed group of revolutionaries in Watts and the Harbor Area. I learned to paint murals at seventeen after being acknowledged for the graffiti pieces I stylishly scrawled on L.A.-area walls. My world was opening up: I participated in antiwar rallies, school protests, and forums against police abuse and other injustices. I even returned to high school after dropping out, joining a Chicano student group, learning Mexika (so-called Aztec) dance, and writing my first essays and what some people called poems.

With all this behind me, I stood at a sharply defined crossroads in the county jail.

By then twenty-five of my friends—including so-called enemies—had been killed by gang rivals, police bullets, heroin overdoses, robbery calamities, and suicides (wasn't it all suicide?). I overdosed three times on drugs and inhalants in those years. I had also faced half a dozen gun assaults, including by machine-gun fire and at point-blank range, although, miraculously, I was never hit.

My problem was that the gang life and drugs as well as the political consciousness and artistic expression were pulling me in widely divergent directions. For some reason, politics and art appealed to me more than I thought they would. Yet, although organizers in the Chicano movement tried to convince me to leave drugs and the gang, I didn't know how or if I could. I had turned my life and everything else I had over to the madness—my identity was so intertwined with La Vida Loca that any appeal to leave felt threatening.

"This is my barrio," I'd declare. "I'll die for Las Lomas—*y qué!*"

Once, a short time before my last arrest, during the funeral of one of my homies, a neighborhood girl warned how I'd end up the same way if I didn't stop what I was doing.

"I can hardly wait to have a funeral just like this," I told her with a far-off look. "To have the mothers crying, the homies and girls missing me, with all this love. That would be the best day of my life."

I wanted to die in a blaze of glory, for the barrio, manacled to those dark streets, those dirt roads, those scrap homes, the marked-up walls— but I wasn't dying. I got close, but every time I somehow escaped death's grasp, just to keep going at it again. La Vida Loca was a web and a lure. Dudes tattooed the spider in the web or the cross with the three rays over it signifying the Crazy Life (meaning you had to carry the cross of this life wherever you went—today this is represented by three dots in a triangle shape). You're caught. You can't let this go. I had to break the chains that pointed to three outcomes—*pinto, tecato, or muerto:* a prisoner, an addict, or dead. These were the three choices you inherited in *la locura*. The three things a *vato* could expect. The trinity. Three dots. No more responsibility. No more caring. All dreams gone.

At the county jail I shuffled through the booking routine: getting fingerprints taken; placing my clothes by my feet; getting checked for contraband/weapons as well as "marks," mostly hidden by tats or in hard-to-find places with scratches and bruises on my torso and face; taking a shower; then getting deloused with a white powder thrown at my naked flesh.

The next day a homie of mine walked up to me in the canteen. Known as Largo, he was dark, huge, with tattoos and bullet holes. Largo helped run things for the main Chicano prison organization in the jail and state prison system.

"*Carnal,* time to think about becoming a *soldado,*" he said, eyeing me as another soldier in the upper echelons of the barrio gang crime organization.

Street *vatos* were making their bones in jails and prisons and some were now calling shots for various cell blocks, yards, and eventually neighborhoods. All tattooed-down Mexican barrio gang members were probable recruits. In those days, however, not everyone was brought in or even wanted. No punks, no rats, no liars, no cowards, no *levas*, as we called them, were accepted. They didn't think I was any of these so Largo tried to bring me into the fold.

Also the high-level *pintos* didn't just ask someone to join. You had to prove yourself. When called upon you had to do things, even stab or kill, without question. You had to develop their trust that you were down over a long period of time. If you had doubts, if you had other ideas, if you hesitated, they didn't want you.

Largo hit me up to demonstrate my mettle. But for the first time I found myself personally conflicted, in a bind, as they say. I had paid my dues in the barrio, doing what Las Lomas expected of me. I accepted this and the barrio rules, which were summed up by the 1963 Sunny and the Sunliners song "Smile Now, Cry Later"—you can hurt me now, but you'll pay later. All affronts had to be accounted for. And if I damaged another dude or barrio, I would expect to be taken out as well.

Largo asked me what I was arrested for.

"Was it a *jale*—robbery, drive-by, burglary?"

"*Chale*, homes," I responded. "It was for fighting with *chotas.*"

Largo looked at me like I had lost my mind. I told him the story of the Chicana being attacked by deputies and how they turned on me when I confronted them.

"Why the fuck didn't you let that *ruca* eat concrete?" Largo asked. "It was none of your business."

"That's where you're wrong, homegrown," I said. "I made it my business. I'm tired of the police, the racism, the unjust treatment. I took my stand so here I am."

Largo didn't know how to take this, so he let it slide . . . for now.

I made a crucial decision in jail. Because of my jones with heroin, there were dudes willing to set me up, *eres* and all. For some reason, I said no. I wanted to get clean. I convinced them, and the same guys who were going to score for me now helped me through the first stages of my withdrawals. I didn't realize how bad things had gotten with *chiva* and me. These dudes served as lookouts, holding the deputies at bay, ignoring me when I hollered for a hit, when I pleaded for them to forget what I requested, while my insides twisted into knots and I withered in cold sweats, cramps, slivers of pain.

Next I had to address this issue of becoming a *soldado* in the joint. Fear had to be pushed down as far as possible—I'd confronted many a fool, regardless of how I felt. But I also had to consider all these dudes from hundreds of barrio gangs now uniting as Raza (the Mexican people) in the joints.

I yearned for another way to go—unity not for crime or the drug trade, but for real social and economic change. This derived from the political consciousness I had developed and actions I had taken, including the East L.A. school walkouts of 1968 and, more important, the 1970 Chicano Moratorium Against the Vietnam War. My mentor in this work had been a Brown Beret and a founder of the United Mexican American Students (UMAS). Prior to this I had little imagination. The barrio, jails, drugs, and killings were the only concerns I knew and lived with.

"Largo, I don't want to go that way," I told him the next time my homie hit me up to do things like run contraband or stab somebody. Largo tried his best to bring down the hammer with words and veiled threats. At one point he said, more out of concern than as a warning, "If you don't, homie, I can't do nothing to protect you."

I responded, more to make a political stand than to be confrontational: "I'm not worried about what I have to do to be free. This includes from drugs. From 'the life.' *Simón*, I'm all for Raza unity, but this is something else. I don't want to be a part of this."

Largo didn't know what to say. I walked away expecting the worst. Part of me felt I'd signed my death warrant. Raza prisoners were harsh—they were the first to organize strategically for defense and protection, the first to establish the basic rules and methods of most prison gangs regardless of race. They became the most organized, largest, and most ruthless of all prison associations.

To let them know I was no *leva*, even during *las malías*, I stepped out of my cell, not threatening or acting hard. I made my way to the dayroom. I wasn't hiding out, nor was I challenging anyone or playing martyr. I was making clear my position without being a *pendejo* in the process. Largo came up to me as I watched TV, sweat beading on my forehead, itches under the skin.

"What are you going to do, homie?" he asked.

"I'm going to be a warrior for a new world, *carnal*," I responded as if my voice had been taken over by another person, sprouting a new tongue, energized by a new mind. "I don't want any more barrio warfare or early suicide that only hurts our communities and destroys our brothers and sisters. Everybody wants to die for the barrio — how about living for the barrio? I want to finally do something different."

In those days, the majority of Chicano leaders in prison were men of their word. They had *palabra*, which meant they could be trusted to do what they said they'd do. This meant they were the first to be heard, the first to be followed. And for a time these *pintos* were able to hear my words, my ideas, see the contours of a new life. What I said to Largo resonated, but I didn't know how long it would last.

My mentors in the movement wanted me out of jail as soon as possible. They feared political reprisals, not gang ones (although at the time, many such reprisals were linked). They obtained enough funds from the community to make my bail.

Following my release, I was allowed to get my property. On the way there, Largo and a couple of the *locotes* came up to me. For a second I thought this was how they'd get me, before I left, as an example to others who dared to remove themselves from the sturdy net of La Vida Loca.

Instead Largo gave me what I was seeking — a way out with dignity.

"We're going to give you a pass, *ese*, your walking papers," he declared. "Go ahead and be this revolutionary, this Chicano. Do some good for the people — some of us are too far gone to try. But maybe you can, homie. I know you've always been game for the barrio, always *firme*. But you also have something not many of us got. You've got smarts, *ese*. You read books. You already know *chiva* is not for you. Remember once in the neighborhood when I told you that? I know you've been making changes for some time. I've been watching you: the murals, the Chicano school clubs, all that *pedo*. This may not happen again, but for now you have a charge—help the *morros*, the youngsters. Stay out of this life. Don't go both ways. Getting this pass means you can never walk this way again, *me oyes*? If you come back to the county jail for any reason, if we see you inside these walls, you belong to us. *Entiendes, Mendes?*"

I understood. The blood in my veins understood. This was my first big break from the drug-and-crime matrix I had once been so eager to be entangled in. Yet as I walked out, without looking back, carrying what little I owned on my back and the words of my homie, it was the deputy's statement that rang in my ears.

"You'll be back."

These words, now a cliché, heard in movies and TV shows with actors walking away from pretend jails or prisons, were at the time a personal curse, with my name on it, meant to dishearten and disassemble, meant to hold one in the stasis of the criminal world. A big part of me believed I would be back.

The second break came from a judge whose name I don't remember and whose face I can't recall. Community members had organized a letter writing campaign on my behalf among former teachers, fellow organizers, as well as college professors and staff. When I got popped, I was attending California State College, Los Angeles, taking Chicano studies and broadcasting classes. I had no idea this effort would go anywhere.

When I next appeared in front of the judge, I had a pretty *jaina* at my side named Licha—the young woman who had been beaten the night of my arrest. I was looking at more time than she was because of my "assault." Deputies in the stands were clamoring for me to be thrown into the state pen. Yet the judge decided to turn us loose: We both got convicted for drunk-and-disorderly with time served. The deputies were upset. They wanted my hide. I wasn't sure I'd accept this arrangement. But I got those looks from the public defender, Licha, and supporters in the courtroom that said: Don't blow this.

I reluctantly accepted—and Licha and I were freed.

Once out I realized I had been given a chance to begin anew, something I was known previously to throw away. This time too many people had placed their confidence in me, even my homeboy in *la torcida*. For some reason, I matured, which was really an invitation to take life seriously. I needed this weight on me before I made any desperate moves toward drugs, violence, or a street reputation—I needed to finally learn to own my life.

Although I had hardworking Mexican migrant parents, my childhood and youth had been punctuated by an intense and hazardous street life. I was born on the border, in El Paso, Texas, to be exact, although I never lived there. My family resided on the other side, in Ciudad Juarez, Chihuahua—a city with good people, yet few resources.

Prior to my birth, my father had been arrested for allegedly stealing property from the school where he was principal. My mother told me my dad had no access to books or supplies for the students and had to sell the school's wrought-iron fence for funds. He spent six months in an open-air jail with no food except what my mother brought him, which he ate out of a rusty tin can.

Things also happened along the border that may not happen in other parts of the United States. One of my oldest half sister's newborn twins was believed stolen after being born in an El Paso fly-by-night clinic. There was an illegal trade in babies. My sister didn't know she had twins until years later when her daughter contracted a kidney infection that only twins get. My sister then put two and two together. She recalled that while she was still groggy from anesthesia, a nurse inadvertently asked about her "other" daughter, which doctors and staff later insisted was a mistake. This sounded odd, but at the time she didn't think much about it.

We moved to Los Angeles as refugees when I was two. My half sister first found a place in Watts/South Central L.A. with her husband and two daughters. Our family followed. Due to restricted covenants against people of color, Watts was one of the few neighborhoods we could move into. I entered a Watts-area elementary school at age six, speaking only Spanish, pushed from classroom to classroom until a teacher finally accepted me. I spent that year in a corner playing with blocks, and I was scolded and even swatted whenever a Spanish word crept out of me in class or on the playground.

At seven, I began stealing from local stores and markets. At eight, teachers punished me for sticking pins into fellow students *y otras travesuras*—whatever violence or humiliations existed at home, I took it out against my classmates. When I was nine, the family moved to a two-bedroom apartment in the San Gabriel Valley near East L.A. There were eleven of us, with the kids sleeping on blankets in the living room, arguing and yelling all the time, until one family member stabbed another and the landlord threw us into the streets.

With the help of a poverty agency, six of us (Mom, Dad, an older brother, two younger sisters, and me) ended up in South San Gabriel, then part of L.A. County territory that no city claimed. Las Lomas, which means the Hills, was a part of the South San Gabriel barrio with dirt roads, wood-frame shacks, goats and chickens, and stripped cars, surrounded by the mostly better-off cities of Monterey Park, Rosemead, and Montebello.

My mother stayed at home, taking care of us kids. When she worked, it was in garment-industry sweatshops, including doing what was known as "piecework" with an industrial sewing machine wrangled into our small barrio home, rented out of her meager pay. She often labored into the wee hours, rattling the whole place each time her foot pushed on the pedal, her hair disheveled, eyes almost closed, stitching her life to scraps of cloth. I called this machine "the monster."

At ten, my best friend died after we broke into a local school to play ball and the police chased us. He climbed the roof, didn't see a skylight in the dark, and ran across, falling through the glass. That same year I ruptured the lining of my intestines doing rough backyard weight lifting with my brother and a cousin. After I was rushed to White Memorial Medical Center in Boyle Heights, the doctors there also circumcised me, giving me anesthesia for these surgeries. Two years later, I was experimenting with drugs, including *carga*.

At eleven, I witnessed a gang burst through my elementary school chasing after some guys. They arrived in lowered cars and on bikes, with baggy pants and long shirts. Students and teachers ran. I got attracted to whatever power these dudes displayed. That's when I joined a gang. Besides the drug use, at twelve I drank and received my first tattoo. At thirteen I stole bikes, burglarized homes, fought in schools and on the streets—and was getting detained by police, landing in various local jails.

My dad eventually found a job as a laboratory custodian at a community college in the San Fernando Valley that allowed him to buy a house in San Gabriel. I ended up jumping in many *vatos* for Las Lomas to keep this section of San Gabriel out of the hands of our main rivals, La Sangra, a gang named after an old barrio situated around the Mission, north of there. As much as I could, I snuck out of my house to go a couple of miles south to the Hills and hang with the homies.

The rest of the family sort of settled in. My brother and sisters didn't get into crime, gangs, or drugs. My parents, like in many families, were often tired from work, unable to spend "quality time" with us, but they had their rules, their expectations. We were supposed to comply, without question. We weren't allowed to be "bad." But somebody fell through the cracks. It turned out to be me.

At fifteen I got jumped into the hard-core clique of Las Lomas, stabbing someone with a rusty screwdriver that first night. I also got expelled from high school. Soon after this my parents kicked me out of the house. My father declared, "You do what we say or get out." I got out.

I slept in discarded vehicles, in downtown streets with winos and heroin addicts, along church pews, squatting in empty buildings and sitting in all-night movie theaters when I wasn't sleeping on the sofas or in the backyards of homeboys or lover girls. I mugged tourists on Olvera Street and in Chinatown. I eventually returned home to live in a cell-like room in the garage with no running water. I put gang graffiti and murals on all the walls to make it my own.

At sixteen, I was placed in two adult facilities following my arrest during the Chicano Moratorium, what the media dubbed "the East L.A. riot." At one point, sheriff's deputies stowed me away on Murderers' Row in the Hall of Justice jail, threatening to charge several of us *cholos* with the murder of three persons who died in the disturbances, including Rubén Salazar, a prominent Chicano journalist killed by deputies. They threw me into a cell with two killers (and next to the cell of mass murderer Charles Manson). That first night, my cell mates put a razor blade to my neck. I had to stand up to them, even if I was scared to death. They soon smiled, laughed. Afterward, we played cards all night long. I was eventually released with no charges.

After this, my interest in social justice spiked. I realized on Murderers' Row how easily I could be thrown away. If I woke up one morning with my throat cut, who'd care? So I sought teachers, mentors, activists. I returned to high school, catching up on lost units, leading student walkouts that resulted in the establishment of our own Chicano student center, Chicano studies classes, poetic theater pieces, and my short stint as "Joe Aztec," the school's mascot. I also stopped using heroin and other drugs for more than a year when I was around sixteen and seventeen. I don't know how exactly. But for that time I was appraised differently, finally seen as someone with intrinsic value. Unusual as this was, I felt recognized, significant. A whole community rose up to meet my passions and interests.

Just before I finished school, however, I unwound again, in a weird depression. I lost my bearings and went back to the heavy drugs as well as a more intense gang life. I took part in shootings and a firebombing. Then near the end of my seventeenth year, I got arrested for attempted murder after a shoot-out with bikers in which four people were injured. I was released after my homies intimidated all the witnesses.

Because of the pull I felt toward intelligent revolutionary activity, as well as the artistic pursuits I was dabbling in, my relationship to the gang changed again. One of my saving graces was a love of reading. When I first learned English, I turned to books. Even while I was in the gang or on the streets I spent hours in libraries.

Largo had approached me in the county jail because he knew I was a down homeboy, one of the first to rush into battle with fists, knives, or guns. But I also had this book thing. I didn't know it at the time but my destiny was calling me, and a couple of adults, and some of the *vatos*, stone gangsters even, acknowledged this even when I didn't.

I received my diploma in the principal's office since it was too late to take part in the cap-and-gown ceremony. A different persona emerged: I wore my hair long, working out, wearing "normal" clothes instead of *cholo* attire. Going to Cal State L.A. was part of this turn.

But then I got arrested for the incident with the sheriff's deputies. After the judge's decision to give me a lesser charge and time served, I was forced to finally consider another trajectory for my life.

The thing was, my college days were over after my arrest. I missed too many classes and received a number of withdrawals and failures. I wasn't totally out of the woods yet.

Prior to my arrest, the *Los Angeles Times's Home* magazine published a letter on the murals I painted with thirteen gang members and other troubled youth. Next to this they featured a color photo of a section of wall we did at the side of a hardware store in Rosemead.

In the summer of 1972 we put up eight murals as part of the Bienvenidos Community Center, supported by the city of Rosemead and trained by Chicano muralists like Cecil Felix and Alicia Venegas. I took part in mural-making classes at the Goez Art Studio in East L.A. and witnessed the creation of public art at the Estrada Courts Housing Projects. I painted a mural by myself at the Del Mar Public Library and several for the barrio's preschool, alternative school, and youth center.

This mural work happened when a youth organizer saw the intricate graffiti work I was doing with other homeboys. The lettering was precise, unique, cryptic. The drawings were well done and shaded, like the Chicano tattoos and airbrushed images on lowrider cars that were considered the best in the streets and joints. The murals I did included barrio scenes (lowriders, hypodermic needles, *cholos*), preconquest motifs (Mexika and Mayan temples), and abstract images (such as mouths interspersed with raging faces). The biggest mural involved several panels portraying the then 125-year history of Chicanos in the United States.

One day my mother received a phone call from a professor at a major Catholic university on L.A.'s Westside. When I finally got around to returning the call, the professor said he read the *Home* magazine piece and wanted to hire me to do a mural for the campus. He had paints, brushes, scaffolding, students to help, and was offering me $1,000—this was big bucks in 1973.

I traveled to the university, which was in a well-off part of town I was not familiar with. The professor showed me around the campus. He pointed out a wide, clean, and empty wall. Then he took me to a storage area where canisters of acrylic paints as well as equipment were laid out, all at my disposal. I got interested but also overwhelmed. I doubted my skills and questioned whether I deserved this—I often thought good things shouldn't happen to me.

Regardless, I shook his hand and the professor seemed glad we had an agreement.

"You don't realize how honored I am," he declared.

I never painted that mural.

The professor called and called. I never returned his calls. He simply stopped trying to reach me. I was too plagued by self-doubt and deep into the drug world by then.

I left heroin soon after my last county jail experience. Despite those fierce pressures to end the withdrawals, I stayed on course away from family, from homies. I had relapses, complications, but I was nonetheless determined to break this powerful hold.

By then I had been convinced, with the help of others, that heroin and other illicit drugs were part of a systematic way to control the poor working-class communities of mostly blacks and Mexicans, but also poor whites, that began to rebel and organize in the 1960s. The old Chicano gangsters, known as *pachucos*, got hit hard with heroin after World War II when the U.S. government deserted the poppy fields they had set up in Mexico for the morphine required for wounded servicemen. African-American and Puerto Rican neighborhoods also got inundated. The Vietnam War brought in more addicts, more access to heroin. By the time I got into this, there were a few generations already addicted.

I was also filling in the emptiness of my life—which heroin and other drugs had done fairly well until then—with the art, stories, and poems bursting out of my depths, out of my active mind, out of my aches and sorrows. At eighteen, prior to my last arrest and still drowning in *carga*, I walked into my first poetry reading in Berkeley, California. I had won honorable mention in 1973's Quinto Sol Chicano Literary Awards for vignettes of street life I first wrote in jail called "Barrio Expressions." I was invited to the awards ceremony and given $250, a lot of money for a thief and drug user. Later on stage I saw José Montoya, the Godfather of Chicano poetry; David Henderson, one of the country's leading African-American poets; and Pedro Pietri, the Nuyorican word meister. In turn they each stood up to read their works—I was held in a trance of images, stories, metaphors, and passionate feeling.

I had never heard poetry read before. I didn't even know what poems were. But that day their verses and politics called to me, more music than talk, more fevered shapes than sentences, more Che and Malcolm than Shakespeare—I was never the same after this. For the first time, I even imagined my own works on the shelves among those of other writers.

The best way to pull oneself out of a life of crime and drugs is to stop, as difficult as this may be. Being "conflicted" is an important part of the process, which also involves alignment of deep self and ego, the physical with the psychological, the emotional with the spiritual, the individual with the community. Profound knowledge and a therapeutic community were the best ways to pull street warriors like me away from these drugs, a grueling and lifelong struggle. For me, it also involved having a sense of history and political clarity.

I vowed never again to use illegal drugs or to go to jail for any criminal act, a thorny proposition compounded by the fact that, though I had a general vision of a just world, I had no skills or any idea about what I'd be or where I'd go.

Still, I often thought about that mural project at the Catholic university I had sabotaged. Who knows what other offers would have come my way? Perhaps the mural experience was too tied to the combination of drugs and street life. I'm not sure. But when I stopped that life, especially the drugs, I also let go of the colors, the symbols, the shapes, the faces I sketched on paper or imagined in my mind.

I never again picked up a paintbrush.

Chapter Two

A revolutionary mind and a revolutionary life were probably the worst things you could strive for in America. Killers, gangsters, addicts . . . they were all relatively tolerable unless they became "godless commies." In schools and in the media, it had been rammed into my head that opponents of the political and economic status quo were the Antichrists, the precursors of the Apocalypse, the devil's henchmen on this earth.

My parents were against this, too. They railed against the Chicano movement, which involved school walkouts, marches, protests. Once in the United States, and regardless of whatever politics they had in the old country, they became right-wing patriots (even before they became citizens).

They were thus horrified when I let on that I was studying radical political theory. In their view being in a gang, on drugs, and incorrigible were preferable to this, perhaps because they believed my core being was now in peril (they wrongly surmised revolutionaries were against God and country).

"Ya te perdistes," my mother declared. I became rotten, no good, lost.

Worse still was when I tried to enlist my siblings and anyone else who would listen. I was now an instrument of darkness and evil among the family. The sense I got was, "You were always mixed up—now this!"

Forget that these revolutionaries helped pull me off the death road I was on. Forget that they provided something meaningful in the black hole of an existence called poverty, where abuse, sexual and physical, was rampant. Where low-paid and exploitative manufacturing and service work, when there was work, claimed most of the residents. A reality where the wrong look, the wrong color, or walking into the wrong place at the wrong time meant an untimely death.

Forget that I wouldn't be who I am, or have achieved whatever I've achieved, if not for what I learned during this critical period of my life.

Radical politics wasn't the first thing I tried outside the gang and heroin. I once attended evangelical Christian gatherings that were proliferating in the barrio in the 1970s with organizations like Victory Outreach and Teen Challenge.

I had a niece who had drug problems at fifteen. After she was held in a juvenile facility, they released her to a Christian home for troubled teens. I picked her up from there on weekends at her request. She was "born again" and wanted me to follow her example in dealing with my own drug issues. I was a knucklehead, but I had to admit these Christians were turning around a good number of addicts.

I remember being at her church and being asked to accept Christ as my personal saviour. Many spiritually beaten youth walked up to have a pastor lay hands on them. Tears and chants abounded, utterances in tongues, much song. I too approached the pastor, but inside I put up a challenge.

God, if you're for real, you'll save me, I thought. *You'll come in and I'll know it.* If not, I will know that too.

Since around age eleven, a year after I first received Holy Communion, I had turned away from the Catholic Church. The priests, nuns, and laypeople seemed hypocritical. They hated the *cholos* and tried to guilt-trip us into being obedient and chaste. I could not abide by the multifaceted ways they tried to control us. I could not accept the bloody history the Church had in Mexico and other countries—or their power and wealth. The Church was also institutionally abusive, striking kids on hands with rulers, forcing them to kneel on bottle caps while holding missals in outstretched arms, and, as we now know, sexually molesting tens of thousands of young parishioners all over the United States and other parts of the world.

Yes, I'm aware that most priests and nuns did not abuse anyone. I'm aware that most Catholics are decent people. I have worked with Catholics on many justice issues over the years. But the problems with the Church were too many to be denied. So an evangelical Christian conversion was going to be rough, although I knew they weren't Catholics. But I was willing to let them try.

I walked up the center aisle, through a refrain of praises, some of the faithful with their arms in the air, others in deep worship. My niece looked pleased. Finally, as I faced the pastor, I lifted my arms slightly above me and looked up. The pastor placed his hands on the back of my neck then thundered out exhortations, unintelligible phrases, his eyes pinched shut. I waited for the sign, the "feeling," the electricity or whatever I was supposed to undergo.

But nothing happened.

I knew that wonderful words and sincere thoughts were sent my way. But I felt no surge, no opening. Part of me said to myself, *Maybe God doesn't want me. Maybe I'm too far gone to be saved.* Another part said that maybe this was not a "true" way for everyone, a somewhat more reasonable conclusion.

Not long after that day, I went to a church meeting as before. But this time my niece met me at the door. She told me, somewhat dejected, that I was not welcome there. The pastor had declared I had the devil in me. The people at the home were to shun me. I would not turn to Christ so something had to be wrong with me.

That was the end of my dabbling with evangelical Christianity.

Over the years I've seen this faith help my niece, eventually her mother (my oldest half sister), and my other nieces, even siblings. But I demanded something else. I put spiritual matters on hold. I didn't think there was a religious or spiritual path that could quench my thirst for meaning. Science and art became more compelling means to help me "see" again.

I became an atheist by default, shutting off spiritual access, closing doors to what I felt were unwarranted belief systems. Revolutionary politics isn't solely to blame, since, unlike what is generally believed, there are Christian revolutionaries, Buddhist revolutionaries, revolutionaries from every religious leaning.

I personally embarked on a godless path to the mystery.

You could not find an apple as far away from the tree as I was from my father. We disagreed about many things, but mostly we disagreed about politics.

My father made his final trip to Los Angeles from Mexico when he was in his early forties and I was two years old. By then Dad had eight children with three different women (he had also married and divorced another woman, although they had no kids). Embittered with Mexico's poverty and seemingly insurmountable corruption, he brought my mother and his last family to the United States, buying whole hog into the "American Dream."

In Mexico, my father once owned a *jacal* (small woodshed) to sell food products on the street. Another time he peddled *chicharrones* (Mexican-style pork rinds) out of a basket on his shoulder. His first daughter, unfortunately, died of diarrhea when as an infant she crawled and ate a *chicharrón* from a basket my dad inadvertently placed on the floor. In time, and with higher education behind him, he became a biologist and school administrator.

But once in Los Angeles, Dad's Mexican credentials were worthless. He found work in dog food plants, construction, paint factories. On weekends, he sold insurance, pots and pans, Bibles. Despite several false starts—including getting evicted a few times, going bankrupt, losing a home—we finally bought that San Gabriel house, a modest, wood-framed two-bedroom for a family of six, making us one of the few Mexican families to own one in the area. He retired as a laboratory custodian after fifteen years.

The problem was that when we first moved in I was thirteen years old and already in the streets. Something rang hollow about my family pretending to "make it" when I knew otherwise. We may have bought a house, but we had little means for anything else.

Dad fell for the materialistic appeal of American capitalism. He dealt with growing debt by getting into more debt—he had liens and mortgages on the house and bought services, cars, and things we didn't need. He also had little emotional connection with his children. He was a hard guy to figure out, to influence, even to love.

When I first got involved in community organizing, my father and I often debated—about unions (he hated them), civil rights (he felt people should stop complaining), and who should run the country (he loved Richard Nixon).

"What good have unions or revolutions done for anyone?" my father asked one day. "They've only brought ruin and suffering—look at Mexico. What good did the revolution bring there?"

I wasn't learned, but I picked things up quickly.

"The revolution in Mexico was never completed, 'Apa," I responded. "And capitalism, which drives Mexico and this country, only creates a smaller wealthy class and a growing army of hungry and poor. Many in the middle are left without decent schooling, housing, health care, or jobs. People's lives and futures are literally taken out of their hands. A new society has to be about the common person, the workers, *los campesinos*, the artists able to rule themselves, in their own interests, for the common good of everyone."

"*O que* 'common good' *ni que la chingada*," my mother snapped back—she'd been listening in and brought the animosity into arguments my father often failed to do.

One time, my dad asked me to attend a meeting of a conservative political group. West San Gabriel Valley at the time had many middle-class upwardly mobile white communities next to very poor Mexican barrios (which also included poor whites). A high school principal once told me the local school boards and city governments were overrun with John Birch Society members and other conservatives.

My father looked out of place at this meeting. He was relatively short and brown skinned, and wore a buttoned shirt and slacks. The other men were tall, many gray haired, in business suits and ties. I saw how awestruck my father looked among them. I was livid. To me these men didn't deserve the respect of most people, let alone my father. I could see they cared little about his presence. They tolerated him. But he was invisible, as were the many working-class Mexicans surrounding their sterile suburbs. Their words at the meeting were declarations of war against radicals, hippies, and peaceniks.

They were declarations of war against people like me.

When I finally left my garage room, with no more gang ties, no college, no murals, off drugs, I ended up in a run-down federal housing project in the Harbor Area called Rancho San Pedro.

I spent two months there studying Marxist politics, economics, and philosophy. I walked to the local library to do research. Several others were part of this training for area radicals, including organizers from community centers, labor unions, and student groups. I learned that those who gravitated toward politics weren't afraid or off, unlike what my parents were telling me. I could tell the nut jobs from the genuine visionaries (the crazies were often police plants and operatives). Those who provoked violence were often long gone when the trouble came down. These so-called militants often had no community ties—nor had they done preparatory work or taught in the factories and neighborhoods where they brought unnecessary tensions.

The ones I studied with were sharp and principled.

I was introduced to various teachers, including one dude who became my physical trainer. A former boxer, this guy had me rise early in the morning, just as dawn broke, and run around a nearby park. I also, again, used weights, but this time properly. Believe it or not this helped with staying clean from drugs. The endorphins released in exercise are similar, on a different scale, of course, to the release of pleasure chemicals from drugs. He also had me eat right—proper balance of vegetables, fruits, whole grains, and proteins (not necessarily meats, although I found that hard to give up).

This was indeed a formidable remedy, drawing on mental powers I tried to build up with my own forays into books, music, and whatever passionate dialogue I could find. Now, in Rancho San Pedro, I met more than my match. I felt out of the loop, dumb even, but I had to keep trying to comprehend. I made many errors. And there were days I wanted to pack up and leave, only I had nowhere else to go.

To top this off, I wasn't an easy student. I required a heroic amount of patience—it's a testament to my teachers that they remained steady and engaged. In time my interest in the subject of social change, tied to my personal ordeal of self-transformation, compelled me to learn more. When I finally grasped a concept or idea, it became exhilarating. I felt victorious, alive, competent. Books, which were once my escape, both a blessing and a curse, now carried me into this power I didn't know I possessed.

I'd been failed by a system. I could not fail myself.

During the time I lived in the housing projects, I had a girlfriend I'd met at Garfield High School in East L.A. when I was briefly head of MEChA (Movimiento Estudiantil Chicano de Aztlan—the Chicano Student Movement of Aztlan) Central at California State College.

MEChA Central was established to help the Chicano student organizations in East L.A.'s high schools. Besides Garfield, these included Roosevelt, Lincoln, Wilson, Franklin, and others in the surrounding area. I was also editor of the MEChA newspaper at Cal State, which allowed me to go into these schools to talk to students, pass out newspapers, encourage them toward college.

Camila was a self-motivated young woman, unlike the street girls I knew. She was pretty, vivacious, an A student, active in school projects, and into *teatro*, the Chicano theater movement. A high school senior when I met her, she was seventeen. I was nineteen. She seemed to admire my militant stance, my organizing prowess, my older-dude demeanor. It was quaint having status among girls due to my activist politics. But soon Camila drew warm and loving feelings from me, something I had to figure out since sex and love didn't always come together in the streets.

I'd had sexual encounters with *cholas*, homeless girls, and addicts since age twelve. Feeling each other up, oral sex, and the inevitable glory of actual sex, which over time became one of my favorite things until the heavy drugs overpowered even that. I didn't have guidance from parents or older siblings. I learned about sex the hard way, muddling through, making blunder after blunder, until once in a while I got it right.

To add to this, I wasn't handsome or suave or even stable, so most smart and relatively sane girls stayed away from me. This had been true since two *vatos* jumped me at age nine and fractured my jaw. I never had this taken care of, so my chin jutted out. For a couple of years class-mates and girls taunted me. I was unable to make friends. This changed when I joined a gang. I looked hard, older than my age, and the homies gave me a *placaso*: Chin. They embraced my most damaged feature and I learned to accept it, even to flaunt it. So when my parents, at great sacrifice, offered to get my jaw fixed, I refused. I was "El Chin de Las Lomas."

Being ugly was being cool.

So by the time I asked Camila to be my girl, I'd had a number of encounters with women, sloppy and unhealthy as this may have been. Camila, on the other hand, had never been with a man before.

This, too, was interesting, desirable, quaint.

Camila's face held both shame and excitement when I managed to re-move her clothes one late night in the parking lot of Salazar Park while we both sat in the front seat of a blue 1968 lowriding V-dub I'd recently bought.

Earlier Camila had snuck out of the side window of a house near Garfield High, her sister's house, which her mother had banished her to when she discovered I was hanging around, thinking the sister could keep a better eye on things. But like most teens, we found a way around this.

Camila quickly learned the pleasures of intimacy and desire. Once she got what this was all about, she wanted sex all the time. I was more than willing to oblige. Camila became my focus, my lifeline to some-thing decent and good. I had a troublesome time with family, always fighting with my parents, not close to my brother or sisters, and felt disconnected since I had pretty much done what I wanted to do after joining a gang. By this time, I was also removed from my homeboys. The fact is love and relationships were key ingredients for "maturing out" of that life.

Since my dealings with the female species up to that point were spotty and not much to sing about, Camila filled in nicely. She was extraordinarily cute, with honey-brown skin from her roots among the Huichol and Cora tribes of Nayarit, Mexico, where her mother's family came from, as well as her father's Mexican/Native American heritage. She had a healthy body, curved and youthful, and the slanted eyes of indigenous people.

Compelling politics and a gorgeous woman—a good way to start a new life.

Hortencia was a hard-bitten Mexican mother of four girls, two boys, and two "found" daughters ("adopted" after their families couldn't take care of them). She owned property in the Geraghty hills as well as on a street off Whittier Boulevard and several lots in the Maravilla neighborhood of El Hoyo.

For years some of the dwellings on Hortencia's lands were surrounded by cardboard, old tires, car parts, chickens, stray dogs, and other junk and animals she accumulated. She drove around East L.A. in a smoky old Ford pickup and hauled off whatever had been discarded. She also invaded clothing/furniture bins and trash Dumpsters to salvage things she could remake, reuse, or sell.

And she could also twist the necks of two chickens at one time with an agile move of her wrists, the old-country way.

Hortencia assisted fellow Mexicans who landed in East L.A. without knowing where to go or what to do. She found them work and housing, but not because she had money. She had the survivor's wisdom, a way of figuring things out with little to work with.

She was also known for having some interesting ways to make do. She found green meat, bruised fruits and vegetables, and other seemingly inedible food from Dumpsters behind restaurants. In fact, she did wonders with green meat—with enough *ajo, cebolla, y salsa picante.* I once tried a skillet of this stuff and didn't get ill (I don't recommend this, however).

In an attic of one of her homes, she had years of old *telas,* pieces of moldy cloth she swore she'd use someday. Cinder blocks, old bricks, wood pieces, and piping lay next to the house. Hortencia had male companions, but it was clear who wore the pants and the tool belt.

In one of her houses lived Camila, one of Hortencia's actual daughters. Camila had never had a real boyfriend before, so when she brought me around Hortencia tested me to make sure I was right for her daughter—Camila's dad, a farm worker in California's Central Valley, was not involved in her life.

Let me tell you, Hortencia was tough enough.

First, I had to know how to wield a hammer, turn a pipe wrench, and push a saw. I had to prove I wasn't allergic to work. She had me replace broken windows, install new doors, and drive in floorboards. She once convinced me to crawl beneath one of her houses to fix a leak. I was working in a paper mill on graveyard at the time and was so tired I actually fell asleep down there while Hortencia pulled on pipes above me in the bathroom.

In one backyard, Hortencia had built an underground bomb shelter during the atom bomb scare of the 1960s. When I came by at dawn after a full night shift, she let me sleep down there. The place was so dark I was knocked out as soon as I fell onto the dusty mattress. Years later county inspectors forced her to bury the shelter when they got wind of its existence. Like many East L.A. structures of the time, the shelter was built *rasquache* style, with no permits and tons of code violations.

So while Hortencia gave me a hard time at first, I passed her tests. Over time, I learned to honor Hortencia—her strong spirit, her sharp survival skills, the knowledge she got by doing things, making mistakes, and picking up again.

To some, Hortencia may have seemed off her *mecedora*. I, on the other hand, thought she had a profusion of eccentric energy that this world needed to be complete.

After Rancho San Pedro, I ended up in Watts for a couple of weeks. Then I moved in with a woman almost ten years my senior, and her seven-year-old son, for a couple of months in the *White Fence* barrio. But mostly I stayed in the Eastside community of Boyle Heights near

the Aliso Village and Pico Gardens federally subsidized housing projects—at the time, the largest poor people's housing complex west of the
Mississippi.

I met Tony Prince in these housing projects when I attended study
sessions and organizing meetings. He'd been a Jewish-Italian community leader since his middle school days, when he participated in school
walkouts and protests at the predominantly African-American Louis
Pasteur Junior High School in L.A.'s Westside. Tony later moved to
Aliso Village, one of a handful of white people in housing units made
up of Mexicans and African-Americans.

Tony was also one of the funniest dudes I ever met. He actually
learned to imitate me. This irritated me at first, until I found myself
laughing at his uncanny ability to use words and expressions I recognized but didn't think anyone else did. He also did great imitations of
Chicano organizers, African-American preachers, and TV characters
like James T. Kirk of the starship *Enterprise*.

Tony and I became tight despite our pasts being so different. He
was the son of longtime union activists with origins in the radical politics of Chicago and St. Louis. He didn't do drugs or get involved with
gangs. Although he was mostly on his own at thirteen, the one thing
we had somewhat in common was strong work and study habits. He
was the same age as I, although I learned much from him about the
dedication required for immediate *and* lasting social changes in our
communities.

After leaving behind drugs, I found a drive I didn't know I had.
We often didn't sleep, staying up late having impassioned talks, writing, printing materials. Early mornings we passed out flyers in front of
foundries, factories, assembly lines, and schools.

Along with Tony there was a nucleus of young leaders who included
a South Central L.A.–raised African-American intellectual; a Hopi-
Laguna activist whose family lived among Mexicans in Pico Gardens;
and young women like Camila. We were Mexican, black, Native American, and, with Tony, also white. Quite a team.

Most of us worked or attended school, but this didn't stop us. We
met whenever we managed to muster everyone together. We spoke at

government meetings, like at the school board, with well-argued statements. One school board member said the district couldn't be failing that bad if they graduated people like us.

We took on the police and sheriff's departments, which had an extraordinary record of abuse and murder of unarmed citizens, including Danny Garcia (I wrote my first leaflet for a rally after police killed this fifteen-year-old Chicano in the Florencia community of South L.A.). Other cases involved the police murders of Randall Miles, Eula Love, and the Sanchez cousins—all black and brown, all poor and working-class.

Once when LAPD officers at the Hollenbeck Station of Boyle Heights beat up seven Mexican youths in the confines of their basement, we organized an overnight rally in Pico Gardens. Three to four hundred people showed up (years later, Mark Fuhrman, the police officer discredited during the O. J. Simpson murder trial, was exposed as one of the masked officers who took part in the beatings).

East L.A., like South Central L.A., and like most working-class communities of color, was under siege. The mainstream media ignored the rather outrageous government-sponsored attacks and incitements against our communities. While some of our leaders later ended up working for various community-based nonprofits, organizing drives, and trade unions, we mostly connected heart and mind with any community we tried to assist. We weren't paid for these efforts. We became examples of commitment.

And, for this, we were often spied on, detained, beaten.

COINTELPRO, the coordinated national repression machine that targeted movements and community organizations, even those doing good, sturdy work, also intervened in East L.A. At that time this was the foremost weapon the government had in their war against dissent. Their targets included organizations that advocated nonviolence or racial harmony. In particular, these agencies undermined most barrio peace gatherings and actions. They appeared to *want* gang warfare (and there were enough traumatized youths to oblige them). One of our study group leaders, a former hype and gang member, ended up dead in his car one night, shot full of heroin—we figured he didn't do this to himself. Others were forced out of jobs, arrested, deported.

For a year after the Chicano Moratorium, East L.A. was under a kind of martial law, with sheriff's deputies imposing curfews at six P.M. for almost a year. The government tapped phones. We were often followed from meeting to meeting, rally to rally. Once Tony and I had to give police the slip. We were meeting with gang members trying to establish peace. We had people leave in different directions after the meeting to confuse those spying on us. Police eventually stopped the car we were in, had everyone get out, searched us, and held us for a while, but finally let us go.

We had important rules to keep the police from targeting us: No drugs, not even weed. No drunkenness. No weapons or threats of violence. No exploiting, abusing, or disrespecting members of the opposite sex. And we set up a careful protocol about phones, mail, and whom we talked to. We didn't do anything unlawful, but we were still harassed.

We became outcasts because of our ideas, our spirits, our aims. We planted seeds in the fertile ground of justly outraged minds. There was no other reason the government should have messed with us. To a fault, we were Mister and Missus Clean. Yet this didn't stop taxpayer-sponsored repression.

One of the Eastside study circles included a young Chicano named Carlos and his beautiful new wife, Flora. They insisted we meet at their modest home in a run-down neighborhood. Carlos was a UCLA student, one of the first Chicanos ever to attend the four-year institution that had generally graduated generations of Jewish Americans and other white students. He was rather homely looking yet smart.

Flora was attractive, always wearing the best clothes and expensive perfumes, even at our shoddy-ass meetings. She always had a smile for us as we entered their living room, decorated with Mexican masks, rugs, and floral arrangements. The walls were painted in earth tones. The coffee mugs were Mexican earthenware and snacks included guacamole and salsa with chips or sliced fried *taquitos*.

Besides studying, several of us took martial arts training at a nearby park with a former Special Forces agent, a Chicano, who had fought in Korea and Vietnam. His teachings combined the best of different

Asian styles, which gave us varied skills to draw from. I had already been trained briefly in Shodokan, a hard Japanese style, and Limalama, a Polynesian martial art. I also tried amateur boxing one summer. I wanted to learn more.

An interesting thing developed in this study circle: Flora was becoming close with many of the men who attended. In fact, we found out later she was sleeping with a few of them, including those already hitched. She was generally nice to me, but I don't recall her trying to get me into bed. Just as well. Flora was an LAPD agent infiltrating our collective. This was proof that police had sent agents into MEChA, the Brown Berets, various gang peace efforts, and other Chicano organizations, even those with clearly nonthreatening agendas.

Flora would ask many questions of her bedmates, one of whom became suspicious and, to his credit, decided to inform the rest of us. ¡Qué cábula! There was plenty of embarrassment as others copped to being taken in by Flora, although I'm sure there were those who just kept their mouths shut.

We guessed right that Carlos wasn't in on this—he was brokenhearted when we gave him the news. I'm sure he thought she was a dream come true, although I thought it was extreme that any agent would go so far as to marry somebody (whom I assumed she didn't love) just to get information. Talk about deep undercover—or, in this case, under covers.

Many of these circles soon disbanded. We simply didn't know whom to trust.

Because the martial arts instructor was a former government agent, it was also determined that we should not take any more training with him. To close ranks, many of us were asked to pull back from public actions. I felt this was a mistake. We needed to do more—our best and safest place was among the community, properly interlinked with teachings and actions.

Tony walked door to door at the Pico Gardens housing project with leaflets about an upcoming rally. The families, many of whom spoke only Spanish, were sympathetic. A few knew Tony from his association with the organizers and their families. There was nothing to indicate he was in danger. We tried to anticipate such things, to protect our young cadre.

One day Tony turned a corner and strode through a section of two-story housing units. A group of guys confronted him in a narrow gap between the buildings. Tony loosened a brick from a low wall to defend himself. What happened next he doesn't recall. From what can be ascertained, Tony was hit with a bat to his head.

The attackers were a group of antirevolutionaries that were apparently trained in the projects by a police operative. Some were gang members who were willing to do anything for money and/or drugs. They were a goon squad, known to show up to community meetings with firearms and dirty looks. One activist in a demonstration in the projects was later stabbed to death. The message: Don't provide alternative knowledge and organization to the people of these poor communities.

After beating Tony, the assailants left him for dead.

Residents helped get Tony to the hospital. He had a fractured skull and was in and out of consciousness for weeks. It didn't seem that Tony would make it. Yet he survived the attack, though he lost his sense of smell and began having intense headaches. Tony could have given up—nobody would have blamed him. But as soon as he got well, he was back in the projects, doing his best to provide assistance to people who were otherwise kept ignorant, unorganized, and scattered.

For a short time, a probation officer I knew worked at an L.A. County probation camp for adjudicated minors. Many dudes from barrio gangs ended up in these facilities, which they called *campo*, some of which were firefighting camps. These youth were trained to contain vast brushfires, often risking their lives to do so.

This PO interacted politically with the various young men sent to this one camp. They often had nothing to do but lay on their bunks and look at the ceiling for hours on end. It was a shame that most of these juvenile facilities were warehousing offenders, not providing them books or rehabilitative guidance. But the PO learned who the leaders were, the smart dudes, the ones who had the potential to change and to help remake communities.

Since I was doing work with gang members, the PO invited the more *trucha* gangsters to hook up with me when they were released. I helped them with job referrals, treatment, if needed, and sometimes places to stay. Many of them ended up in our study circles, dealing with the motive forces of society—not as a condition of our help, but as an option if they were inclined to political matters.

We had dudes from Wilmas, Primera Flats, and Monte Flores, among other barrios. It was part of the gang intervention and peace work I was doing, which also included truces, late-night calls to stop retaliations, visits to hospitals and morgues.

One of the *vatos* who showed an interest in our grassroots "program" (it was never part of an official organization) was Roberto Gutierrez. Roberto was from Sangra, my barrio gang's main rival. He was eighteen years old.

I actually knew Roberto's family. Prior to our splitting up into rival gangs, I visited once or twice with Roberto and his brother Ernie. In middle school, I liked their sister Corrine, who later became a Sangra homegirl (unfortunately, Corrine succumbed to gang warfare in her teens). Sometimes in close neighborhoods dudes who were buddies as kids would end up bitter enemies as teenagers.

Although I was a former rival, Roberto agreed to come to our street knowledge sessions. I had already talked to a couple of other Sangra dudes about peace and social action, so I was prepared to work with Roberto. Despite my previous gang involvement, I felt the gang violence was destroying our communities and was highly manipulated by police. We discussed this and other pertinent topics at the meetings.

Yet Roberto never made it.

One afternoon in February 1977, Roberto confronted a former San Gabriel police officer named Bobby Ray McPhee. McPhee, in his early thirties, apparently stalked Roberto for several weeks, making threatening phone calls to his mother and even spraying gang-type graffiti in support of the police on the sidewalk in front of his house. At one point someone firebombed the Gutierrez home. Roberto wanted to find out why this dude was harassing his family. According to news reports, McPhee displayed his police badge, handcuffed Roberto, and forced him into his car. Roberto's friend Jorge Gomez, who witnessed what happened, was not taken and he called the family.

Later, McPhee contacted authorities from his West Covina home claiming Roberto Gutierrez and another gangster were holding him captive, supposedly for sending another Sangra member to jail. Police for two hours surrounded McPhee's home. Reportedly hundreds of rounds were fired at the officers, including with an alleged submachine gun that was also leveled against a news helicopter circling above.

Police supposedly believed Roberto was the gunman. Finally, McPhee called back to say he shot Roberto with a pistol he had hidden in his boot when the teenager got distracted. McPhee was hailed as a hero. However, when police entered the home they found Roberto "shot to pieces" with at least six shotgun blasts—hardly a pistol. McPhee, it turned out, had kidnapped Roberto, held *him* hostage. It was McPhee who made police believe the opposite had happened. Law enforcement officers arrested McPhee and charged him with kidnapping and murder.

Transcripts and news reports during the subsequent trial described an environment of virtual war between San Gabriel police officers and La Sangra. Supposedly, new Sangra recruits were told to beat up or shoot police officers—however, this was denied by Sangra members I talked to. And one evening gang members had allegedly ambushed McPhee near his home, shooting him in the stomach and groin. McPhee reportedly shot at his assailants, killing one of them. Again, one Sangra *veterano* said McPhee set this all up, even shooting himself, to make this claim in court to justify his actions.

Nonetheless, disabled, McPhee was forced to retire—accounts claimed this was the catalyst for Roberto's abduction. The police department, like others in the area, was saturated with right-wing members. Many of them saw Mexicans, Chicano gang members in particular, as the scum of the earth. They harassed and beat Sangra dudes. After McPhee's arrest a number of police officers set up a legal defense committee on his behalf.

I visited with the Gutierrez family a few times after Roberto's murder. I talked with his mother and Roberto's girlfriend at the time of his death. They both testified to the ongoing harassment, phone calls, threats, and more from Bobby Ray McPhee.

Then a few weeks after Roberto's murder an alleged gang rival shot and killed Jorge Gomez, the sole witness to the kidnapping. Many speculated police paid the gunman, since whoever killed Jorge somehow disappeared and was never arrested.

Visiting the family, writing about this case, and taking part in meetings was my way, I suppose, of making up for my former role as enemy to Roberto and the Sangra barrio. I was no longer at war with them, even if for years a few families never wanted anything to do with me. I understood their ire, and I never bothered them or insisted on their forgiveness. In trying to help his mother and this case, I moved beyond some inescapable barriers that generations of barrio warfare created. It was to the family's credit that they allowed me into their home.

McPhee was eventually convicted of the kidnapping and murder of Roberto Gutierrez. He was sent to prison for life. Reportedly no other police officer in the state up until then had been convicted for killing a civilian. McPhee's sentence, however, was commuted in the 1990s by then-governor Pete Wilson.

Chapter Three

The graveyard shift at St. Regis Paper Company buzzed with machine gears and loud whistles. The plant produced paper products twenty-four hours a day, the menial labor mostly done by Mexicans and African-Americans and a few whites.

I was hired as a utility man—bringing in massive rolls of brown or white industrial paper, taller than I was, then maneuvering sharp tools to cut the metal bindings, preparing the paper for insertion into a bag-making machine, moving the roll to the machine, and pushing the paper through the rollers without getting my fingers crushed.

On the other end was the bag man, who caught the re-formed and glued paper bags coming out of the machine, bound them in set numbers, and placed them on pallets. Burly forklift drivers moved the pallets over to another section of the plant. The paper bags were made for major market chains and fast food outlets.

Simple enough. The problem was the monotony of doing this over and over for hours on end until the dawn broke through the line of windows at the ceiling and a whistle signaled an end to the shift. I was nineteen years old. I had learned to work at nine when my mother—who picked cotton in Texas when she was the same age—insisted it was time for me to contribute to the family's finances, which were always in dire straits.

There were times at St. Regis when I felt so tired, I'd wander over to the restroom and then catch myself sleeping on the toilet after trying hard not to close my eyes. After I stood up, I'd pour water on my face, squat once or twice, and bend over so the blood would fill my head. I drowned myself in coffee. This was better than the illegal amphetamine pills that were available to all-night employees throughout the area, usually sold by *cholos* in parking lots.

When the paper rolls were not readily available, I had to sweep in and around the paper-bag-making machines. Once I found myself sleeping standing up—I didn't know this was possible. I woke up when I almost toppled into the gears of the machine.

St. Regis was one of the impediments to falling back into the barrio and the craziness this would lead to, because the drugs, the homies, the homegirls, the excitement, and violence often called me back. For so long they were all I knew. I didn't return much to the old neighborhood, but when I did I fell back into the hole. Back to slurring and fighting and drugging. It turns out that heroin is hard to leave. The relapse rate is the highest of any drug and the quit rate the lowest. This was quite an undertaking. I had to keep myself occupied, away from the barrio, away from anything that could pull me back again. The best thing for me was to work.

I also had Camila in my life. This liaison took up much of my nondrug moments, only now I was drinking. Alcohol, I felt, was okay. Everyone drank. I could handle it. It wasn't hard drugs, right? The beer was fine for during the week. On weekends I binged on the hard stuff. For now, I was safe with Camila—at first she didn't drink or do drugs, but the drinking began for her as well, I suspect, largely because of me. Again, this was normal for working people. No biggie. Right?

The activists went underground, but also into industry. Camila and I—and leaders like Tony—were already working-class. We entered our parents' world. But there were some organizers, mostly from privileged white communities, who also began doing industrial work. They wanted to get near the working class, labor next to the working class. Become the working class. But they stood out like sore thumbs. Even though we were radicals like them, we didn't connect with these out-of-the-flow activists. Many workers pulled their leg or simply ignored them.

Working hard was also part of the deal. A few organizers were actually lazy, as if their principles kept them from making surplus value for the plant owners. But nobody respected you if you didn't pull your own weight. Working-class people judged others by certain standards, no matter how smart you thought you were: You worked hard. You didn't complain. You always stood up for the other guy.

Our work ethic was top-notch. We didn't complain, although we did politicize (complaints with a plan). And we maintained respectful relationships. Acting as if you're better than others is not a good move in industry. The bosses had their own tactics, as if they'd all been schooled in Boss 101. For one, they never praised you, even if you worked your ass off. They wanted to keep you on your toes. At St. Regis, the shift boss talked to the new workers after about six months, just prior to the end of their probationary period, mostly to fire them (so that no benefits had to be paid).

They kept many "short-timers" around just to save on costs. If they planned to hang on to you, the boss gave a speech about how bad you were doing, how you needed major improvements, but that you could stay on if you wanted. I got one of those speeches, not knowing what this was about. So I said yes, that I'd try harder, thank you.

I found out later this was the "you've got the job" speech.

Eventually I got pushed out along with others for organizing among the employees. I applied for unemployment benefits. You had to know how to deal with unemployment insurance (it was also a part of the "working" life). I also wanted to keep working, so I'd check the job board every day and go to various job sites for applications.

I sought work in construction, assembly lines, even day labor. To find day labor work you congregated (often late at night, which makes calling it "day labor" a misnomer) in east downtown's warehouse district to get picked for a day or night's output. Many Mexicans lined up, but also a fair number of unemployed African-Americans and whites. I learned to wear a heavy coat, lined with newspapers, so that I looked hunkier than I was—and to keep out the L.A. desert night cold.

I removed boxes from freight trains or big-rig containers. I had a sturdy back in those days. Once I hosed guts and blood into a large hole in a meatpacking plant. I dug ditches or crawled through oil-plugged piping. You had to be willing to do just about anything for a paycheck.

The wages stank. But you worked hard. No complaints.

For a short time, I operated a smelter at National Lead, one of L.A.'s big foundries. I worked in the blast furnaces that separated the lead from other metals and junk, heating the furnaces with oxygen and other materials. The molten lead layer sank to the bottom of the furnace while the other layers, including the top layer, which we called slag, bubbled to the top.

Every fifteen minutes I had to "tap the heat," which meant I held a jackhammer perpendicular to my shoulders and hammered away at the concrete slag hole until it busted, forcing the top-layer slag to pour with sparks into slag cars beneath it. I'd then pour the more or less pure lead from the other side, using handheld electrical controls, into cast-iron containers to make bullion.

When you breathe in lead the poisonous mineral stays in your body, mostly in the bones, potentially damaging the brain, nervous system, stomach, and kidneys. National Lead employees had to wear hazardous-material coats and pants as well as masks that covered your whole head. We looked like poor versions of astronauts. It got so hot in there that I was often tempted to lift the bottom of the mask to get some air, which would have been a big mistake. We also had to take a shower in company locker rooms after every shift.

We'd get regular blood tests. Still, the company wouldn't let you know how bad lead had gotten into your system until you reached a perilous level, and then they'd let you go. Lead could also be taken home, to the wife and kids. Lead air pollution was a problem in the area around the plant as well. While there were some regulations at the time, the major safety regulations didn't take effect in the industry until the 1990s.

I'm sure I still have lead in my body from that time.

There were some real characters who worked there. There was Dolly, a gay man who worked as hard as anyone, but during the break periods (we had to take breaks every half hour because of the lead), he'd revert to "His Queenness," flirting with other dudes, using a high voice, and fluttering his eyelids. Nobody seemed to mind. He was one of the crew, one of us.

There was Popeye, who had muscular forearms like the cartoon character from cutting the top of car batteries all day in the battery-saw section of the plant and picking the batteries up to remove the lead plates.

There were jokesters, storytellers, knuckleheads, radicals, and outright racists. Just like in the rest of the world, only concentrated in a small place.

I even became one of the characters. After every heat, I placed a wire rope sling in the molten lead. Soon after the lead hardened, I'd get a forklift and pick up the lead bullion with the sling and take this to a section of the plant where the lead was stacked. One day, I placed a particularly large wire rope sling in the molten lead inside the cast-iron container. After it hardened, I raised the forks of the forklift to their highest level to clear the bullion for transport. I drove around carefully but failed to see the top of the forks strike the overhead water piping, busting them and spraying gallons of water all over the place.

I never heard the end of it, becoming the butt of jokes when a safety instructor one weekend used this incident to demonstrate what *not* to do.

Camila and I were becoming serious fast. I remember the first dance we went to as a couple, sponsored by MEChA at Cal State L.A. We were on the dance floor, swaying to a slow number. Camila held on to me, smelling lovely, her arms around my neck, my arms around her waist. Suddenly she whispered in my ear, "I think I like you."

This was the way it should be. I had feelings for Camila I'd never had for anyone else. Sometimes I came into the high school for lunch, before security prohibited this due to gang violence. I drove up in a ten-wheeled, double-clutch truck (I worked briefly as a driver for a lamp factory). I held Camila's hand as we sat on a graffiti-carved bench, carrying on with small talk, stealing kisses.

Soon Camila and I began addressing our future. Somehow the topic turned to our getting married. This sounded good to me, just what I needed to begin a new life, a family, to be on track to something healthy and correct—key to mending after a formerly noxious existence.

One of Camila's favorite teachers was a white woman named Miss Daniels. Miss Daniels had a particular interest in getting Camila out of the poor barrio life. She saw potential in her. Camila was an honor student, active in theater, in community service. I could see why Miss Daniels took a liking to her.

One day, Camila, in her excitement, told Miss Daniels that we were thinking of getting married. For some reason, Miss Daniels went off. She sat Camila down and sternly told her not to get married. Camila got confused, bothered. So a day or so later I went to the school to talk to Miss Daniels. She gave me a dirty look as soon as I walked into the classroom.

"Miss Daniels," I said, "I assure you my intentions are honorable with Camila. I'll take good care of her. I'll work and help us have a good family."

Convincing words, I thought. But Miss Daniels wasn't having it.

"No, you're just going to ruin her life, her chances," Miss Daniels said. "She's smart, she's pretty. She should get out into the world and make something of herself. Do you know how many young women I know in East L.A. who've gotten married, pregnant, or ended up in dead-end jobs? They're lost, wasting their lives away. No, don't do that to Camila. You should both stop this talk about marriage."

"Listen, miss," I answered. "Young people get married in the barrio all the time. Life isn't going to stop. You shouldn't worry about this."

Miss Daniels became enraged.

"What about her schooling, her future?"

"This doesn't have to stop if we're married," I retorted, holding my own. "She can go to school. She can still do what she wants. We just want to take the next step as a couple. We're in love."

"Love, what do you know about love?" Miss Daniels spat back.

The truth is, I got what Miss Daniels was arguing. Women were being funneled into a nothing life all the time, even when they were smarter than guys. Many would then lose their shape, their beauty, their personal authority—and they'd never truly be alive after that. Their silences were deafening. Especially in working-class neighborhoods, especially in East L.A.

But Miss Daniels's anger and belittling of our desires wasn't helping.

How dare Miss Daniels think she could control Camila's life? She could counsel her. She could guide her, and even, with respect, challenge her. But the way she came at Camila and me only got me angry.

Camila at the time represented my salvation. I felt Miss Daniels was stepping into my happiness, trying to stop it cold. Young and impulsive, I began to control something that was not in my hands to control. I reverted to a kind of gangster stance. I had to force things to happen or they wouldn't happen at all. I couldn't let anyone stop me from being with Camila.

Camila was only two months out of high school, a month after turning eighteen, when we married in August 1974. I was barely twenty. The ceremony was at the Guadalupe Church on Hazard Avenue.

When I asked Camila to marry me, I went to Hortencia and, in my best Spanish, asked her for Camila's hand. Hortencia by then had taken a liking to me and she agreed.

It was a typical East L.A. wedding. We had a caravan of lowrider cars from a car club that had cousins as members from both our families. I wore a black velvet tuxedo and stood next to chiffon-laden bridesmaids and uncomfortable formally attired ushers waiting for the caravan with the bride-to-be.

Although I had not set foot in a Catholic church in years, it seemed appropriate to the new stage of life I was entering. I was being reeled in, tying the knot, getting anchored—all the holding metaphors that are about either getting caught in a web or getting a grip on the world.

Camila arrived late—the pinstriped and hydraulic-pumped cars were being washed. Also one of my ushers got busted and couldn't be in the wedding. I found a substitute in Tony. Then Camila's brother, with the wedding rings, had yet to show up. And the priest—who had an assembly line of weddings that day—threatened to push us aside for the next couple.

This was nothing compared to the day before when Camila and

I had fought about the bridesmaids' dresses and the escorts' tuxedos. I also discovered something about Camila: I was immature, that's a given, but emotionally she was a child.

This hit me as we argued—I almost called it off. We were leaving with our wedding outfits on downtown L.A.'s Broadway Street. I don't even remember why, but before you know it, Camila and I were yelling in the street, a crowded and already noisy street. Simply down each other's throats. She had a way of belittling people when she couldn't reason with them. She brought in other issues, other arguments, past reproaches. I had more life experience and could be more reasonable, but Camila could swat this aside with inane points, dramatic accusations, manipulations. She, more than anyone I knew, could get under my skin.

We made up that night or I wouldn't have gone to my own wedding.

The moment when the heaviness of what I was doing fell on me was as I knelt in front of the altar, Camila at my side, and I wondered— *Should I really be getting married? Maybe I should wait. Have more long-range girlfriends.* I ended up marrying the first decent person I found, feeling fortunate that I had someone at a young age, but still wondering, always wondering: *Maybe it was too fast. Maybe Miss Daniels was right.*

No matter, in minutes it was a moot point. I looked over and saw the most appealing woman I could imagine—gorgeous, enticing, and, in my mind, in love with me. I'd be crazy not to marry her. We voiced our vows. The rings—which had finally arrived—were exchanged. The priest, cagey and harried, pronounced us man and wife. We stepped back down the aisle with people smiling, cameras flashing.

If I had misgivings, it was too late.

I called it newlywed poor. We moved into the Florencia barrio of South Los Angeles. This destitute area had fabrication plants in and around the housing and railroad tracks. It was also home to one of the oldest and largest Chicano gangs in the city—La Florencia. The apartment we had was a one bedroom situated behind an old 1920s wood Victorian with several Mexican families occupying it.

Just before I got married, I also had to leave the lead foundry, due to the danger of lead poisoning my friends warned me about. They also worried I'd be maimed for life. I finally agreed to quit, even though I loved the work—it was fast, hard, and exciting. Now I had to go around the city looking for another job, which was often as much work as work itself.

I searched for employment every morning. I preferred to be working rather than unemployed again, worried about the idleness this produced. I walked from one factory and warehouse to another, sometimes getting swollen feet and blisters in the hot sun. Soon I found myself putting lies on the applications, like about my arrests and conviction. I didn't have too many skills, so I pretended I did. So what if I'd never worked a lathe machine or table saw? I put down that I had, and if hired, I'd figure it out. Of course, my lies got the better of me when I stared at a relatively complicated machine as other workers waited for me to get started. They kicked me back to the curb as soon as my deception got exposed. But this was worth it if it meant I might actually get a job.

One time a pickle factory hired me as an electrician. The first day the manager assigned me to rewire a workshed. I had a little knowledge of this. So I measured what I needed. I stretched out lengths of wire. I cut conduit pipe to size. I figured out the positive and ground lines, putting everything in place in the outlet. The problem was I failed to file the ends of the conduit. The burrs ended up cutting the wire, exposing it and shorting the whole setup. I also forgot to turn off the power—a good electrician knows this is rule number one.

I went up an aluminum ladder to change the wire and inadvertently touched the exposed wire and got electrocuted—I fell off, onto my backside. I wasn't hurt too badly, but, needless to say, I was out on the street again.

Camila also looked for work on assembly lines, in light industry, in all-night diners as a waitress. We woke up early to hit the streets.

I remember the morning love songs on the alarm radio that popped us out of bed. How sexy and beautiful Camila was on those days—her skin, her eyes, and her incredible lips. When she smiled the whole world bloomed. She used to sleep with an arm and leg draped across my body and I felt complete there.

My homeless nights, my heroin days, the long periods without a woman, without friends, without family, were beginning to feel like long-lost memories. Except there were times when I woke up distraught, anxious. There were times when a fury burst out of me. Anything could trigger it. A certain look. Someone not paying attention to me or talking in an irritating tone.

Camila didn't know what to make of my behavior. I'd yell at her for no good reason, throw a face cloth at her while she was bathing. I didn't hit her with my fists. But I'd get close. She'd say something that would be normal for anyone else to say, but for me it was an affront. I was paranoid. On edge. I didn't know it then, but I was experiencing post-traumatic stress disorder. The effects of my street life hadn't totally left me. I was hurting yet asleep to my pain. It came for me at the strangest times: in the middle of the night, at the dinner table, glancing sideways from a doorway.

In the midst of my job-searching adventures, I got accepted into the Millwright Apprentice Program of the Brotherhood of Carpenters union under a Mexican/Native American consent decree. There were quotas so I barely got in before the openings were closed. For decades they had allowed only whites in those jobs. This program gave me a chance to attend local community colleges for the carpenter and mill-wright trades. It also allowed me to serve as an apprentice with journey-man millwrights on actual job sites.

The process of opening up these jobs involved protests and campaigns on the part of black and brown organizers over many years. We were denied opportunities that others for generations took for granted. Men of all races, ethnicities, and classes fought in Vietnam. Because of the draft, however, a large number of black, brown, and Native American soldiers were killed or wounded. Now it was our obligation to continue the struggle of those before us who had been killed, jailed, and derailed.

A millwright is a highly specialized mechanic who builds, rigs, and repairs machinery in mills, in smelters, on construction sites, and in factories. As an apprentice, I worked in water treatment plants, in manufacturing plants, in refineries, installing or dismantling machines, or as part of repair teams in existing plants like GM's auto plant in South Gate. When a plant retooled, millwrights were brought in as needed.

This was all new to me. I was okay with the basic tools, helped by what I learned at St. Regis and National Lead. But these skilled positions demanded a sound foundation in geometry, heavier tools (large wrenches, channel locks, ball-peen hammers) as well as delicate measuring instruments like micrometers and dial indicators.

However, this sudden admission of people of color to the skilled trades was not welcomed. We were often despised and relegated to the most menial work. I'd be assigned a job through the carpenter's union hall with a journeyman. The journeymen were white. Now, there were some decent white journeymen. Not all were racists. But I knew a few who were dog asses.

On one construction assignment they had me carry large steel beams up and down several floors of a work site. This wouldn't have been so bad, but they had this tall, young white dude order me around. He didn't talk to me with any respect. When I sat for a break, he was told to get me back to work. When I finished one job, he'd have another one at the ready. I worked as hard and as fast as I could, but it was never good enough.

I finally had it when we were instructed to tow around a large I-beam. The young dude was in front holding one end of the beam. But the full weight fell on me since he was almost a foot taller. We walked around with that beam, which we carried up scaffolding and stairs, my shoulder hurting, my face contorting, but I didn't say anything until it was over. Then I turned toward the dude.

"Don't ever fuck with me again," I said.

"What are you talking about?" he responded with a smirk on his face. "I didn't do anything."

"You may not like me, but I'm not stupid." I stared at him hard—I didn't care if he was big or not.

"Ah, you're just a baby," he dared to say, but he stopped looking at me.

The other workers stood around but did nothing. That's when I punched the dude in the face. He shouldn't have stopped looking at me. He fell like a tall tree after the ax, straight back. I then pounced on him before he got up and gathered his senses. The others yelled, but nobody pulled me off. I stood up with bloody fists and walked off the site.

I almost lost my apprenticeship. I related to the site boss all that led up to the incident. They were trying to set me up and I argued my case. Finally, they decided to give me another chance. One thing I learned, even if it cost me—I had to stand up to these guys. They'd learn to respect me one way or another. I wasn't going to be mincemeat for any of them.

Meanwhile, word about what I did made the rounds. When I showed up to the next job and millwright classes, the sneers, inside jokes, and people just plain ignoring me stopped. I let down my guard and felt some relief. But I should've known better. I should've known it wasn't over.

The apprenticeship program one day assigned me to a bottling plant where giant machines and what seemed like miles of rollers and tracks were being installed. I thought this would be a job where I could really learn the millwright's craft.

This time I had an older white journeyman to work with named Steve. He hardly said a word to me. So I didn't say much either. "Come here," "Do this," "Hold that"—simple commands were all Steve uttered. I watched what Steve did, rigging with wire rope and signaling overhead cranes where to put things and how. I tried to extrapolate as much knowledge as I could with a minimum of conversation. If you asked these guys questions, they looked at you as if you were E.T. on crack.

I didn't know they still had it in for me. It turned out that Steve knew the guy I'd beat up—he was a friend of the dude's dad or something. They should never have assigned me to Steve.

One day, Steve asked me to work with him on an arc-welding job. I had never done this before. I knew about acetylene torches and how to cut metal, using goggles to protect the eyes from sparks. But arc welding used a power supply box to create an electric arc between an electrode and metal to melt the metal at the welding point. This created a strong bond that proved useful in high-end building and mechanical work.

Steve had me hold pieces of metal he then welded together. However, he had a full arc-welding mask and a leather coat over his torso and arms—the electric arc was a powerful current that could burn skin and destroy eyesight. I didn't know this and Steve failed to tell me. I held the metal in my gloved hands and looked at the arc's intense spark, not thinking much about it.

After a few hours, lunchtime arrived. Soon I felt inklings of pain. Lint, dust, even just air struck my eyes and caused them to burn. I didn't know what was going on at first, but then I thought about the electric arc and how I stood there without protection. I hated to say anything about this, but it became unbearable. I stepped up to Steve and told him what I was going through. He asked if I had stared at the arc with unprotected eyes.

"Yeah, Steve, you were there. You saw me looking at it," I responded.

"You shouldn't have done that—this will damage your eyes," he answered, knowing full well that I didn't know.

"Why didn't you tell me? You stood there the whole time and didn't say a word."

"Hey, you should have known this already. How am I supposed to figure out what you know or don't know?"

I told the site boss I had to go to the hospital. He didn't question me. He didn't even offer to call an ambulance. I ended up driving to a nearby clinic, having a hard time seeing the road since my eyes were now in full-throttle pain. The electric arc had burned off the lubrication. This made my eyes supersensitive to everything. By the time the doctor ended up seeing me, I couldn't keep my eyes open.

It took around a week before my eyes were back to normal, fully lubricated. It was a price to pay for daring to enter the skilled trades, for daring to find a better way of life, for daring to break the obstructions that held back generations of Mexicans and blacks.

I thought about this as I lay my head on Camila's lap one night in front of the TV, bandages over my eyes, as she stroked my face. I heard the vacuum-tube voices and music, my wife's melodious breathing, the sounds of the street pressing against the windows. And I sensed my anger rising.

Chapter Four

Soon the first few months Camila and I had together developed into despair on the fast track: unemployment, tons of political work, then coming back to our drab apartment and pretending we weren't around when the landlord knocked for the rent.

We argued a lot.

"What are you doing?" I asked one hot day after coming home from job searching.

"I'm cooking, what do you think I'm doing?"

What she was doing was frying the minute pieces of meat from a can of soup in a pan. All you had to do was heat the soup, but she felt the meat had to be cooked separately. A minor matter. But I was too tired and mean to let this go. I looked at her like she was crazy. I may have called her that. She took this badly, of course. We yelled at each other. Then I waved my arm and struck Camila on her shoulder. Really slightly. That's when the drama escalated.

"You hit me," she yelled.

"N-no I didn't—it was an accident," I stammered.

Camila didn't see it that way. To her, I struck her. I had broken a law of revolutionary politics—don't ever strike a woman, don't put her down, don't belittle her. I argued with her, but now I was a "wife beater." Bullshit. But Camila did what she often did—exaggerated the whole thing. She rushed out of the house, dropping the apron and straightening her hair on the way out, and ran down the street, yelling that I hit her. Neighbors stuck their heads out of windows, readily accepting Camila's story.

Later the community elders had a sit-down with me about nonviolence and the importance of women in the world and the movement. I agreed with that. I was no woman beater. I never did that—and I never liked others who did that either. Even in my most rage-filled moments, and I'd had many, I wouldn't lift a hand against a woman.

On the other hand, I was emotionally abusive, controlling. I pushed too hard, too fast. Camila had to duck for cover when I got into combat mode. This would eventually rip into our young love, a love that also tried to blossom with little water, like millions of other couples starting out with no money, no security, lots of outside stress.

Looking back I can see why we had such a topsy-turvy relationship. This would have been a shame except that we often made up, kissed with tears in our eyes, and made love. Our moods were always on a high or low flame, hardly ever in between. We were erratic: One minute I pinched her booty and the next minute I wanted to wring her neck.

The lack of money didn't help.

Soon enough, I began to outline armed robberies in my head. This was something I knew about. I'd done a few heists with homies at convenience stores or food stands, with a gun in hand, held to the head of clerks and counter men. Knowing I'd shoot them if they resisted. I tried not to think about this anymore, but when times were tight, my thoughts just went there. I didn't tell Camila. She wasn't about this. This was something I'd have to do myself. Just do one job. Bring home some dough. *Where'd you get this?* Camila would ask. *I got lucky at a friend's poker game,* I'd respond. Just lie.

Then one day, I ended up at the Bethlehem Steel Plant's hiring hall in Maywood. I heard from others that the steel mill was looking for a new crop of employees. This was a big deal in the Southeast, South, and East L.A. neighborhoods. Bethlehem Steel was one of the key plants, like the plants in the auto, tire, aluminum, brass, defense, meatpacking, garment, shipyard, cannery, and aerospace industries that were all over L.A.'s almost five-hundred-square-mile sprawl.

That day I lined up behind hundreds of dudes, most young like me—former dopers and gang members, bikers and lowriders, farmers' sons and perennial factory heads. Also a few older guys with tools in tow, in worn-out work clothes, spitting crud on the sidewalk. All races, all types. Men.

I filled out the application form, making sure I didn't include the jobs I had gotten fired from or into a fight at. With so many people applying for work, I felt this was going to be a waste of time. While I sat waiting I kept going over a possible robbery in my head. That would be exciting. I almost didn't want this job.

Then I heard my name on the intercom.

A personnel officer scrutinized my application, looking at me every couple of minutes. He was dressed in a wrinkled white shirt and plain-colored tie. I looked around and noticed nothing but white people behind the desks, although most of those applying were people of color. This dude searched my face. My hands. My answers on the form. A few of my previous jobs showed promise, especially my time in the mill-wright's apprenticeship program.

"We got some openings we think you'd qualify for," White Shirt and Tie said. "It requires mechanical aptitude. You seem to have this. Are you interested?"

"What do I have to do?"

"The position I'm thinking about is called 'oiler-greaser,'" the dude replied. "You'll work in the repair unit, oiling and greasing all the machines throughout the plant, including overhead and scrap yard cranes."

I didn't like it already. The "oiler-greaser" part sounded derogatory and I could already see the tons of grease and oil I'd have to wade through. I didn't want this job. But the dude insisted—he had quotas to fill.

"The good thing is that in a short time you'll be eligible for our in-plant millwright training program," he said, continuing. "We have our own millwrights and skilled craft employees. It so happens we have a consent decree with the United Steelworkers of America to bring a certain number of minorities into these trades. The pay is great. The benefits are great. What do you say?"

What could I say? Camila and I were drowning in unpaid bills. Utility companies were threatening to cut off our gas and lights. The marshals were probably already amassing at our door to remove us from the abode. I said yes. They still had to check out my jobs, my record, other details. Perhaps they'd discover my lies and I'd be back looking for work. But, to my surprise, I soon got called to come in for an orientation. They probably didn't bother to check anything. They needed these quotas filled, and this was good. We'd have been on skid row if it weren't for those darn consent decrees.

Camila and I moved into a cottage among a row of cottages that faced each other in another Florence neighborhood. It was a one-bedroom, one-bath matchbox. The place needed work. I redid the plumbing in the bathroom. The landlords, an old Mexican couple, decided we were okay. They reduced our rent when I agreed to fix whatever needed fixing. My work skills proved to be handy over the years.

Also Camila had a surprise for me: She was pregnant. Yes, we fought often, but we also made up. A baby. Everything seemed to fall into place as soon as I heard this. A baby. My baby. My dream.

Working at the steel mill was a fiery initiation — heat, racket, exhaustion, drinking, people killed. This was Bethlehem, an icon in industrial L.A. Many generations had already lived, worked, and died with steel in their blood. I was hired in the fall of 1974, a couple of months after getting married. I began to mull over the generations that would follow me.

Three shifts with thousands of workers kept Bethlehem's L.A. plant moving. I entered the mill's high gates with a metal identification plate on my key chain. This got me a time sheet with my name and employee number. I was able to get paid every two weeks, the kind of pay people like me only imagined.

My job was to enter every nook and cranny of the greasy monster machines, forges, furnaces, rolling mills, and pumps armed with a grease gun and copper piping day in and day out, eight hours a day, and make sure every fitting, button, oil line, roller, and gear was properly oiled and greased. This was the promised oiler-greaser job.

But the danger level—that was another matter.

We placed locks on the electrical switches to all the machines, locks with our names and employee numbers on them to inform others who was working where. No one could pull those switches on without breaking the locks. We had to go deep into pits, like below the forging mills, which had miles of grease and slag from the red-hot ingots of steel that were rolled through.

We often climbed eighty feet up the electric furnaces—most of which were about three hundred degrees despite hours of cooling down. To grease what they called the "eccentric" wheels of the ingot cranes, a fellow worker, whether he liked you or not, had to hold on to your feet as you stretched out under railings, praying that this dude wouldn't let you go by accident or a sour disposition.

Camila's water busted one night at home while we sat around the living room. She felt the warm stream run down her leg. "It's time," she yelled. I hesitated for a bit, like "What time?" I was such an idiot.

Once I realized what was happening, I jumped up. "It's time, man, get your bag, I'll get the car . . . where are the directions?" I was a mess. Camila remained focused. We had actually driven out to the hospital— located a few miles southeast of us—a couple of times to get familiar with the route. The clinic where she was being taken care of was in another direction. I was so nervous, I started to drive her to the clinic.

"No, Louie, we're going to the hospital," Camila gently reminded me. "It's *time*—that means the real thing. This is it."

This child, with my wife, Camila, now filled me with joy, with visions of a father walking hand in hand with a young son. I felt a strong link, beginning with the baby's first stages of life inside its mother.

Under the Bethlehem health plan, everything was covered: the doctor visits, the medicines, the shots (Camila had iron-deficiency anemia), the Lamaze classes, and everything at the hospital. I mean everything. I had to pay for the TV and phone calls, which amounted to around $4. This particular hospital had a birthing room with wood drawers that mothers pulled out to hold their babies and pushed back into a nursery when they got tired. I thought this was the coolest thing.

Camila held her own during the labor. We heard a mother-to-be screaming bloody murder down the hall. Not Camila. I tried to make things comfortable. I told lousy jokes. I'd learned card tricks and messed up a few times while demonstrating. Camila was patient, although I'm sure she was annoyed. When it was time for the infant to come out, I was there behind Camila, encouraging her, wiping perspiration off her brow, breathing with her rapidly, and then telling her to push when the doctor told me it was time.

I watched the baby being born as if in a trance. He came out reddish-purple, with a milky substance all over. But he was tiny. I could carry him in one hand. He had a huge bald head and a large tummy. He turned out to be underweight—he was less than five pounds. This was a problem. They had him in an incubator. I provided Camila encouraging words about how this was okay, it was normal, he'd be fine. But inside, I worried. For a couple of days, while Camila rested, they kept him under close watch. He had a hard time latching on to the nipple, but he finally did. Things looked better. When we left the hospital, our baby came home as well.

We named him Ramiro Daniel. It was June 1975.

Ramiro slept so much. One night, with Camila resting, I held him. He had been out for hours. I wonder now if he had symptoms of fetal alcohol syndrome, but there was no way to know at the time. Camila wasn't a drinker like me, but she did drink during the pregnancy. But, again, we had no idea.

As I gazed upon Ramiro, I began to cry. I'm not entirely sure why. It was a mixture of happiness and concern. The boy looked stern, even with closed eyelids, and he had hardly any hair on his head, like an old man. For a few minutes I thought Ramiro wouldn't wake up. I put the infant next to my face and tears streamed down. Even though I had no God to appeal to, I prayed. *Save my son. You can do anything to me, but save Ramiro. He deserves a better life than I ever had. He deserves to be something.*

When there was a new father at Bethlehem, it was as if all the guys had had a baby. There were slaps on the back. People handed out cigars.

Deaths and births, these were the most important happenings in the mill. Yeah, we lived for a payday, for the weekends, for the beer joints. But deaths and births stopped everyone cold.

Something was different about me, too. I began to care, to fret. To call home. Camila was alone at the house taking care of Ramiro. I felt anything could happen. And one day something did: A burglar burst through the front door after breaking the lock. He stopped in the living room facing Camila, who froze there with the baby in her arms. She didn't know what to do but scream. Luckily for her, he panicked and ran off. Neighbors rushed out of their homes. One of them tackled the burglar to the ground. The whole world stood up for Camila and Ramiro.

When I got the news, I couldn't believe it. I thought about my stupid burglaries as a youth. Now I was part of the decent working-class world. The crime world was all around us. But most of the poor there worked hard for their money, even if it didn't go far. I happened to work in the big mill, in a job few managed to obtain. I was no longer a criminal. Planning robberies? That would have to stop. I was now a regular working stiff. Some people may not think much of this, but for me, this was truly making it.

Again, however, like in the construction trades—remember, we were the first people of color to work in the mill's skilled jobs—racism reared its pockmarked face. Mr. Branford was the head of the repair crews during the day, including the oiler-greasers. He didn't seem to like the consent decree and all the blacks and browns coming in. When white kids got hired, he automatically gave them the prime assignments. In a few weeks, they would move up to millwright's apprentices. I stayed on as an oiler-greaser along with other dark-skinned folks.

In time, many of them quit or were pushed out—African-Americans, Chicanos, Puerto Ricans, Native Americans. The mostly white millwrights and shift bosses made our work harder, more unsafe—and they talked to us like we were pieces of crap. I even got to train the newly hired whites to maintain the machines. Then I saw them move up to better-paying positions. I'd still be there in the oil gang, going nowhere.

I stayed so long in that job—three years—that I got to be the best oiler-greaser that mill ever had.

The racial tensions heightened in the plant when jobs were scarce and the company wanted to keep the workers off kilter. Whites were the principal instigators and benefactors. African-Americans and Mexicans were also prejudicial, hard on whites, a few thinking they were better than others. But most of this was in response to the system of racial division that most industries instituted—providing whites with the management jobs and the best-paid skilled work, and having them manage the finances. The lowest-paid and most difficult work got pushed onto blacks and browns.

Yet, as revolutionaries, it was our job to unite black, brown, and white despite these divisions, to turn people toward their class interests, especially among the mill hands. They may have walked into the plant with different-colored skins, but when they exited they were the same color—the color of the dirt, oil, and grease on their faces, clothing, and hands.

Bethlehem Steel was struggling in the mid-1970s, especially on the West Coast. Supposedly this had to do with Japanese imports of better-quality steel: They had the newest equipment, including computer-run mills, and government subsidies. We heard gripes about large union contracts, about environmental cleanups—how the international and domestic demand for steel had fallen.

My first big layoff happened just after Ramiro was born. *Híjole*, what a setback this became. Community leaders also invited Camila and me to move to Pasadena—a good-sized city northeast of L.A.—that had issues with court-ordered integration, a municipal bus strike, and urban redevelopment. Pasadena at the time had a thriving ghetto of African-Americans and Mexicans, with all that entails—poverty, unemployment, crime, but also organization, churches, and leaders.

I only remembered Pasadena from the New Year's Day Rose Parade. Once when I was a boy, my dad woke us all up early in the morning—it was still dark and foggy—and drove us there to find good seats along Colorado Boulevard to watch the parade. Years later, I partied there during the annual affair, drunk and drugged out, meeting girls, getting into fights. Now Camila and I were moving to Pasadena to push forward civic participation and social action.

We also *had* to move. Our once-welcoming landlords started to get into our personal business. The old Mexican couple accused Camila of having men over for sex during the day. She was actually holding meetings with activists. And they claimed we were hosting too many parties. We got into shouting matches with them, even while we packed our stuff and loaded a truck with furniture, appliances, and boxes.

We decided to take the nice curtains these people had in the cottage for the grief they gave us. The couple called the police on us as we were carrying our things into a borrowed truck. After hearing everyone's version of the story, the cops sided with Camila and me.

"They're already leaving—what are you going on about?" one officer told the couple. The landlords fumed and insisted we were up to no good. The cops shrugged and stood around.

We left under the watchful eyes of the police.

The first place in Pasadena we found was also a cottage, in worse shape than the one we left in Florencia. There were six wood-framed cottages facing one another, with a bedroom, a bathroom (and one of those old four-footed, although stained, porcelain tubs), and a small kitchen. The only heat came from a woodstove. The "air conditioner" was an open window or door. An African-American Holy Roller church lay next to the cottages. They often congregated into the wee hours singing, praising, banging tambourines.

Our cottages were filled with Mexicans, largely undocumented. There was a young *cholo* and his girlfriend who lived in the cottage next to us. A family across the way had eight kids in a tiny place like we had. A truck driver, his wife, and their kids lived in one cottage closer to the street.

The first day we moved in, we placed Ramiro in a corner of the bedroom so he'd be safe. He was sound asleep like usual, only a few weeks old. Then we brought in the boxes and a few furniture items. The place was so small it didn't take much to fill it up.

Pooped, Camila and I opened a couple of beer cans and sat down on the creaky wooden floor. But we had forgotten about Ramiro. We realized this when we heard whimpering and couldn't figure out where it was coming from. We got up and started to move boxes around. We finally found him in the corner where we left him. Poor little guy—by then he was crying mad tears. Camila soothed him with a breast and he sucked up the milk like it was his last meal.

Because we had no dresser drawers or closet space, we nailed cardboard boxes to a wall and put our clothes, linens, and towels in them. I also had one of my favorite guns—a sawed-off shotgun—which I placed beneath the bed. Camila knew about this. I couldn't hide it. It was the one armament I kept from my barrio gang days. In my new life, only the shotgun made sense to keep since it was relatively easy to conceal and devastating (you couldn't miss much with the buckshot spread). It was a prized possession at the time.

Being laid off from Bethlehem, I lived on unemployment benefits for a while. I continued to look for other work, but I often stayed with the baby during the day. Ramiro grew quickly. I sat him down on the floor, propped up by stuffed animals and plastic toys. Since he couldn't sit up, he'd eventually fall to one side and then look up at me as if thinking, *What do I do now, Dad?*

We got to know the neighbors. The dirty-faced kids across the way loved to take Ramiro in his baby carriage back and forth through the middle corridor between the cottages. One time I sat on the porch on a warm day and watched as several of the girls, ages five to nine, pushed the carriage, talking in rapid-fire Spanish.

Then I noticed Ramiro making faces, scrunching his eyebrows, and keeping his eyes shut tight. I looked closer and realized that Ramiro's bare feet were scraping the cement walkway. The kids failed to put his feet on a footrest below the carriage. I stopped the girls and looked at the baby's toes. They were bloody. I couldn't believe it. Ramiro didn't cry. He just made faces, as if this was the way things were and he just had to take it. Amazing.

Another time, I took Ramiro to a park on Fair Oaks south of Colorado that at the time was known as "Wino Park"—with *un chingo de* derelicts, junkies, winos. There was a set of swings for infants. I placed

Ramiro on one of them and swung him. Then I sat back on a bench. Nearby on another bench sat a scrappy-looking wrinkled woman. I didn't think much about this. But soon I noticed the woman move closer to the swing set, like she was up to something. I eyed her for a few seconds and then got the notion she was going to grab Ramiro. I pulled the baby off the swing, lifted him to my shoulder, and walked away from the park.

At one point, I volunteered as one of the community organizers for the municipal bus strike. I also assisted a number of teachers in schools where there was an active MEChA student organization. At our home, Camila and I started an activity center with gang and nongang young people. On weekends, we'd play in the park, football, mostly. We'd go to the beach, to the mountains, or in the winter to Frazier Park, about an hour or so away, with snow everywhere. For the first time, I went on a toboggan run down snowy slopes, almost busting my butt.

We also had house meetings, talking about society and the power of organized and educated people to change the world. The youth, mostly Chicano, some black, ate this up. We even held parties where their parents showed up. They saw there were no drugs or booze. We honored the young people's spirits and ideas. Camila and I weren't far removed from these youngsters. I was twenty-one and Camila nineteen.

One night Camila and I were sound asleep, Ramiro in a crib next to us. We were suddenly awakened by loud noises, glass breaking, yelling. I already knew what this was—somebody was getting the living shit kicked out of him. I walked out to the front room and in the dark peered through the window blinds. I barely made out what was happening, but soon realized that three big *vatos locos* were stomping on my next-door neighbor, the *cholo* next door who was always cool with us.

One of the dudes doing the stomping was a gangster they called Samson. I had seen him come in and out of the *cholo's* cottage a few times. They were friends, but this particular night, they weren't. I couldn't just let the *cholo* get beat down like that. I saw Samson wield a bottle and start hitting our neighbor on the head as he lay on the ground. Soon the dude stopped moving, unconscious or dead. I rushed back to the bedroom and retrieved the shotgun. I turned around toward the front door and just then, out of nowhere, Camila stood in front of me.

"No te vayas . . . you ain't leaving, Louie," Camila shouted.

"What are you talking about? I can't let them kill him," I shouted back. "Get out of the way, mujer."

"I'm not moving. You're going to have to shoot me if you want to get through this door."

"Shoot you? Are you kidding? Just move before it's too late."

"I'm not going to let you get mixed up in that shit. You shoot somebody, the police come and they get you. You have a son now. You can't just go out and shoot people. I need you. Ramiro needs you. I can't let you do this. Remember, you don't live alone. You have to think about us too."

Darn if Camila didn't make sense. The adrenaline rush began to wind down. I heard police sirens getting closer. Somebody had called the cops. Sure enough Samson and his boys got arrested. The cholo was taken to a hospital and survived. Why did I need to get into this? The excitement hurried through me like in the old days and I went for the gun. Camila was right. Ramiro was in my life now. I needed to think before I reacted. I had to figure out what was best and safe for my family instead of hastening to battle.

In a few months, we moved again. The slum landlords were ripping off all the tenants in several vecindades, including ours. Because most of these tenants didn't have their U.S. status papers, they were treated badly. We organized a tenants' union to address building violations, unreturned deposits, lack of response to our needs. One family got burned out when their wood heater malfunctioned, forcing them into the streets. When the landlords finally got court approval to get rid of us, we turned on the water in all the bathtubs and flooded their places—we were going, but not without a fight.

Camila and I found a bigger and better place in one of those old homes that Pasadena is famous for. It was a former two-story building that got rehabbed into apartments. Our space had a porch with a painted wood railing where I sat and read. There were flowers, vegetation, and a garden in the front yard. I thought this was what southern-style houses must look like.

Again, as in East L.A., Camila and I became targets of police operatives and informants. During one meeting concerning beatings of young black and brown youths, the police chief and his underlings gave us dirty looks and said things to provoke us. We raised our issues but remained calm. It turned out we had a friend in the police department who got involved with us when we worked with the young people. He knew about our meetings and activities—he actually liked what we were doing. One day, he called me.

"You're being watched."

"What do you mean?" I asked.

"The police department is tracking your moves."

"You sure?"

"Yeah, I shouldn't be telling you this, but I happen to think they're wrong about you guys. You're helping people. You're teaching people. I see how well you work with those kids. But you better be careful."

"Okay, what should we do?"

"Just stay clean. You're not breaking any laws, but don't do anything that will draw the attention of the police," my officer friend advised me. "Also, that dude Tony Prince . . . they know when he comes to Pasadena and when he leaves. He has to be careful, too. Pay your parking tickets. Get your car registered. Don't be out late at night. I don't know what they'll do, but you're definitely on their radar."

One afternoon there was a knock on the door. I opened it and a twenty-two-year-old Chicana named Trini stood there. She had a slender body, long straight hair, smooth skin. She could have been Mediterranean or Middle Eastern, but she was Mexican, naturally good-looking and sweet-natured.

Trini was from the San Fernando Valley and came to buy books. I sold books out of the kitchen pantry on political philosophy, organizing, and other social change topics. This place soon became a mecca for activists, not just in Pasadena but also throughout the L.A. area.

Young people met there. Striking workers. Overworked teachers. Police abuse victims. We were getting known for our community work and study materials.

I recalled Ramiro in his crib, already standing at one year old, looking at us from the bedroom. Trini looked over at him. Ramiro, who still couldn't talk, just smiled. He liked to meet new people.

Trini became our friend. She took part in our organizing committees, even though she lived near California State University, Northridge, where she eventually graduated cum laude. She was active in La Raza Unida Party, in folklórico dance, in MEChA. She was also part of Operation Chicano Teacher, trained to be among the first corps of bilingual teachers to enter L.A.'s schools.

I didn't know this at the time, but Trini suffered for her education and activism. She grew up in a strict but stable family with her mother and father and a total of eleven children in a barrio called Pacoima in the northeast San Fernando Valley.

For a long time the Northeast Valley was known as the "Mexican" side of the valley, although it had a significant African-American population and some whites. This was in contrast with the West Valley, which was highly developed and consisted of mostly European Americans. In the Pacoima community of the Northeast Valley there were federal housing projects, railroad tracks, a brass foundry, and other industry. It had its share of gang and drug violence.

Pacoima's claim to fame was the first Chicano rock and roll star, Ritchie Valens (Richard Steven Valenzuela), who brought the Mexican standard "La Bamba" into the rock world in 1958, transforming the sound of rock music ever since.

Trini's parents grew up in a *pueblito* in Jalisco, Mexico, and crossed the border as farm workers in the California migrant stream. When they settled in Pacoima in the 1950s, Trini's parents made sure their children knew the value of work, study, and family cohesion. With great effort, all her siblings did well in school, refusing to join gangs or use drugs (sadly, one brother accidentally drowned at Rosarito Beach in Mexico when he was sixteen).

But there were still some old-country values that Trini's parents clung to. Like in far too many Mexican households, girls were expected to grow up, get married, have children, mind the home. However, Trini was of that first generation of Chicanas who attended college in critical numbers, who wanted to realize a fuller life of work, creation, and self-development beyond just marriage and children. The mind-set of many traditional Mexican homes clashed against these possibilities. Often the father had the last word, held up by hundreds of years of patriarchy, peonage, and poverty.

Trini didn't do anything wrong. She attended a poor barrio school and excelled. She didn't get into drugs, gangs, or early sex. And because of her grades and good behavior, she was sought as college material, even by Stanford University. Although Trini was grudgingly allowed to attend college, she was not allowed to leave home. By her last year of college, she felt she needed to move out. Trini wanted to immerse herself in study and university life. She raised this with her parents, but they didn't want to hear it. Her father forbade her to leave. She did leave and was summarily disowned.

This was an extremely painful choice. A determined Trini, with the threatened loss of her relationship with her parents, decided to take the leap for her own development as a young woman. She devoted herself full-time to her studies, community work, and career. She was never able to come home again as long as her father forbade it. Trini's siblings were also hurt by this development, but none of them was able to alter their dad's position, a stance that lasted almost twenty years.

Trini became a disciplined, learned person, but she paid a big price for doing so.

Chapter Five

Camila and I then moved to Watts in the neighborhood between the Jordan Downs and the Imperial Courts housing projects. The plan was to concentrate organizational work in this crucial part of town. However, it was hard to leave Pasadena with all the connections we'd made. Others were assigned to follow up, which didn't pan out, and much of our labors bore little fruit.

Despite this, I was okay with moving to Watts. I had lived in and around there as a kid. And it was only a few miles from the steel mill. Camila, on the other hand, often missed her Eastside stomping grounds. With our experiences in Florencia and Pasadena I hoped she felt more at home away from home. But there were many days when I knew she didn't.

The poverty in Watts was extreme and painful. The house Camila and I moved into had two mold-infested bedrooms, a living room, a basement, and hardly a kitchen or bath. A fire had destroyed a house next door, and nobody bothered to clean it up—the blackened wood-frame structure and charred furniture stayed there for years. Abandoned cars filled many a lot and curbside. People stole from each other every day. The housing projects were gang-run and many people were dying in escalating turf wars. At the time there were no grocery stores, cultural centers, or movie houses in Watts—but liquor stores abounded.

In the 1960s and 1970s, Watts was the heart of L.A.'s black community. It was also the city's most intense battleground for social equality. The Watts Rebellion of 1965 was the deadliest and costliest of the many uprisings of the time. There was already an old and active Mexican community in Watts called La Colonia. Mexican railroad workers settled in Watts soon after it was incorporated into Los Angeles in 1926.

Ten years after the '65 upheaval, community leaders were earnestly organizing among the populace. From the time I first got involved in revolutionary work in East L.A., I attended meetings in Watts. Among the people I met there was Nelson Peery, a bricklayer by trade in his midforties.

Nelson was a longtime African-American communist and World War II veteran who also fought in the Philippines' liberation struggle. Nelson lived in Watts with his Chinese-Swedish-American wife, Sue Ying. Before and after the rebellion, they trained a theoretically sound cadre of leaders.

Nelson looked like your callused working-class uncle or local street corner storyteller. He had a beer gut, a black and gray head of hair, and a goatee. He'd actually close his eyes during our talks, as if sleeping, but then open them and answer our many inquiries and misperceptions—he knew exactly what everyone had said.

A word about the people I studied with: They were salt-of-the-earth folk. They looked like America—white, black, brown, red, and yellow. These leaders were mostly women, people of color, and working-class. They embodied the ideals of freedom, social justice, and democracy that this country uniquely contributed to the world, while fighting the empire that the U.S. ruling class was hell-bent on constructing for world dominance. They were independent *and* beholden to all humanity while carrying forward the most radical trends of the U.S. historical process.

And they were into armed struggle. But this wasn't about guns. Their "arms" were ideas, science, music, art, theater, and organization. Nelson personified this more than anyone. He could break down complex ideas in clear and comprehensible ways. He used to say the key to explaining difficult concepts simply was to understand them profoundly.

"Clarity on the burning issues of the day is the most important thing we can offer the American people," he often stated.

Nelson had us all delve into current affairs as well as history.

We opened meetings with clippings from the daily newspapers and magazines. We analyzed the economic/political situation and how to respond in the most effective way possible. This period of growth as mature and serious leaders was difficult—it wasn't for everyone. Many fell by the wayside. I hung in there, despite my agonies in learning.

One facet of Nelson that intrigued me was his speech-making. He often soapboxed on street corners and spoke in storefront church-type halls in the most impoverished sections of town. Twenty to thirty people would show up most of time. Every once in a while a larger presentation brought around two hundred. He had a mastery of facts, of the daily pressures to survive, but he could be funny and grave, in your head and in your heart. He moved like a southern preacher but also like the coolest college professor.

I loved to read, to study, but up to that point I was not a good speaker. The barrio life, the streets and jails, didn't prepare me for that. The less said, the better. The Chicano movement pushed me to become vocal, speaking at student walkouts and rallies. But I was ill at ease, too often pausing to catch a thought, and unable to get a rise out of anybody. But with Nelson, I found a model and mentor. I wanted to do what he did—bring thunder down with words and ideas, be an ocean and a river, and move people to think, learn, organize.

Around the same time as the move, Bethlehem Steel called me back to work, I thought for good this time. The company assigned me to the wire mill as the sole oiler-greaser. I had to maintain every machine in that part of the plant, some difficult, others not. I had computer-generated tasks that I checked off. I had regular rounds to do and had to make any new repairs as well. I was still not asked to be an apprentice. I figured I had to work hard and thoroughly in the wire mill to prove I was ready for the millwright crew.

Camila was working in an assembly plant but quit so she could take care of Ramiro after I returned to the steel mill. For community work, we showed politically charged films on the wall of the house one night a week that drew many of the local residents, both African-American and Mexican. On Saturdays, we had a youth talent day when kids danced, sang songs, jumped rope, and even staged "dozens" battles (spontane-ous well-versed insults between teams, one of the precursor arts of Rap).

It wasn't long before Camila let me know she was pregnant again. This seemed perfect with my job back and a new place to do our com-munity work. By then, Ramiro had become a happy and energetic tod-dler. He got bigger and stronger despite his low birth weight. He loved to wave at strangers. And, taking after Camila, he had the cutest face and brightest eyes.

It was also during this time that I bought myself a 1954 Chevy Bel Air for $800. It needed a lot of work, but I was game. The Bel Air was a popular model for lowriders. My brother as a teen had a 1957 Chevy Bel Air with fins on the back fenders. I helped him work on it in San Gabriel, although once, when I was eleven, I accidentally dropped a transmission he had disconnected on his chest, which could have crushed him. I ran off to avoid a beating. My brother still talks about that incident.

On my days off I worked on the Chevy. It was stock with original seats, visor, skirts, and engine. In those days one could take an engine out of a car and put it back in without much trouble. I removed and rebored that engine to get it into the best shape possible. I put in a kill switch. I washed it every weekend. I even lowered it the old-fashioned way—cutting the springs on the differential over the back tires. The Chevy now became my most prized possession.

Camila appeared jealous of the time I spent on the car. I think she hated having it around. She got on my case about it all the time. I didn't pay any mind to her when it came to the car. If it was a vice, it was one I was willing to have. I didn't neglect my son or our time as a couple. I just loved doting on the Chevy. One day, during one of our regular fights, she finally said it, out of nowhere. Even if it was over-stated, the words stung.

"You love that car more than me!"

Several weeks into the pregnancy, Bethlehem laid me off—again. Bad timing. This meant the new baby had to be born without the company's health plan.

This time Camila applied for food stamps and general relief. She also qualified for a government medical card. For pregnancy checkups she went to the Watts Health Center, which at the time was on 103rd Street—one of the positive outcomes of the Watts Rebellion. We had to do what we could to make it with a small child and a new one on the way.

One day a fellow organizer came up with an idea. The battle for school integration and having a say in the education of our kids was heating up in Los Angeles. One of the old-guard school board members, closed off to our communities, was up for reelection. Our friend proposed to Nelson and other leaders that I run for a school board seat against this dude. We needed a more vocal presence in the community battles, especially from places like Watts. I could campaign on a program that most of the community was already fighting for but also bring in some longer-range substantial concerns. The fact was class and race were dominant factors in determining whether someone received a decent education or not.

I would be the only working-class school board member—and only the second Chicano—if by any chance I should win.

I agreed to run, not that I had a clue what campaigning was about. This was also a political risk—I became part of a "Vote Communist" electoral campaign, which also took place in cities like San Francisco, Detroit, and New York City. Getting on the ballot took a court battle: A San Francisco-based case involving whether communists could run for public office was won based on First Amendment rights. The local press mentioned me in their pieces.

I didn't think twice about repercussions. I liked the concept of having a politically marginalized Chicano steelworker from Watts speak for the millions not being represented or heard. Eighteen candidates signed up. I put in $1,000 with the help of others and filled out the paperwork. I asked Tony to be my campaign manager.

We rented offices next to the railroad tracks in the Southeast L.A. city of Huntington Park, not far from my Watts home (and near the Florencia barrio I once lived in). A young Chicana helped with the phones. With hardly a prayer we began the campaign.

The L.A. school board race was citywide and beyond, not in districts as they are now. This meant we had to travel the wide expanse of the Los

Angeles Unified School District, which also included cities and communities outside of L.A. I'm talking about a lot of ground to cover.

Now, someone might think it was bizarre for a community-based organizer like me to run for school board in the second-largest school district in the United States. But this is L.A., man. Nothing's strange here. For example, here were a few of the candidates: A prim and proper teacher with the profile of a bird—"Miss Birdface." There was "the Sergeant," a crew-cut tough-talking police officer who pushed for safety in the schools. Then there was the prerequisite Nazi, who often showed up at events with a bullhorn, as well as a former student representing the youth vote. In addition, there was the elegant anti-busing lady from the Valley who actually believed her interests weren't racist (at least the Nazi was up-front about his). And, of course, the incumbent who'd held this seat for years, with receding hairline, politician's paunch, and very little patience for the rest of us—he was a shoo-in for reelection so he rarely showed up for candidate nights or interviews.

For once, I seemed to be the "normal" guy.

Still, Tony and I made quite a spectacle driving from one candidates' meeting to another in a lowered red 1954 Chevy Bel Air. Most of these meetings were in the well-off Westside and Valley enclaves. No barrio or ghetto meetings were organized. We changed that when we got a Watts middle school to open up one evening for the candidates. I didn't think anyone would show. Interestingly almost all of the main candidates made it—despite long-held fears that Watts was dangerous to whites.

Of course, something was bound to happen: As the panel of candidates talked and answered questions from the audience, somebody rushed into the school's auditorium to announce cars had been broken into. Sure enough, two or three of the other candidates' vehicles had busted windows, including a limousine, although not my Chevy. I felt bad, but this is what we went through on a daily basis in Watts. They got a taste of something they didn't often experience in their highly secured fancy homes and gated communities.

One of the candidates even accused me of arranging this.

I also attended a West Valley house meeting in a predominantly affluent Jewish community. There were snacks in the living room as the candidates took seats on couches and sofas. Guests stood around to listen. I tried to make my speeches sensible, full of facts and passion but not over the top.

That particular day the Nazi showed up with a bow tie, an amplifier, and a microphone. When it was his turn to speak, he pushed up the volume and began to scare the bejesus out of the guests—talking about how African-Americans, Mexicans, and Jews were destroying the American way of life. I was flabbergasted nobody attacked him. This was polite society. But you could see the upturned eyebrows.

In time people began to ask me more questions than the other candidates. I also did my homework, researching topics so I knew what I was talking about. For instance, at a meeting downtown the elegant Valley lady railed against bilingual education.

"Mexicans are the only ones who've ever demanded bilingual education," she declared. "But they're not special. Nobody else gets this. My grandparents were immigrants from Eastern Europe and they had to learn English like everybody else—the hard way. They weren't given any privileges or programs. Mexicans shouldn't be treated any differently. Who do they think they are?"

Then it was my turn to speak.

"I have to respectfully disagree with the statement that only Mexicans want bilingual education. It turns out the first bilingual education programs were among German immigrants in the 1800s. The Chinese were some of the first to struggle for bilingual education in public schools in this century. We should also note that in the Valley—where my opponent presently resides—Vietnamese and Laotian refugees are being taught in their languages with public funds as we speak."

People applauded. The Valley lady had no response to this.

Also the fact that I was Mexican with relatively good English skills seemed odd to some of the audiences—people actually thought all Mexicans spoke only Spanish.

More and more people listened, however, as I articulated in the best terms possible our plight, but also how we could be fair for everyone. Education for most whites was being pushed down because the education for African-Americans and Mexicans was so bad. I argued that lifting it up for everyone helped whites as well. This wasn't liberal politics, and it wasn't totally against conservative politics (Nelson often said we were more conservative than liberal but always for revolution).

I even seemed to get the Sergeant on my side. Once at an auditorium where the candidates were to speak, Tony and I stepped outside to get soft drinks and didn't pay attention to the time. The Sergeant went around to find us so I wouldn't miss the introductions. Perhaps, compared to the Nazi and others, the Sergeant thought I was a breath of fresh air.

I actually liked the former student, who seemed to be a sincere young man. He'd get up onstage in a nice suit, announcing how he had spent hours working on his notes. Then he'd chuck them so he could "speak from the heart." Tony got suspicious one day and retrieved the paper with the alleged notes. The paper was blank.

Overall the campaign was fun. Tony and I met interesting people wherever we went. Most were okay that I was radical. We received support from the black and brown areas—as well as among poor and progressive whites. People came by our small office to help. One newspaper article even seemed favorable to our cause.

But we had a couple of difficult turns. At one event on the Westside, someone handed me a written question that said, "Why don't you go back to where you came from?"

I could have ignored it, but instead I stood up, read the question aloud, and said, "I'd be glad to go back to where I came from—anybody willing to spring for a ticket to Texas?"

And once we had a run-in with the Ku Klux Klan in the Valley—the KKK were active in those days in mostly middle-class white communities. They sat in the back of the auditorium as everyone else patiently heard from the candidates. They carried antibusing and antibilingual education signs. They heavily applauded the Nazi. The more liberal candidates hardly said anything and quickly took their seats. They were scared. So when I got up I didn't back down. I talked about quality education for everyone, regardless of race. How busing wasn't the whole answer but a major first step. And how we needed bilingual education and sustainability in the poorest schools. The KKKers abruptly stood up, yelled out racist slurs, and walked out.

I looked at the audience and remarked, "Good, I didn't come here to talk to them anyway. It's you I want to address—the people whose children are most affected by the failure of our schools."

This went over well with the remaining participants. However, when Tony and I returned to the Chevy, one of the KKK members had placed a death threat note under the windshield wiper.

In the end, after several months, I cleared up many misconceptions, eased many fears. Of course, we didn't have the funds to wage a major campaign in such a large area. I had no fancy brochures or mailers or lawn signs or TV and radio ads. We had a few cream-colored offset flyers. And my voice.

In the election, I received the second-lowest votes of the eighteen candidates. Still, this amounted to 22,500 ballots. Also Tony and I later checked the numbers and discovered we actually won precincts in three communities—East L.A., Watts, and, to our surprise, the West San Fernando Valley.

Soon after the end of the school board campaign, Andrea Victoria was born in late April 1977. For the birth, the Watts Health Center assigned Camila to a hospital in Gardena, one of those bedroom communities adjacent to South L.A.

I witnessed Andrea's entrance into the world, which was faster than Ramiro's but no less miraculous. She came out with a full head of hair that stood straight up on her head, at an adequate weight, round and bouncy. She had slanted eyes, like her mother, and looked like an Inuit baby. The only issue was jaundice—her skin was yellow due to liver complications. The hospital held on to her a little while, but soon we were able to bring the baby girl home to meet her brother. They were only a year and ten months apart.

That spring was joyous. Being a father seemed to fit me. I loved holding the babies, taking them to parks, to shop, or just watching TV. They were good children. On a nice day, I'd take Andrea to the yard and put her belly-down on a blanket, where she took in the new world with fresh infant eyes. Ramiro was kind to her. He was no longer the one and only, but he didn't seem to mind.

Camila was worn out, but again as with Ramiro she quickly lost the pregnancy weight and got back to her nice full-figured body. With the babies I fell in love with her all over again.

I also returned to Bethlehem Steel. This time, finally, the company moved me into their apprenticeship program, with higher pay and more hours. The mill also clobbered me with rotating shifts—working days one week, nights another week, then afternoons the next. This was an ass kicker to get used to. But it was proof I had moved up.

My assignment was to assist the journeyman millwrights on the toughest, noisiest, and most complicated sections of the plant. I learned the meaning of real mechanical labor. We had to repair and replace what was needed even as the furnaces melted the scrap metal or forges pounded the ingots into sheets, rods, or beams. On repair days, we tore things up—big machines, cranes, and the furnaces themselves.

Every once in a while the furnaces needed to be rebricked, rewired, and repiped due to the damage caused when they were fired up. Bricklayers, electricians, and millwrights worked side by side on those days to get everything ready for production. If we needed to work double shifts—sixteen hours in one day—we'd do that. No matter how tired I may have been, I still volunteered to work a double—you got double pay on double shifts. Of course, this kept me away from home much too often. Sometimes, I'd barely get out of a shift, make it to the nearest bar to hang out with other mill hands, then end up back in the plant, not going home at all.

Something was also happening with Camila. Perhaps it was postpartum stress. Perhaps it was my absence from home. She became hard to deal with, arguing petty points. This also brought out the worst in me. I also noticed she liked to dress up and go to parties and dances: *pachangeando*. She loved to laugh, be with friends, boogie. The happiest I ever saw her was when she partied. When she danced.

During the day when I worked nights or afternoons, everything had to be quiet and totally dark so I could sleep. We put aluminum foil on the windows to keep the sunlight out. We finally had money for bills and nice extra things, but we weren't good at making ends meet. I didn't feel we were doing all that much better.

My Chevy got neglected. I had problems with the solenoid and other parts and didn't have time to take care of these. The Chevy sat in the yard like many old cars in Watts. We did get a new VW, topaz in color, which Camila used when I didn't need it for work. Many times she'd drop me off at work if the hours were decent.

Early one morning, Camila and I awoke to a loud crunch of metal and glass. A drunk had fallen asleep and crashed into our new VW Bug parked in the street, crushing it between a pickup truck and his car. I put pants and a shirt on and ran outside but then stopped. The Bug was compressed like an accordion. When I went to check on the guy, he was dazed, with an expression like "What happened?" Although bleeding from the forehead, he tried to start the car to pull out and drive off, but part of his vehicle was stuck to the back of the Bug. He wasn't going anywhere.

Police arrived and arrested the dude. He had empty hard-liquor bottles in the front seat. They also arranged for his car to be detached from mine and towed. An officer stayed behind to get a report. Everything was fine until one of our neighbors, an older African-American woman, asked me in Spanish what was going on (over time many African-Americans in Watts picked up the language). But the white cop went off on her.

"Hey, speak English!" he shouted.

"Officer, she's my neighbor. We're friends. We're just talking here," I said.

"Well, don't talk Spanish around me." He looked at me with disdain. "I don't know what she's saying."

The woman and I acknowledged with our eyes what a racist asshole he was.

The Bug was totaled. In the meantime, the auto shop lent us a 1968 Chevy Impala for a couple of days while the adjusters determined damages. The first night the Impala was parked in the yard somebody stole the damn thing.

Our insurance company just *loved* us.

The dude wore a large Pendleton flannel shirt, baggy starched khaki pants, and a dark blue beanie cap down over his eyebrows. He stood on the front porch and knocked. I opened the door with baby Andrea in my arms. He looked at me hard, goatee and *pinto* mustache covering his mouth. I didn't recognize him. Then he smiled.

"*Órale*, homes," he said, a couple of missing teeth flashing back.

I then realized who it was but couldn't believe it. It was Chicharrón. My old hang dog from Lomas. I hadn't seen him in five years or so, about a year before I left that life. That was when Chicharrón and a couple other homeboys were arrested for the murder of a rival gang member. Chicharrón was seventeen at the time. He was given prison time in the California Youth Authority—allowing him to get out before his twenty-fifth birthday. He was now on YA parole.

I invited Chicharrón inside. Camila stepped out of the kitchen and stared at him, expressionless. He had a toothbrush he used to comb his thick mustache. His dark face had a spiderweb tattoo on the side of one eye and a *pachuco* cross below the other eye. He extended a heavily tattooed hand to Camila, who took it reluctantly. I told him to sit down. Ramiro toddled by, friendly as always.

Soon we related stories—of the barrio gangster life, the drugs, shootings, robberies, but also funny things like the time we snuck into a convent boardinghouse and partied with the good Catholic girls, who then tried to hide us when the nuns got wind we were there. Or how we'd go to various high schools around the San Gabriel Valley and pretend to be students (we would promise the administrators our parents were coming later to sign us up). We met many a pretty girl . . . and an equal number of infuriated boyfriends.

At first we talked and laughed and it was all in fun. But I began to feel uneasy. A twinge of the feeling that I was falling back struck me. Still, he was my closest homie. I needed to at least show him some hospitality. Then the other shoe dropped.

"Homie, I need a big favor," Chicharrón whispered when Camila stood up to get more beers, brushing his mustache with the toothbrush nervously. "I need a place to stay, not for long, until I get back on my feet. I just got out, and my *jefitos* moved out of the 'hood and don't want anything to do with me . . . you know how it is. Just for a few days, *carnal*."

Part of me knew this was a mistake. Another part felt I owed my *camarada*. Perhaps because of all that we did and saw in the old days. I got picked up a few times for crimes and shootings and didn't rat on anybody. But then again, homeboys ended up doing time for crimes I was party to—and they never ratted on me. I felt this was the least I could do for the homie.

We had Chicharrón sleep in an open pantry area that was long enough for him to lay down and put a few of his things. He brought with him a worn sleeping bag and some clothes, little else.

A few days? This turned into weeks.

I went to work, worried about Chicharrón with Camila and the kids. But they seemed fine so I tried not to let it get to me. Chicharrón was supposed to look for a job. He said he picked up vocational skills at the Youth Training School at Chino, a YA facility. But he never did find a job. Chicharrón, we learned, was a PCP user. "Angel dust"—totally nuts on that stuff. I tried PCP in my druggie days. It racked your brain and seemed to give you extra strength—really it was your brain acting as if your body had extra strength. Paranoia gripped you from the inside. I called it the "zombie maker."

At the time, we began to assist members of the local neighborhood gang. They came around the house during our film nights and talent weekends. They were Chicano youngsters who should have been in middle school or early high school but were already dropouts with rough tattoos all over their bodies and usually under the influence of something. Chicharrón began to talk to them. They in turn started to look up to Chicharrón. He appeared stone gangster—his jailhouse tats were elaborate, up and down his arms, back, stomach, neck, and legs. Before he got popped, he had only a few tattoos, including one that said LOMAS that I did on his arm years back. Now he was a walking canvas.

When I was off at work, he began to get these *morrillos* organized. I didn't know it then, but he was selling PCP out of the house—he had his connections, which is where he went during the day instead of seeking work. One day, he brought over a part–Native American girl, about fifteen. She seemed too young, but he somehow fitted her into his pantry room, with blankets over the open doorway. Her name was Lurlene—she had a light-skinned Indian face. They called her Lula.

Camila took the babies out during the day but would come home to find Chicharrón and Lurlene sleeping or having sex. Camila got tired of this real quick. One night as soon as I got home from the mill, Camila grabbed my hand and took me outside.

"What's up with your fucking homeboy?" she said, not mincing any words.

"What do you want me to do?" I whispered. "He was my best friend. I can't just throw him out on the street."

"And why not? Why do you feel like you have to do this? I don't get it—he's messing with bad stuff. We got kids in the house. Something's not right with him and that *puta* getting it on all day long in the pantry. You need to get rid of his ass."

I couldn't tell Camila why I was of two minds about booting Chicharrón out. How I felt some kind of homies-till-the-end thing. I was no longer involved in the barrio, but I never actually got jumped out. I had left because the barrio politics, along with police operatives, changed things for me there, not because I lacked love for the homies. Again, part of me felt I was still tied to the barrio—even though I hadn't set foot there in years.

Every day I went to the mill with jumbled thoughts. I wasn't paying attention to the *jale*. One day, I failed to properly connect an air hose to a pipe with supercompressed air flowing through it. Air hoses powered huge ratchet wrenches, grease guns, and other equipment. There were pipes with compressed air all over the plant. So I turned the flow dial with a wrench (it had arrows on it to indicate if the fixture was closed or open, like gas pipes). I had grease on the inside of my right arm so when the hose popped out, a tremendous amount of pressure drove the grease under the skin like a thick black tattoo. I rushed to the mill's clinic.

They said I was lucky no air bubbles penetrated a vein, which could've traveled to my heart and burst a valve or two. Still, they used a hard wire scraper to remove layers of skin and get the grease out. Man, this hurt. I tried not to wince as the nurse scraped away for what seemed hours. When they were done, my arm was bloody and torn up. Another nurse bandaged it and I went home to recuperate for a few days.

Meantime, Camila would not let up with her grumbling. Yeah, she was concerned about my arm, but she had other pressing matters on her mind.

"Things are getting out of hand here," Camila said. "I don't know all that's going on, but those young *cholos* are into something bad with your so-called friend. I'm telling you, Louie, you have to put your foot down. You have to get rid of the fucker. Right now I can't even stay in my own house. I take the kids to my sister's or to our friends'. That's not right, you understand me? It's not right for me and the kids not to feel safe in our own house."

Then a few of the local gang dudes asked me for a ride in my Bug. They said they had some business to take care of in another barrio, not far from Watts. My intuition said, *Don't go*, but I went anyway. Again, I wasn't thinking straight. I drove over the tracks with these dudes, my arm in gauze and tape.

We came into a barrio-looking street with graffiti everywhere and small homes. Several *cholos* were standing on a corner. As I approached, one of the dudes in the car drew out a handgun and yelled out the barrio name, then began firing. I realized what was happening and sped off. I looked in the rearview mirror and saw dudes scrambling in all directions, but nobody was hit. I yelled and cursed at the dudes as we raced back to Watts, practically tearing up the Bug's undercarriage on the railroad tracks.

At the house, I told those dudes to scram since the police would probably locate them there. But I also told them they shouldn't come back. They had no right to pull me into a drive-by like that. They felt bad and apologized. I advised them to get going. Then I went to the pantry and told Chicharrón to come out, we had to talk.

When Chicharrón emerged he had on a wife-beater T-shirt and boxer shorts. I told him to sit down. Lurlene wasn't there so I didn't have to extract him from the poonanny.

I told him about what the local dudes had done. How this situation was endangering my family and community work. Chicharrón agreed. He said those dudes were fuckups. How he was getting tired of them anyway. I didn't believe him. But instead of throwing him out, I ended the talk with an understanding that those dudes weren't allowed at the house, unless they were genuinely looking for help. It turned out not all the guys were messing up. I continued to deal with the motivated ones. They were like homeboys everywhere who just needed viable ways to go. But that day I had to keep all the local gangsters from bringing trouble to my home. Chicharrón readily accepted these terms. Again, I didn't trust his words.

Sure enough, the PCP sales continued. Lurlene supposedly turned tricks for cash.

It was Camila who resolved the whole freakin' mess. It should have been me, but I was stuck in my own bullshit. One day when Chicharrón and Lurlene were out, Camila gathered all their stuff—they had accumulated a few things by then—and threw it to the curb: blankets, sleeping bag, pillows, toiletries, a radio, a black-and-white TV, and other junk. The drugs she flushed down the toilet.

When Chicharrón returned to the house, he got the message. I had to speak to him, though—I couldn't just let him leave like that.

"Homie, I'm sorry how things worked out," I stated. "But you and I are on different tracks, *carnal*. You didn't change after getting locked up. You're still the same *vato* I knew from the old days. Well, I'm not the same. Yeah, we were once crazy together. We were into the same crimes, same *babosadas*. But I've got a family now, a job. I tried to help you but you were only bringing the old stuff back. I can't do that anymore. I hope you finally get it together. If not, *ese*, your future will be behind prison walls. Look at your body—it tells the tales, man. If that's what you're about, *órale*, I can't change that. All I'm asking is don't drag me along."

Chicharrón looked glum. But I think he knew the road he was on. He knew I was on a completely different course. If I couldn't bring him my way, at least I wouldn't let him take me to his.

One of Chicharrón's cousins came for him in an old beat-up Ford. They somehow stuffed his things in the trunk and backseat. He left a few things that were Lurlene's. I glanced over at the car as they sped off. Chicharrón still had his toothbrush, smoothing out his *bigote*.

Lurlene made it back to the house later that day. We told her she had to find another place to stay as we presented her with a box of her things. She said she had nobody but Chicharrón. She had no family, nowhere to go. Camila and I reiterated that we couldn't do anything about that. I pressed her for a phone number, any phone number, of people she knew. She finally gave me a number she claimed was her mother's.

We called this number, but nobody answered. She cried but soon grabbed her box and walked out. I walked out with her, saying I'd drive her wherever she needed to go. But she kept on stepping, not responding. It was still daytime so I figured she'd get a bus.

That night, after we put the babies to bed, we received a phone call. It was from a nearby sheriff's station. They asked if we knew Lurlene Saint Marie. "Yeah, sure, but—" Right away they wanted me to pick her up from the station. I asked what happened. The deputies said she was found down a busy street talking with herself, acting weird. They brought her to the station and it was evident she had taken PCP. She yelled, screamed, fought—she even overturned desks and chairs.

The deputies wanted her out of there and the only number she gave them was mine. If I didn't get her they would take her to the Central Juvenile Hall, where things would be worse for her. I couldn't let them do that to Lurlene. So I told Camila what I was going to do. She rolled her eyes, but I still went to claim the girl.

I brought Lurlene to the house—the deputies were happy to get rid of her. She was in bad shape. We kept calling her mother's number. Again no answer. Then Lurlene went nuts. She started throwing things around. I tried to stop her, but the PCP had muscled her up—she was stronger than I'd presumed she'd be. I told Camila to take the kids to the neighbor's house. Camila held the sleepy kids in her arms as she took off down the street.

I went to grab Lurlene, but she easily peeled my arms off her. She went to the bathroom and closed the door. I heard glass bottles of cologne and perfume crash onto the floor. I hammered at the door and yelled for Lurlene to get out.

"Lula, Lula, you're destroying our stuff," I roared. "Come out so we can get you home."

Lurlene opened the door and jumped out, forcing me back. She darted into the bedroom and began to go through my record collection. She busted up vinyl LPs like Santana; Earth, Wind and Fire; Marvin Gaye; and Malo before I could get to her. I pulled her out of the bedroom, which I then closed. She scampered to the kitchen just as Camila returned. Lurlene picked up a butter knife and started to slash her wrist, but the dull knife didn't cut anything. She screamed that she wanted to die.

"Lula, please, don't hurt yourself." Camila tried to reason with her. "Just calm down, *m'ija*, we only want to help."

As Camila talked, Lurlene hesitated for a moment. I then grabbed her from behind. She yelled and began to thrash about to shake me off. But I didn't let go, even with a bandaged arm that smarted like hell. I placed my arms under her breasts so she couldn't slip away. I sat down the both of us, my back against a wall. Her blouse by then had opened, exposing her bra, but I kept holding on. Camila went to the phone and called Lurlene's mother. No one picked up, but she kept trying. I held on to Lurlene all night long. She rested in intervals, then would suddenly stir again, but to no avail. It was near dawn when she finally fell asleep there with my arms around her.

I carried her to the couch and laid her down. She was out. A PCP downslide.

Sometime that morning, we reached Lurlene's mom. Her mother lived in a white suburban section of Downey. She said her daughter had run away some time ago. She was half native but grew up among whites. Her father was a drug addict and nowhere to be found. We asked her mother to come get her—there was nothing more we could do. Later that day, Lurlene's mother arrived. She was tired-looking but young. She must have had Lurlene when she was a teenager.

Lurlene finally woke up in the afternoon. Utterly tame, she didn't quarrel when her mother fixed her clothes and brushed her hair, or walked her to the car. Lurlene's mom said thanks to Camila and me as we looked on from the porch. Then they drove off.

We never saw Lurlene—or Chicharrón—again.

Chapter Six

I was finally given the graveyard shift full-time instead of rotating shifts. Assigned to the furnaces, I worked with a dour old millwright from the Deep South named Curly, a white dude who regularly complained about me. I did the work, but he liked to boss me around as if I were a high school kid. Again, if I didn't fight for respect, I'd never get it. I stood up to the dude. Told him off a few times. I took my time getting things for him. This drove him up the wall.

When I finally got home in the early hours, I was beat. Camila often got on my case about something or other. She didn't seem happy anymore. I understood that having two babies in two years was a whale of a load. She didn't have to work, but dealing with the kids without having me around much became a burden.

One day, we met a new neighbor, Kendra, a young single African-American woman with three kids. She was copper-skinned, big-bodied, but cute. Camila and Kendra became friends, conversed, shopped together. I thought this was good—that she had somebody to spend time with while I worked or rested.

I also took a machinist course at the Watts Skills Center on 111th Street, not far from where I used to live as a kid. I wanted to move up in the mill and felt I needed more proficiency. I particularly wanted to be a higher-paid full-fledged millwright. I found a friend there, Marcus, a light-skinned young Watts dude trying to find new skills in a changing job market. We began to hang out when I wasn't working. Marcus became my only friend outside the political circles.

Camila and I would party with Tony or our other friends, even a few times when Tony and Trini, our young friend from the Valley, dated for a while. When the bump became a dance craze, Camila and Tony got on the dance floor and bumped the night away. I liked to dance, but Tony and Camila really got into this, making a commotion among other dancers. Once they won a dance contest. When Trini was there, we'd just sit and talk. Trini danced very well, but she wasn't flamboyant like Camila or Tony. Neither was I.

I was known for the "Louie shuffle," from my old barrio days, keeping my arms up by my chest, moving my body and hips slowly, and sometimes stomping my feet to a beat. Not a pretty sight.

It didn't take long for Camila and me to stop having fun. I found fault with almost anything she did or said. As they say, we got on each other's last nerve.

My initial approach was to reason, to make sense, to bring out the dialectic, to decipher what was happening and what to do about it. She tore through that shit. Facts were nothing to her. Instead she wrapped you into an emotional headlock, and you were a goner. When I became frustrated I threw fuck-yous around. No more subtleties. But she knew there was no violence behind those words. I felt discouraged, worn out, after our fights. She didn't respond to the "sound" points I came up with. She became like a tight spring, bounding from one wall to another. And my furious releases didn't help. They only fed her outrageous responses.

My anger was her gasoline.

One warm weekend afternoon, I informed Camila I'd take the kids to the park.

"What are you going to do?"

"What does it matter what I'm going to do? They can play in the playground, the swings or slides. I'm just taking them to the park."

"How do I know you'll return? That you're not going to take them away? How do I know I'll see them again?"

She was serious. I looked at her like she had just landed from another planet.

"I'll be back with them in a couple of hours—you know very well I wouldn't do anything to harm the babies."

Camila's face changed—the ready-to-scuffle expression left it. She relaxed, looked out the window, to nowhere in particular, and said, "I know." She turned around and walked away.

Something was bothering her. I just couldn't figure out what.

Camila and I often sought counsel with Nelson or Sue. They were wise in life and relationships. And I sort of adopted Nelson as the father I didn't feel I had.

One day, Camila said she'd had it. That was it. She wanted to leave. This didn't seem like a totally bad idea. I, too, was drained. But I also felt we had more love to give, that not all was lost. So I talked Camila into having Nelson and Sue over to discuss our possible breakup. That night they came to the house, Nelson making light of things before getting serious. Finally, we sat across from each other and talked.

"We know it's been hard," Nelson said. "You've both endured much. Don't let the difficult times determine *all* the times. There will be hard and happy moments. Let the happy times carry you through the hard ones, not the other way around. Believe me, you'll have more good than bad."

"You are both young," Sue interjected. "You need to stretch out the relationship over many years, decades. Someday you'll look back at these times and laugh. Right now you're caught in the moment, with many uncertainties. I know you both love each other. Build on that, not the hurting, not the quarrels."

"And remember, if you move on to another relationship, you'll only be trading one set of problems for new ones," Nelson told us. "No union is without its challenges."

Nelson and Sue provided sage words, advice, warning. I knew they were right. We were letting the bedlam of the hard times pull us along. Of course, we had good times. But I didn't know at the time that Camila felt trapped, a slave to circumstances—growing demands with the kids, a husband constantly at the mill, and thinning romance. Perhaps she felt her issues with my temper weren't being heard.

Anyway, Camila wasn't going to argue with Nelson and Sue the way she argued with me. They made sense: Why destroy a marriage after only three and a half years, with a son of two and a half years old and a daughter of ten months? Yet this wasn't about what made sense. It was about what Camila felt. She wanted to get away. She was determined to find a way out. She couldn't provide a rational argument to break up the marriage, so she'd go for the irrational. One way or another she was leaving.

Work kept me from thinking everything through. I should have known that Camila was serious. But I had my delusions. I actually thought we had a chance. That we just needed time to adapt and adjust, to expand into stages of loving and being loved. For despite the arguments and uncomfortable moments, I wanted a family more than anything. I left my original family for the streets. Now I felt compelled to have a family even when the conditions didn't seem to exist for one. We would have to change the dynamics of how Camila and I related, but it would be worth it to preserve this family. I got sideswiped because I wanted to believe that maybe, this time at least, something could work out.

One night, Camila and I had dinner at a Chinese restaurant on Florence Avenue in our old neighborhood. The place was actually one my father took the family to when we were children. When I was five or six years old, my mother had me in a white shirt and slacks whenever we went there. I had fond memories—of carved Chinese images on dark wood enclosing the booths. Gold-thread-embroidered hangings on the walls. Elaborately decorated vases by the doors. We always seemed happy when the family ended up there, which wasn't often, but enough that I'd remember.

I held Camila's hand as we ate, talked, smiled. I tried to salvage whatever we had left. Curiously, Camila didn't argue. Didn't oppose anything. Didn't demand anything. I wanted this so bad I made myself believe we were going to be okay. Unfortunately, I wasn't aware she had already given up, was just going through the motions, planning how she'd make the break. Still, for now, she went along so it appeared we were on the same page, the same train ride, with the same objective.

I've been wrong many times but never as wrong as I was about that night, that dinner, that marriage.

I came home from the mill after a particularly busy shift. It was still morning, and Camila appeared cheerful yet distracted. I had a couple of days off before I reentered the mill so I was in a good mood. I woke up after sleeping from morning to midday in my room with the aluminum-covered windows.

It seemed Camila didn't expect me to stay that evening. I asked her about going out, but she said she was busy. Instead I went out, like I often did, for a few beers. Camila expected me to return late, something I'd do when I had the night off. But for some reason, the bar was quiet. I stuck around for a while but sensed the need to get home.

I parked the V-dub in the yard and wandered into the house. To my bewilderment, Marcus, the friend I met at the Watts Skills Center, was sitting on the living room couch. Camila sat next to him, showing him a copy of the political newspaper we passed out in the factories and neighborhoods. I didn't think much of this.

Camila explained that Marcus was interested in our community work. I sat down for a while and talked politics with Marcus. Camila left this to me while she went to the bedroom, I thought, to put the babies to sleep. Marcus showed interest. We exchanged ideas. Then he said he needed to go.

I stood up to take him home. Camila, out of the blue, offered to drive Marcus, adding that I should rest. I wasn't tired, but still, I didn't sense anything was wrong. I said I was fine with taking him, but Camila insisted, not in a desperate way, but still making a good case. Okay, sure, why not. Marcus lived not far away. She'd be back soon.

I went to the room to check on the babies. As soon as I turned on the lights, cockroaches scrambled, including a couple on my kids' faces. I squashed one on the floor. The babies slept together in a small bed at opposite ends, their feet touching. They looked soft, peaceful, bundled in frayed blankets. I turned off the light, closed the door.

I read a book for a while and perused a couple of magazines. I turned on the TV. A clock over the mantel ticked the minutes away. Sometime that night I became aware that Camila had not come home. Did she stop off to see a friend? Did she get into an accident? Soon a terrible feeling crept over me. I began to contemplate the impossible—was Camila having an affair? With Marcus? I shook my head in disbelief. How could this be? Nothing in Camila's demeanor suggested anything of the sort. Was I *that* blind? I denied everything. The kicker came when it occurred to me to check the bathroom for her diaphragm. I knew where she kept it and how she'd clean it and put it back there after we made love.

That was the most dreadful moment—when I searched for the diaphragm and it was gone. Something sank inside me. My heart felt like it had fallen out of my chest. My mind raced. Could she have put it somewhere else? But then the smell, ever so delicate, wafted toward me. It was the scent from the cream used in the diaphragm. I knew it well—nothing else was like it. That's when it struck me, like a ton of bricks, like a hammer blow to the head: Camila had put the diaphragm inside her to be with Marcus.

The accelerating emotions held me in a grip so tight I could barely breathe. They inundated me, a flood of rage, of revulsion. I thought over and over again of Camila with Marcus. It was a madness with its own mind, its own heart, murderous, confused, grotesque, with its own blood. I ran into the living room and rummaged around without knowing for what. It occurred to me to locate my wife and friend. I dashed to the yard and realized that Camila had taken the V-dub. I pivoted toward the Chevy but then remembered the solenoid was broken—the car hadn't worked for weeks and there was no time to fix it.

"Damn it, damn it all to fuckin' hell," I yelled.

Everything was betraying me, abandoning me, kicking me in the face.

I scrambled back to the house. I then thought about running down the street to Marcus's place to catch them together. I should've been thinking of not leaving the kids alone, but at that instant the kids were the least of my worries.

I went to the bedroom closet and reached behind loose boards. I pulled out the shotgun. I hurried to the pantry and grabbed a few shotgun shells next to boxes of cereal and a bag of flour. I loaded the weapon and then loped down the street, not even locking the door. I went past a handful of homes when it hit me that a man with a shotgun hastening through Watts was going to rouse neighbors and police. I wouldn't get far. I trotted back.

I reentered my place, pacing back and forth, the shotgun in my clutches. I was a man possessed. Everything closed in on me, all doors shut, all paths cut off. I wound up at the back porch, where Camila would most likely enter once she returned with the Bug. I sat down with the shotgun across my legs, gazing at a section of yellowed grass spotlighted by a streetlamp. Heavy salty tears squeezed from my eyes as I closed them. I was going to wait for Camila and then shoot her. The madness now controlled every nerve, muscle, limb. I was drowning in its bile. I stood up, I sat down, I stood up, deliberating again and again about killing Camila, killing Marcus—killing me some *vatos* . . . killing, just killing, anybody.

At some point, I stepped back into the house. I entered the kids' room and an insane thought rushed through me—of shooting the babies, then Camila. Then myself. I know how repugnant this sounds. The memory of having the idea will haunt me forever. It was a red-eyed monster tearing through the viscera, sinews, and skin. I glanced over at the sleeping children and at that instant I fell apart, crying like I had never cried before, crying for allowing this poison to pulse through me, heartbeat by heartbeat.

I staggered out of the kids' room, dropped the shotgun, and fell to the floor in the living room.

Sometime that morning, without sleep for hours, I stood up from my wilted position, took the shells out of the shotgun, and placed the firearm back in the closet. I was in a numb floating state that one gets after a terrible accident, after witnessing someone die or after being shot at—things I had been through.

But not this. I had never been through this before.

I sat back down on the porch. The light of day sprayed over the rooftops, telephone poles, power lines, dirt yards. The sun appeared bright, cheery, as if what I had just been through wasn't even a blip. The V-dub finally arrived. Camila emerged out of the car and looked at me like nothing had happened. I knew she had a story in her head. That she was going to try to pull one over on me. But she considered my face for a second and must have seen the mirror I held to her. She must have perceived what I knew. Instead of a clever excuse, she said something ridiculous like "I'm no longer a virgin."

It didn't matter. Something died in me that night. It didn't matter what she said. I grabbed the keys from Camila's hand, slipped into the Bug, and took off.

I drove to Imperial Highway and then east to the entrance of the Los Angeles River near Interstate 710 and the South Gate and Downey city limits. I parked and climbed over the chain-link fence, stumbling down a slope to the concrete riverbed. A line of water rippled through the middle, graffiti on every cement slope and pillar. From the time I was a child the river and its veins of canals were places for me to think, to play, to get loaded, to sleep. Places to heal. Once on the riverbed, I began to cleanse.

I ran.

I ran with taut muscles into the mist of morning, carrying the heat of emotion through the sun's rays, thoughts muddled, touching upon choices and lack of choices, wrong turns, false moves—mostly where I'd fucked up. I was twenty-three years old. I'd already lasted longer on this earth than I ever thought I would. I began to question why I even left the gang, the jails, the heroin. I might as well have ODed or been shot, or walked headlong into all the interesting ways people can die in the barrio. I might as well have gone Chicharrón's way. Why did I leave all that to end up in this hideous anguish, of all things, tied to love?

I ran past scrawled-on warehouses and factories, past bland apartments, strewn garbage, rusty market carts, past alleys with overturned trash cans and mounds of tires. Debris underfoot. Overgrown weeds scraping my legs.

My world ended that night. My worst self cracked through along with whatever fiber of decency I still possessed after mutating into animals, germs, vibrations. At a certain level it wasn't about Camila. I was in battle with myself, with some mixed-up chemistry, explosive, implosive, trying to reconcile my steamroller side—which tended to roll over people, family, friends, kids, enemies, those I loved and hated—with something like grace. I had to see what mud I'd been formed from, what personal arithmetic summed up the chaotic numbers, what logic wound around the illogical impulses, even to imagine for a second, for excruciating fractions of a second, that I could destroy my children, my wife, myself. Somehow, I managed to overcome the most searing lunacy, realizing—as I stared at the babies, as I housed that reprehensible thought—that I'd wake up, that whatever good I still had still stirred, that I could stop myself.

Even in my teens, in the streets, I found a rationale, a block, so as not to plunge all the way down the web's entrails, the layered abyss of a deadened life. I wandered along downtown's back streets and alleys and witnessed many things, too many humanly rotten things. In those years, I was on the worst drugs of the time and losing myself in the process. But I also found out what people were capable of—I mean anything—for that next fix. I got there at times, believe me, but I also stopped before I totally spiraled downward.

Now I continued to run—beneath bridges, under overpasses, next to train tracks, splashing rainwater as I trod, heels hammering against the pavement. So much momentum propelling my legs, and just like the river, going on for miles. I finally turned around and ran back to where I'd left the car. I didn't know why I had the strength. It was a form of depression I didn't comprehend, so much adrenaline pushing me. I ran and ran. It would take weeks before I fully fell asleep. Even in my attempts at slumber, at finding some rest, I kept running.

Chapter Seven

When Camila and I next encountered each other she was prepared to move out of the house with babies in tow. No explanations, no answers, no apologies. I said good-bye to the kids. Ramiro must have sensed we were embroiled in a terrible tale. Andrea was too tiny. When I held her, tears fell and my body shook. Andrea laughed—she thought I was playing with her.

Camila took a few items and said she'd be back to get the rest of their things. Camila's sister arrived to scuttle them back to East L.A.—no words exchanged between us—and soon they were gone. I dropped down on a chair next to the dining table not knowing what to do, where to gaze, what to feel. I looked across the table and noticed a crumpled piece of paper. I opened it—there in Camila's handwriting were the words "I love you," written over and over.

I went to work as usual, not really there, like a ghost, disembodied, dispirited, every motion with no vitality, every thought stripped of flesh. A few of the guys figured out something was up. I didn't laugh at their teasing. I didn't push back when they jostled, punched a shoulder. Curly became less bothersome, less abusive. People knew. I didn't know how, but they knew.

One morning, I came home and found the back door unlocked. I went inside and saw that Camila had taken several things—a crib, bed, drawers, clothes, bathroom items, kitchen utensils. This was fine, but she apparently ran off with the TV, the stereo, a camera, and other good stuff. This wasn't right. I called her at her sister's but it turned out Camila didn't take those things. We finally deduced I'd been robbed. After

I hung up, I rushed to the closet and stuck my hand through the loose boards. Damn if they didn't take the shotgun. Damn.

The first person I talked to about the incident was an activist whose husband had recently been killed during a labor dispute. I needed to open up to someone who had it worse than me. She would understand. She knew about loss. Although at one point she said something that made me look up.

"What you've gone through is worse than what I've experienced," the activist said after a long silence following my painful account. "My husband was killed, but Camila left you—it's a different heartache when choice is involved."

Damn.

Soon word got around. I received a couple of phone calls. One of the first to visit was Kendra, Camila's friend, who lived in a one-room apartment two streets down with her children. She hugged me, strolled into the house, made dinner. We went to a drive-in movie, held hands. That night, with her kids in bed, we made love on her couch.

Kendra was nice. She was always friendly with me. I enjoyed the intimacy. But it was too early for anything serious to happen. Kendra wanted a man in her life, and she didn't waste any time when Camila left. I'm sure she thought I'd be her man. But it didn't work out this way. She came over several times, helping with the chores. Again, making things to eat. I didn't know how to tell her I needed to be alone for a while.

I then decided it was time for me to leave Watts. Being in that house was torturous. Every room screamed treachery. The phone rang, but I didn't answer, assuming the calls were Kendra's. She left notes on my back door that I ignored.

One night when I wasn't working, a fellow steelworker and I quickly packed my stuff and piled whatever I had left into the truck. I stored most of my things, including the '54 Chevy, and stayed with friends, slept on sofas, continued to work. I shouldn't have done this, but I left without saying anything to Kendra.

I did break down and call my mother—we hardly spoke until then. The only thing Mom managed to say was, "M'ijo, don't drink."

———

Not long after, I took part in a study circle in Southeast L.A. Many of my friends were there, talking, laughing, munching on chips and fruit. Somebody brought a tequila bottle. People took swigs and made faces. Most of them were not big drinkers. I kind of spaced out. When the bottle came around, I slowly chugged it. No lime. No salt. It felt good down my throat, warm in my gut. Without thinking, I held on to the bottle.

Nelson started the meeting with a political report. Others asked questions. I kept drinking. At one point Nelson stopped midsentence and said, "Please, somebody, take that bottle away from Louie."

I must have looked as if I thought I was the only one in the room. For a while I was inside the drink. Nelson turned to scold me. I got embarrassed that people saw me this way. But then I concluded, *I'm not going to drink in front of these people again.*

Many things were changing in the political circles. Nelson and Sue were moving to Chicago to set up central offices. Others, good friends of mine, were leaving to assist them, including Tony Prince.

In L.A. community leaders asked me to lead local organizing efforts. I didn't want to. I felt useless. Uninspired. Crushed. But, to their credit, they didn't let me *not* do this. I didn't quite get that I needed the stability and focus of these circles. As I broke into pieces, they helped gather me up, find the internal infrastructure to build from.

Bethlehem Steel kept money in my pocket. I found a studio apartment in Maywood above a garage. It had a room and bath. I used a hot plate to boil water for coffee, make soup, fry eggs. It was a few blocks from the mill. I spent most of my time working or organizing. Revolutionaries were being drawn from factories, foundries, and small shops. We now had young leaders at Bethlehem. We studied when we found the time to come together (hard to do with many shifts in the plant).

I tried dating but mostly fell on my face. I asked out women friends who quickly reminded me we were just friends. The one or two who did go out with me failed to get any spark from the occasion, including my friend Trini. We went disco dancing once, Trini and I, but at the end of the night made no moves on each other.

The year Camila and I broke up, 1978, became a year in which disco ruled the dance floors. The sixties and early seventies were about urban revolt, student protests, new ideas, and new music. Then the government, along with weakened leadership in the radical groups, demolished or made ineffectual organizations like the Black Panthers, the Brown Berets, the Young Lords, the American Indian Movement, and Students for a Democratic Society. Key personalities were assassinated—John Kennedy, Malcolm X, George Jackson, Martin Luther King Jr., Robert Kennedy, Ruben Salazar, Fred Hampton, and Harvey Milk, among others. Not to mention cultural icons dying from drugs and personal drama, such as Jimi Hendrix, Jim Morrison, Janis Joplin, and Brian Jones.

By 1978 everybody was dancing.

The loneliness drew me into the bars, dark hangouts, strip clubs. I sought solace in dance halls around town, including the *charro* migrant bars along Brooklyn Avenue in East L.A. or on North Broadway in Lincoln Heights. I particularly fell into the disco set. When *Saturday Night Fever* popped up in movie houses, most of us were already strutting the polyester life—we were all Tony Maneros.

Then I met a young woman named Sarita while driving along East Sunset Boulevard in Echo Park. She was hitchhiking, a strange thing to do in those days after a number of high-profile killings stopped this practice. Sarita was Filipina-Mexicana, in her midtwenties, tall, curly-haired, with chestnut-brown skin. I thought she was too foxy to be risking rides, but when she spoke in a raspy voice and I checked out her steely look, I knew she'd been around. She could handle herself, was barrio-bred. No lightweight.

We became friends. She lived in *Echo Parque* (before parts of it became known for artists, yuppies, and gentrification). Sarita was a total party girl. That's all she wanted to do. She became my disco queen. We'd go dancing, often with a couple of her friends. I didn't mind— they were attractive Chicanas or Filipinas.

I soon moved into the basement apartment of a house in the Geraghty Loma barrio in East L.A., Camila's old hood. I made this move largely to be close to the babies—I missed them so much. They now lived in an old one-room apartment near City Terrace Park. It had a broken windowpane at the bottom of the door. One night, Ramiro, almost three years old, woke up his sister, Andrea. In pajamas and diapers, they slipped through the opening thinking they could walk to my basement apartment, although rain was coming down. They had no idea where to go. Luckily police found them and they ended up nearby at Camila's sister's place downhill from Camila's.

By then Camila and I talked more. I still desired her warm, sweet body next to mine, still craved her smile and fingers. But others were now involved in Camila's life (Marcus was long gone from the picture). She went out at times and would drop off the babies with me. I drank and there were moments when I banged a few walls, kicked over chairs, boiling over inside liked a mixed-up kettle of soup.

I found out about some dude Camila was seeing. I even followed Camila one afternoon—she had recently bought a small car—to where he lived. Another night, drunk, past midnight, I went around to his block. Camila's car was parked in front of his place. I got out and paced the street. I wanted to break through the door and choke the dude. I built myself up into a furor. Then the sidewalk opened up and I fell through, descending past the rebar and cement, through miles of earth, layers of sediment, past granite, into a molten core. Weeping, I walked to the car and drove away.

One thing I did was write on an old funky typewriter I had. For some reason, as I did in my teens, I began to pull together sentences, stories, thoughts. Mostly it was feelings, but soon they became complete anecdotes. I did some of this in Watts—Camila used to leave food by the bedroom door when I wrote, even getting the kids to be quiet, as if I were a mad scientist who couldn't be disturbed. But with the mill's schedule I pretty much left this alone. Now I managed to juggle work and writing.

I often went to a Laundromat on Soto Street. Many Mexican mothers and single dudes like me spent time there. I had a journal and wrote rambling verses while washing my clothes. One time, a teenager, small and compact, sat around while getting her clothes dried. I decided to talk to her. She was game, not annoyed or scared. I helped fold her clothes along with mine.

Her name was La Leti and it turned out she also lived in Geraghty Loma, one of the homegirls. A couple of evenings we sat on the steps leading up to my room and swigged quarts of beer or rotgut wine. One night she knocked on my basement door. She had three other homegirls with her. We drank, partied, threw up, passed out. The girls slept on the bed while I lay on the floor.

I drove the girls once to the Santa Monica pier, drinking the whole time, raising a ruckus. The girls were also angel dust freaks. Of all of them, it was La Leti I got close to. She told me a terrible story about how her brother died from rat poison that somebody put in a batch of heroin. She was seventeen, I was twenty-four. She was too young, I know. I just didn't think about it.

One night, Leti came to my room by herself. We made love several times that night—she was well shaped with creamy skin. Good-looking, but with acne (she *was* a teenager). The only problem was that in the middle of the night she peed on the sleeping bag I had placed over the bed. I had to hang it outside on a fence to dry. We showered together and then got breakfast at an all-night Mexican diner on First Street.

A number of weeks later, Leti asked me to pick her up from a women's health clinic on Whittier Boulevard. I had no idea why. I entered the place and Leti was sitting there, waiting for me, jovial.

"I'm pregnant," she declared. I didn't know what to say. It was something I didn't want, didn't need. But words failed me—a man of words with no words when I most needed them.

The next week, she applied for general assistance. I drove her to the welfare office and fidgeted in a seat while waiting for her to finish. She looked at me through a large window when the social worker turned away to get something. She mouthed the words "I love you." I glared back, mortified.

Leti received government aid for being an unmarried pregnant teenager. Apparently she told the social worker the father was an undocumented Mexican who ran back to the old country.

It was a sad hard day when I finally told Leti I didn't want this baby. She called me a *cabron, pinche . . . hijo de puta*. I didn't blame her, but

I had to tell her. I did say if she insisted on having the baby, I'd help take care of it. But this was little comfort. She threatened to stab me in the heart, to blind me with a fork, to burn the house down. She stormed out, angrily talking to herself as she climbed down the curbless hill from my basement room.

One day I drove around the bend toward the house and saw Leti fighting with another girl in the street. I stopped the car and pulled the girls apart. A few barrio dudes and girls began to congregate. Leti screamed at me, calling me out. I got along well with the Geraghty *vatos*, but I wasn't sure how this would go over with the homies. Leti began to punch her stomach, saying she wished she didn't have this baby. I held her. The girl she fought with tried to get some blows in. People pushed her away, leaving me with Leti in my arms. I didn't know what else to do.

My troubles with Leti ended on the day she miscarried. I visited her at the county hospital. I tried to be soothing, but she was withdrawn, distant, tired. She acknowledged me and we talked a bit. Then she asked me to leave. I didn't argue. I walked out of that room and out of Leti's life forever.

My writing became an obsession. I wrote whenever I had the chance in the midst of all the drama, with rotating shifts and even sixteen-hour days at the mill. Before I knew it, I had hundreds of poems and a book. The book was a true account of my life as a gang member that I called *Mi Vida Loca*.

One of my friends was a writer and editor. He agreed to edit the manuscript and did a good job. I began to send the manuscript to various publishers, not really knowing what to do but picking up tips from books and magazines. I started with the big boys, the New York City publishing houses. I received almost two dozen rejections. I got depressed. Nobody commented on why they didn't want the book. They sent me generic rejection letters.

I seriously considered giving up on writing.

Only one publisher managed to address a personal letter to me. In that letter, the editor said the publishing house had already produced a "Hispanic" book about ten years before and they felt they had done enough as far as "Hispanic" literature was concerned.

I realized they hadn't read what I wrote—they looked at my name, Luis Rodríguez, and turned it down. I stopped getting depressed and started getting pissed.

My kids were small in those two years after Camila and I separated. I visited when I could but found myself busy with work, political activity, writing, relationships, partying. Although I now lived close to them, it was hard for me to be with them more often. Camila, instead, dropped them off with me when she needed to get away or take care of business.

One Saturday, I came by their apartment on Hazard Avenue. I walked Ramiro and Andrea to the park nearby. I took them to the play area. Ramiro frolicked in the sand and I pushed Andrea on a swing. All of a sudden I heard the familiar crack of a firearm—I looked up and saw a *vato* with a gun running down a hillside street shooting at some dudes behind us on the other side of the park. I grabbed Andrea and then rushed up to Ramiro and pushed us all to the ground. I could feel the bullets pass through the air I had just been standing in. The babies were terrified, perhaps a little sore from my abrupt grabbing and dropping. I didn't get up until I knew no more bullets were flying.

Another time, when Andrea was two and Ramiro was four, I decided to go to their home when Camila had to leave for a while. I fed them, changed Andrea's diaper, and play-wrestled with Ramiro. Another *vato* from the apartment complex came by. He had beers. We sat on the small cement porch, guzzling *chelas*, talking, while the kids occupied themselves. After a while, the dude went to the store to get more.

I had a problem of drinking until I passed out. When I next became conscious, I found myself peeing into a toy box I had built for the kids. Andrea looked at me befuddled, in a soiled diaper, and Camila called me every name in the book from the doorway. She had just walked in, and, man, I was out of it. Camila pushed me out of the apartment and slammed the door.

The worst time with my babies, however, was a night Camila dropped them off to go out with a teacher she met at a technical school she attended. I was in my overcrowded kitchen, drinking at the dining table, looking at an old black-and-white TV with aluminum foil pressed around the antennas.

The kids laughed and fought. Ramiro was four—loud, ornery. The way a kid should be. But I was in a foul mood. I put them both on my bed. I planned to knock out in a sleeping bag on the floor. I turned off the lights. I went to the kitchen, lowered the TV volume, and kept drinking. I heard talking, giggling, from the main room.

"Go to sleep," I yelled. "I don't want to hear a peep from you two."

Sure enough, more talking, more giggles. This went on for a while, but at some point, I reached my limit. I stood up, stomped into the main room, and threw off the covers. Andrea and Ramiro were startled. I then picked up four-year-old Ramiro and threw him against the basement wall.

Something had snapped and I lost it. Ramiro hit the wall and fell to the floor. I didn't hear him cry. But I ran up to the boy, picked him up, and said, "I'm sorry, *m'ijo*, I'm so sorry." He didn't appear physically hurt, but a bond was broken that day. This showed on Ramiro's face, a look like "Dad, how could you!" His expression tore me up—it was a cowardly and stupid thing for me to do. I held Ramiro in my arms, painfully aware I had wrecked something between us. As a toddler, my son always looked up to me, always wanted to know what I was doing, was always interested in my talks with him. After that day, things weren't the same.

It was now the summer of 1978, and I was fed up with my life. Fed up with always thinking of Camila with her boyfriends, with the women I went out with, mostly party partners, teasers, more insecure than me. I was fed up with the four-cornered room I slept in, the way it seemed to get tighter, leaving me barely able to breathe. I was tired of my temper—being violent with those I didn't know and hurting those I most loved.

I also hated my work. That steel mill that once saved my life and provided me with consistent checks now drained my passions. I had a sense I belonged somewhere else. By then plant closings had picked up steam. We were all in the beginning stages of an extraordinary shift in the U.S. economy, from mechanical production to electronic/digital production. In a few years, large companies would close down, some moving to cheaper labor areas like the South, Mexico, Central America, or Southeast Asia.

Bethlehem held on, but by a thread. The company kept everything running on overtime, as if they knew they better make as much steel as possible and whatever bucks this might bring—the industry simply wasn't going to last. Newer crews were laid off. No new guys were hired. I had enough seniority to stick around, but this meant we had to work harder, longer. I should've been glad I worked. I should've been glad I was around with skills under my belt. But I wasn't.

I got desperate once, needing more alcohol, maybe a new lousy disco shirt, and without thinking, I sold my '54 Chevy. For two hundred bucks, man. I had stored it in my parents' garage. I hardly came around to deal with it. Mom got tired of the thing sitting there. I was hungry. It was more like spiritual hunger, a hunger for something momentous to happen, to come get me, to pull me out of this rut, this drudgery, this boulevard to nowhere. Then the hunger became a fever, the fever a pain in my head. And as soon as a dude came along with the money I sold it.

Oh, I thought this would get rid of my wife's reflection in the chrome, memories of late-night jaunts, other bronzed women's faces in my coffee cup. I thought this would end the curses in my head, the blank stares from friends, the *pinche* lonely nights.

God almighty, I sold my lowered red Chevy. Prized possession. Two hundred bucks.

One night, I stood on the bridge of a shut-down overhead crane, overlooking the electric furnaces, thirty feet above the furnace floor. Curly and I were working on the motors. I took a break while Curly went to get parts, my blue hardhat scuffed, my tools and uniform greasy, stained, my face dark, dirt in the developing creases, eyes squinting.

One of the furnaces was pouring molten slag into heavy cast-iron cars on tracks. The sparks went everywhere. The widening wisps of sulfur dust built up like thunderclouds. I felt I was in mourning.

The poems I tried to draw out of me weren't coming. I had difficulty writing. My journals were mostly scribbling, meaningless notes, scattered images, a few lines of a poem, unfinished. I felt the poetry dying inside. I faced another crossroads—do I continue this mill life, the disconnection with words, the pathos of a sunken existence? Or do I go for the images, the words, the stories, regardless of the costs? One meant I'd have bread on the table, bills paid, my estranged wife less upset. The other meant I'd be out of work, struggling, getting rejected . . . everybody around me resentful.

Somehow with no more love, no more intact family, few political pressures to do more, I had to choose between the barely-making-it survival mode . . . and the graceful anguish of an artist.

Chapter Eight

I walked away from Bethlehem Steel. It was a crazy man's walk, the proverbial plank walk, the walk of a determined fool. I had no other job prospects, no knowledge of the writing life or how to find it. Still, I stopped by the main millwright shanty, where Mr. Branford sat behind a rectangular metal desk, and declared, "I'm quitting. I'll work for another two weeks, then I'm out of here." Mr. Branford didn't have any expression, pro or con.

"All right, turn over keys and company tools at the end of the two weeks," he muttered. And that was that.

Most people I told shook their heads, as if I had fallen off a high tree. My parents totally gave up at that point. They didn't harbor an ounce of hope for me as it was. When I was in the gang, on drugs, I was no good. Then as a radical I stood at the mouth of hell. Now this writing thing?

Olvídate.

Fellow organizers pointed out the impracticality of letting this job go—a couple even insinuated it was antirevolutionary. Camila only cared if I sent her money. And without the mill, this looked extremely unlikely.

I had no defense against any of this.

I did a few things of note after quitting the steel mill. In one of East L.A.'s throwaway newspapers, I saw a minuscule ad for a writer's group meeting in an old 1920s building on Figueroa Street in Highland Park. They called themselves the Los Angeles Latino Writers Association and offered writing workshops in a largely empty upstairs space.

I also enrolled in East Los Angeles College, a community institution in suburban Monterey Park, a city that at the time consisted of mostly whites, Asians, and upwardly mobile Chicanos. The college, however, straddled the unincorporated, densely populated barrios of Maravilla, including the Maravilla housing projects. I signed up for classes in topics I was interested in—journalism, creative writing, speech. It wasn't to get a degree. I didn't care about the required courses.

In addition, I strolled through the doors of a "Mexican-American" community foundation that provided jobs and training referrals for people living marginal existences—ex-cons, the unemployed, the disabled. They helped me obtain work as a carpenter on nonunion construction sites in the San Gabriel Valley. It was for day shifts, which allowed me to take night classes at the college and attend meetings of the L.A. Latino Writers, including on weekends.

I used to get top pay in the millwright unit of Bethlehem Steel, along with health insurance and other benefits. In this nonunion position, I worked ten hours a day for minimum wage and got no benefits. This particular crew framed structures for new warehouses, restaurants, and cheaply built tract homes.

I worked with mostly undocumented Mexicans and ex-cons, many still on "paper" (parole). I learned to hammer in sixteen-penny nails in no more than two strokes, eight-penny nails with a set and stroke. This required at least a thirty-two-ounce framing hammer.

One day I had to make 350 roof panels in a single day. I smashed my fingers to make the quota—bandaging them with paper towels, my hands looked like they belonged to a mummy. I had to learn how to let the hammer do the work, not my wrist. This meant unlearning my longtime use of ball-peen hammers in mechanical jobs. You could hear my curses for blocks. But I didn't back down. My hands ruined, I still finished the job.

The Los Angeles Latino Writers Association was a small group of emerging writers that years later established a number of published and award-winning Chicano poets, short-story writers, novelists, editors, and journalists. The well-known writers, editors, and artists who emerged out of this group include Helena Maria Viramontes, Roberto Rodríguez, Naomi Quiñones, Victor M. Valle, Guillermo Bejerano, Marisela Norte, J. L. Navarro, David R. Diaz, Mary Helen Ponce, and Barbara Carrasco.

When I came around, we were all unknowns, upstarts, trying to make a name for ourselves in American letters, although we were some twenty-eight hundred miles removed from the publishing hub in New York City. And Hollywood, on the other side of the L.A. River and downtown, ignored the Mexican people in their own metropolis. Still, we had this yearning, this need to be heard, to write, to break through any hindrance—to be men and women of words.

Although the group lasted less than ten years, in that time it published a literary and art magazine, *ChismeArte* (also spelled *XismeArte*). We also facilitated the Barrio Writers Workshops in Echo Park, at Self Help Graphics in East L.A., and in prisons and juvenile lockups. And we sponsored an author reading series that brought notables like José Montoya, Gary Soto, and Lorna Dee Cervantes to East L.A.

I submitted my mangled and badly composed poems, short stories, and journalistic pieces to the workshops. These were writings I hadn't previously shown to anyone. I feared criticism and snickers. But in the Barrio Writers Workshops I found a nurturing environment in which to share. The group pushed me to work harder, smarter, to consider the rigor of craft and the uniqueness of voice.

Here was a world I had been far removed from, yet as soon as I entered the books, the stories, the poems, went into the libraries and bookstores, I felt at home, with a long aching in my bones. But I also realized something of immense value, essential if I were to enmesh myself among these stalwarts of story: I needed to learn how to write.

After about six months, I got fired from my framing jobs when I refused to be pushed around by the nonunion company boss. This dude yelled at and humiliated the hardworking Mexican nationals—the *paisas*—but I wouldn't allow him to do that to me.

With luck and some connections, however, I managed to find a day-shift job as a maintenance mechanic at a chemical refinery not far from the Ramona Gardens housing projects in Boyle Heights. The company produced oil-based chemical products for industry. The pay was much better than the nonunion carpentry work but nowhere near as well paying as Bethlehem Steel—leaving the mill now weighed on me. But I didn't want to go back.

My goal was to work for a while at the refinery until I could get enough writing down to enroll full-time in journalism school, or to possibly write for newspapers or magazines. It was unclear how this would happen, but I had to try.

The place was located so close to my basement apartment that I heard the air whistles in my sleep. The chemicals it produced were toxic and flammable. Many of the machine operators were Mexicans, some of whom were visibly affected by the chemicals—one guy's face appeared to be slowly streaming down his skull. The company also contracted highly skilled undocumented laborers to do the heavy work. They were paid far less than their skills warranted. And they had little say about the lack of safety precautions against the deadly and volatile fumes. If any of them complained, they were promptly fired.

The maintenance crew, of which I was the newest member, concentrated on the daily repairs. There were miles of piping to check and change. There were boilers to fix and weld, electrical motors to mount and align, large compressors and pumps to keep running or remove. What I learned at Bethlehem served me well. I cinched all the repairs and showed the crew I could work with the best of them.

One day I got a whiff of the perils that lurked there. While wearing protective gear, another crew member and I were wrenching apart a flange on an enormous pipe that normally carried a highly toxic chemical. The rusty bolts were practically melded into the metal. I got the largest pipe wrench and placed a "cheater" bar at the end of the wrench to add leverage. I pulled on that sucker with all my strength. Slowly the bolts creaked open. At one point, the perspiration in my suit caused my skin to itch. Like a dummy, I picked up the bottom of my face mask slightly to scratch my neck. When the fumes struck me I fell back several feet against a safety rail and then on my back, knocked out cold.

In a few weeks, I began to champion the undocumented guys. They needed someone to speak for them, particularly about unsafe working conditions. They needed help with their immigration papers. They needed someone to go to the union on their behalf. This I did, including referring them to people who could help. But I was not yet a member of the Oil, Chemical and Atomic Workers International Union, which represented most of the plant's employees. So just before my six-month probationary period was up, without union protection, I was fired by the company.

They had to set me up to do so.

A few days before Christmas in 1979, the plant manager accused me of violating a long-standing safety rule: Whenever two welders were on a job, they were to alternate positions as safety watch to make sure no sparks ignited flammable materials (and possibly destroy a good ten square blocks of East L.A. in the process).

The incident occurred when I worked with another welder whom I had suspected of being a company lackey. We were inside an emptied boiler tank, welding "beads" along cracked seams. We swapped safety watch every fifteen minutes or so. At one point, as I was supposed to, I told the welder I was going to the restroom. He had to stop welding until I returned—that was the rule. He acknowledged my request, and I left.

When I came back, the shift boss stood there, fuming. The welder claimed I departed without saying a word.

"You're lying, man," I responded. The dude looked away.

But this had no effect on the outcome. The shift boss escorted me to the manager's office, where he pronounced that I was terminated. There was no hearing. No warning. I was out. I knew the company was doing this because I was helping the undocumented guys. They were exploiting, as in most L.A. industry, the rigorous but low-paying labor of recent migrants. Still, I needed the money. It was Christmas. I wanted to provide presents and a tree for my children.

"Let's stop playing games," I told the manager. "You know I was set up. You don't have to get rid of me. I'm prepared to work. It's Christmas, man. I would like my job back."

The manager contemplated this with a smug grin. He seemed intoxicated with the power he held over me.

"No, sorry, it's too late," he remarked. "You are to remove your tools and work clothes from your locker and leave the premises immediately."

I scowled at him. There were a few more words between us, but in the end I told him, "Fine, you can have your stinking job."

On the way out a security guard checked my bag to make sure I didn't steal any materials or tools and walked me to the gate.

Since I was still on probation the union refused to help. It was my worst Christmas in years. Ramiro and Andrea seemed to understand. But that was not good enough for me.

Right away the company blocked me from getting unemployment benefits. I decided to fight them on this. I took my case to the state appeals board.

One day, dressed in a suit and tie, which was rare for me, I presented my case to an appeals judge. The company brought in the plant manager to testify instead of the welder who claimed I left him alone in the boiler tank without letting him know.

The judge looked sternly at the manager and demanded to know why the welder wasn't present. The manager claimed the welder had work to do and the company felt the manager could more than adequately convey the details surrounding my alleged violation.

The judge didn't allow this. Without hesitation, he ruled to reinstate my unemployment benefits since I was prepared to testify in person while the company had sent a proxy who could only report secondhand information.

The manager turned red with embarrassment. He tried to squirm out of it but the judge had made his decision. I knew why the company wouldn't allow the welder to show up—he would have had to perjure himself at the hearing.

Afterward, I waited to take an elevator down to the building's first floor. When the elevator doors opened, the plant manager was inside. I didn't say anything as I stepped in. But after the doors closed, the dude began groveling. He managed a weak apology and stammered about how he was only doing his job.

Then, out of nowhere, he blurted, "Please don't hurt me."

Yeah, right. He actually thought I was going to cut his throat or something. I looked over at him and felt contempt. The man's true character had shone through. Behind his desk at his office, he played God. Tough guy. My supposed "superior." But he made a mockery of the power he wielded. A power he never earned in my eyes. There was more courage, more integrity, in any one toe of the Mexicans he so willingly subjugated than in his whole body.

"Get rid of me at Christmas, will you?" I said with a smile.

He looked scared out of his wits.

Then the elevator doors opened and I strolled away.

I wanted to be with my children all the time, not just on a weekend or when Camila had other things to do, or to babysit. It was hard to be totally there when the kids came and went, when I couldn't be around for all their baby issues, baby firsts, baby changes.

The world made it easy for a man like me to lose touch, to find other partners, to leave the past behind. But I didn't want to go away that easily. Yet for almost twenty months, talking and relating to Camila became torturous. She didn't care about my obvious concerns and feelings. She wanted the basics—money, say hello to the kids, money, take the babies somewhere, money. She smelled of other men. Every once in a while she glanced over at me with disdain.

And the children witnessed a couple of our drunken brawls— Ramiro once entered Camila's living room dancing and laughing with tears in his eyes to get us to stop.

I understood. Camila was a single mother. She worked. She went to school. And she dated. But I often didn't handle this well. There were days I was fine. And then there were days I was torn to bits—I wanted Camila and the babies back at my side.

She didn't want me except for the basics.

I started the divorce proceedings when things looked darkest. I didn't fight for custody (joint custody wasn't available in those days). I couldn't take the children away from Camila. I thought they needed a mother more than a father. She seemed fine as a mother. The only contentious point had to do with the monthly child payments. But the job turmoil kept changing my status. I didn't mind child support—of course, I needed to do my part to help with the children's needs. But I was now eyeing a new life and career. I was still in that limbo state of starving writer. At some point I had to face a judge to determine the final child support payments.

Then just before I lost the refinery job, out of the blue, for a fleeting interlude, Camila came around, flirty, eyes radiant. I held my babies and Camila beamed. For a moment, I was caught in an echo, inside an old dream, in something that used to be. This reenergized my heart, made me believe again. That's what I wanted. Family. Kids. Camila. Loving me.

I didn't know what insanity gripped us—we even went so far as to consider houses to rent. Ramiro and Andrea joined us on those days, and I'm sure they thought their father would be home again. I know I did.

I was still taken by Camila's good looks. Once she considered modeling and had professional photos taken. When she showed me the large color and black-and-white photos I was entranced. Many were of her remarkable face. A few had her in silk gowns. Then she got bolder and had some taken in sheer lingerie. I couldn't help but appreciate what the universe conspired to give her.

The thing was, the ideal beauty for most Hollywood modeling agencies consisted of pale flesh, bones through taut skin, tall stature, light-colored eyes. Camila was small in size, wide-hipped, and brown-skinned—natural and enticing to me. But she didn't have a chance in the "industry," receiving rejection after rejection as she tried to stretch her options in the working world.

Still, we found a house in the San Gabriel Valley. Camila and I walked through the rooms. There was sufficient space for Ramiro and Andrea. The yard wasn't big but was big enough. The rent was within our means. It was in a poor working-class area, but compared to some of the dumps we lived in, it was nice and clean.

That night, Camila and I talked it over. We both looked at each other and the world seemed to say yes. But there was something gnawing at us, something that wouldn't go away, that seemed to pull at our hearts like a kid tugging on a dad's shirt at a carnival. Something we couldn't get through by going under, above, or around it.

The next day, Camila brought it up.

"We can't do this," she uttered, exhausted. "Louie, I think I'll always love you. You'll always be the father of my children. But there's too much hurt between us. What I did I can't get over with the snap of a finger. I know you'd like to forget, but it comes to me all the time. In my sleep. When I look at the kids. At work. Sometimes things get broken and there's no way to put them back together. I don't blame you. I blame myself. But I can't look at you and not be reminded. I'm sorry, baby, but I can't move in with you. I can never go back."

I stood blank-eyed inside an obese and oppressive silence. I didn't know what to say. Truer words had never been spoken. Again Camila managed to find the most compelling argument. Once I heard it, I didn't get mad. Or even hurt. I realized right away what I was failing to consider: There was no way around the gulf between us. I would always remember that night when I tasted the devil's breath. Maybe not every day, but something would happen, a look, a word, a posture. And I'd be back in that house, the kids' room, my nightmare.

I loved my children. I wanted to be with them more than anything—but not with Camila. I had done so much damage with my verbal attacks, outbursts. And she did what she did, childish and hurtful as it was, to get out of this insufferable web I spun. Now the love between us was gone. What we were going for was not love—maybe it was something to assuage guilt or live out some fantasy, but it was not love. Soon enough I worked out the child support. When the final divorce papers arrived that winter of 1979 I didn't have tears or regrets. No more ghosts. No more hanging on. Camila and I were done. I was twenty-five years old.

A friend suggested I try out for a security guard opening at a warehouse complex in the City of Commerce. I wasn't sure about this. I was tired of these nowhere jobs with nowhere bosses who often put my dignity on the line for a nowhere check. Most people took a lot of nonsense for a wage. I worked hard. I tried to come through, but I also had my limits. I had a difficult time whenever people bossed me around or tried to diminish my contributions. I felt dismissed and unappreciated much of my life and was perpetually at war because of this.

Nonetheless, I applied for the job. My heart wasn't in it, yet I couldn't see any other way to go. There was a stodgy 1920s office I had to walk through. An older woman sat behind a desk with piles of folders and an array of phones. She gave me an application and told me the extent of the position. I'd learn to use a gun, get a permit and a bond, and I'd work nights making rounds to various warehouses and truck hangars. I got interviewed that same day.

I figured there was a lot of built-in sleep time. I thought about the many years I'd sit there, with a growing beer belly, reading, watching TV, snoring, walking around to find nothing wrong, and doing this night after night. I hoped they didn't want me.

I also applied for a phone company job, when it was Ma Bell and the general perception at the time was that these jobs would last forever. A friend set me up good: He had answers to the test for a tech job, not a pole climber, but one that involved high-end applications. Better pay and security. I didn't know anything about this kind of work, but I went to the testing center just the same, answers written on my arm, and promptly knocked out the questions. Nobody caught me. And, sure enough, they called a couple of days later to say I received the highest score.

Later I got a call from the warehouse complex—they wanted me for the security guard position.

I turned down the phone company. I actually felt bad. I got the job by cheating. Not long before, I would have gone for it. But many people, smarter than me, took those tests. It was wrong for me to take their spot and I knew it.

I showed up at the warehouse complex office with the lady at the desk. The people were happy to see me. Individuals I didn't know shook my hand. The guy who interviewed me left a note welcoming me to the firm. And the lady had already printed up a tag with my name, setting me up with a uniform, shooting range classes, and work schedule.

Overwhelmed, I sat quietly in an old wooden chair as papers were typed, people called, and others moved about, making sure I'd be taken care of.

The desk lady grinned, said I'd be happy working there. Said she was glad to have me on board. I was lost in my thoughts, eyes vacant, for a long time. I knew I couldn't keep going from job to job. If I took this gig I'd have to stay. The pay was okay. The hours at night were not what I wanted, but I could handle it. And there were all the voices in my head about being practical, fulfilling obligations.

After what seemed like forever, I stood up, turned toward the nice lady, and said, "Sorry, but I can't work here."

The lady's face jerked up, jaw dropped, brow scrunched—hurt, confused. She looked like a loving relative had just smacked her.

I placed the papers and name tag she had handed me on the table. I expressed my regrets to everyone and walked out. I still recall that face—the disappointment, dismay, disbelief. But for all the seemingly accommodating people at that warehouse complex, I made a destiny decision. No more industry. No more wasting time. No more drudgery in jobs I didn't have any interest in.

The day had come when being unheard, staying clear of risk, hidden among work, family, or politics, were more inner-destructive than whatever I'd lose by letting myself go, angled toward the pull of stories, writing, poetry.

Chapter Nine

I entered the Eastern Group Publications offices on Soto Street just north of Brooklyn Avenue in Boyle Heights. It was shortly after the first day of the first year of the new decade—the 1980s.

This organization had taken over from a newspaper chain that for years produced several weekly throwaway newspapers in and around L.A.'s Eastside. EGP's principal publications were the *Eastside Sun* and the *Mexican American Sun*. The owners were Dolores Sanchez and Jonathan Sanchez. I took a gamble they'd talk to me, let alone give me a job. The secretary said Dolores and Jonathan were in and I entered their small offices. They were younger than I might have thought, perhaps in their midthirties. Dolores was confident and professional. Jonathan looked like a creative designer at a small fashion outfit.

I asked for a writing/photography job. I showed them a few things I'd published—in my high school newspaper, for Cal State's MEChA newspaper, a letter to the editor. They seemed impressed. People poised toward writing were rare finds. They also asked if I'd work the darkroom, developing film and operating a halftone camera, a large mechanical contraption that resized photos and made halftone reproductions for the layout editors. I said sure, I wanted to learn.

Not long after I started, I worked on a story about the decapitated head of a Mexican migrant found in a nearby alley. I also followed up on the shocking murder of Miss East L.A.—the killer was a jealous fellow employee who knifed her to death, then stabbed himself, not too deep, claiming gang members did it. And I ended up thigh-high in mud when intense rains brought mudslides crashing down on poor barrio homes in the hills and ravines (as well as expensive multilevel houses in the Monterey Park hills).

With a camera and a notepad, I covered car accidents, gang shootings, weddings, and graduations. I overworked at this job, which paid hundreds of dollars less a week than I had made in industry. As the only photo developer at EGP, I also spent many hours a week in the darkroom, set up next to the layout room. I developed rolls of black-and-white film in canisters. We used the old method with chemicals—developer, fixer, running water. I made contact sheets that Jonathan used to pick out the pictures I then developed for the newspapers. And I worked closely with the copy editor, a former Mexican journalist who also did a gossip column under the name Tía Tita (Aunt Tita), although he was a dude.

In 1980 Manuel Gamboa was a forty-six-year-old Chicano poet who had spent seventeen years in prisons—San Quentin, Soledad, and Folsom, among them—and some twenty years as a heroin addict. He was around during the latter era of the *pachuco* gangsters. He grew up in the Chavez Ravine neighborhood with its three barrios: La Bishop, Palo Verde, and La Loma.

Chavez Ravine was also the site of the city and developers' decade-long battle with the mostly impoverished Mexican community to build Dodger Stadium. People were hurt, many arrested, but in the end the stadium got built in 1962.

Back in the day, Manuel Gamboa turned to drugs and crime, like many of the jobless and stigmatized Chicanos of the 1950s, especially those uprooted by so-called urban development. His addictions led to many arrests. Behind bars, like other convicts, Manuel sought refuge in books. He learned to read in prison and eventually to write. He stocked up on reading material, including works by Shakespeare. For Manuel Gamboa books freed his mind.

In prison Manuel met a Brazilian writing teacher who gave him the nickname of "Manazar." I heard various stories about the meaning of the name: "man on fire," "man with a message," "the man who helps." Regardless, this became what we called him.

Due to the efforts of this teacher and others, Manazar was paroled in the late 1970s. He got assistance for his work outside prison at the Beyond Baroque Literary Center in Venice, California, briefly serving as its director. He also started *Obras* magazine, which featured new voices, including Chicanos and African-Americans. Among these was a young and not-yet-ready writer—Manazar published a few of my vignettes, some of my first literary pieces to appear in print.

I met Manazar at a meeting of the Latino Writers Association after they moved downtown on Spring Street. Manazar was a dark-skinned, wavy-haired *vato* with a Chicano *pinto* accent, but with a long, bushy gray beard that made him look bohemian, poetic, like cool smoke. Soon we helped reorganize LALWA. Manazar became a mentor and friend in this new world of metaphors, of lyricism, and this fervor for writing I couldn't shake off.

After the divorce, Camila and I didn't talk much, except when I visited the kids. I continued, however, to relate to Hortencia, her mother.

She was a hard person to let go of.

Once I went to Hortencia's house in Geraghty Loma. I was supposed to use her truck but one of her daughters said she was down on Brooklyn Avenue at one of the bars and asked if I would fetch her. I didn't think much of this.

I ended up in one of those East L.A. dives where migrants found solace after days of work and family strife. When I walked into the place, there was a commotion in the center of the bar. I went over and saw a crowd gathered around two people, one of whom was Hortencia, in a beer-drinking contest. The other person was a drunken laborer. I couldn't get close enough to attract Hortencia's attention, but I could tell she was drinking this dude under the table.

When Hortencia finally noticed me, she called me over and then instructed me to gather the ducats on the bets being taken. She was persuasive, I must say, and I got into a lot of trouble with her family when it took us hours to return.

———

I enrolled in a journalism night class at East L.A. College. The teacher was a Japanese-American named Mr. Takagi. There were around fifteen students. I was excited to begin this training. I wanted to be a journalist, which I felt was the best way to make a living as a writer. Still, I was well aware, even with the on-the-job experience at Eastern Group Publications, that I needed a command of syntax and grammar.

Unfortunately, as in many night classes with working people and heads of families, by the second class I was the only one in attendance. This forced Mr. Takagi to proclaim he had to cancel the class for lack of students. I must have had a deeply disappointed look. Mr. Takagi realized how valuable this class was for me and tried to explain.

"I'm sorry about this. But I don't get paid if the number of students is below the limit we need to keep these classrooms open. I hope you understand."

"I understand," I answered. "It's just that I was looking forward to this class—I really want to be a journalist. But my writing skills aren't as good as they should be. I need the basics. There are no other classes like this in East L.A."

"Well, again, I apologize—please sign up for the next semester."

"Yeah, okay . . . thanks, Mr. Takagi."

I picked up my bag and a couple of books and tried to make my way out of there. But Mr. Takagi stopped me before I reached the door.

"Listen, let me see what I can do," Mr. Takagi said. "Are you willing to come every week, this same time, and do the work? If you are, if you don't skip one class, I'll be here. What do you say?"

I never welcomed a better idea.

A man of his word, Mr. Takagi showed up every week for about three months to assign writing pieces, drop quizzes on the Associated Press and Strunk and White's stylebooks, and listen to my analyses of newspaper articles. I made sure to be there on time and to keep up with all assignments. The poor guy came a long distance, on his own dime, to provide me this opportunity.

I'm sure he preferred to be home, relaxing with family or reading a book. Yet he always showed up, with more directives, tests, procedures. One time, while reading out loud an article I wrote, I looked up to spot

Mr. Takagi fighting sleep, closing his eyes, then opening them. I kept reading as if I hadn't noticed.

Mr. Takagi apparently liked the work I turned in. Before I finished the class he offered me another opportunity—he recommended me to the Summer Program for Minority Journalists at the University of California, Berkeley. This was an eleven-week intensive training that included actual reporting and writing of real news, as well as lectures, so writers of color could enter U.S. newsrooms. At the time, people of color made up less than 5 percent of all TV, radio, and print media, although they were almost 20 percent of the population. He wrote me a recommendation letter and helped me with the application.

Manazar and I began driving out to Chino Prison, about forty miles away in San Bernardino County, to conduct writing workshops with prisoners.

For me this was my way of giving back. I had escaped a state prison term from my gang and drug days, unlike my homies. Now, entering a locked environment, I helped convicts find expression in poetry, fiction, essays. I could not turn my back on the growing numbers in our communities pressured in so many ways to feed the prison industrial monster. Chicanos were becoming the single largest group in the state's corrections system. Around 80 percent of prisoners were people of color. Some 60 percent were from Los Angeles.

At first, the clang of locks and metal doors took me back to those days. An anxiety rushed over me, as if I would not be let out, as if somehow the system had gotten ahold of me and I'd fallen for their scheme. But this was not the case.

Manazar facilitated the discussions, asking each prisoner to read his own work, as I watched, made comments, and read a poem or two from my journal. The group was Mexican, black, and white. Also in attendance was Susan Franklin Tanner, an actress and theater director, who helped the writing projects through L.A. TheatreWorks. When it was over, I left with Manazar and Susan.

Those steel bars weren't meant for me.

Six months into my tenure at the *Eastside Sun*, I told everyone I was leaving to attend the Summer Program for Minority Journalists at UC Berkeley—yes, I had been accepted. Dolores and Jonathan Sanchez were pleased. The other newspaper and clerical staff were also supportive—if not for this job I might have taken another job that I'd have learned to hate.

Robert Maynard and his wife, Nancy Hicks, founded SPMJ. They brought in leading print journalists as teachers from the *Wall Street Journal*, the *New York Times*, the *Los Angeles Times*, *Newsweek*, the *Washington Post*, and other publications. Maynard and Hicks looked for the kind of desire that words on an essay or an application couldn't demonstrate. One concern was my lack of full college preparation. But, to their credit, this obstacle was overlooked in favor of my experience in obtaining work and doing freelance pieces. Only a rare few passed through SPMJ without a degree.

Being selected for this program made me feel like I was on a long, winding road that had reached a summit. It did mean, however, I had to leave Los Angeles for the summer, live in the UC Berkeley dorms, and work my tail off. I was ready.

I packed my worn Bug with clothes, journals, books, and my weights and lifting bar. I worked out often, trying to stay relatively buff. I knew I had the misnamed "fat" gene. It was mostly on my mother's native side, the Rarámuri side, and it afflicted most of her siblings, nephews, and nieces—and some of her kids. The Rarámuri—also known as the Tarahumara—are a native tribe from southern Chihuahua, the largest cohesive tribal grouping after the Navajo north of Mexico City.

This gene hadn't always meant the Rarámuri were prone to fatness. Traditional natives were some of the healthiest people when they stayed within their natural environment and consumed traditional staples of grains, vegetables, fruits. They were also known as runners in the rough terrain of their homeland—the "fleet-footed people."

Those natives who ended up outside these traditions, including in the United States, often ate badly, mostly processed foods and animal products, and soon became diabetics, victims of heart disease and cancer, alcoholics. My family was one of those who left the land of our ancestors, ending up in U.S. barrios and ghettos, trying to survive in an environment largely toxic to our health, our minds, our spirits.

So working out, something I learned in the barrio, including dabbling in boxing and martial arts training, kept me in good shape. Although, I must say the booze and all the junk I ate was bound to catch up with me.

In a day or two I began the thirteen-hour drive up Highway 1—the Pacific Coast Highway. I took my time sliding past Malibu, through the central coastline, across foggy wine country, among majestic redwood trees, next to the splendid cliffs of Big Sur. I rolled through picture-perfect curves intermingled with incomparable scenes of waves smashing against mammoth rocks, ninety-degree cliff drops, and rolling hills that stretched beyond the sunlit horizon.

Green, rocky, misty . . . the landscape may as well have been a woman's body: lips, breasts, belly button, round behind. Then, finally, I hit the dense Bay Area communities.

One of the first stories I rushed out to do as a writer for *Deadline* (the SPMJ daily newspaper that we had to "put to bed" every night) involved a so-called riot between Mexicans and African-Americans in the steel town of Pittsburg, California, in Contra Costa County—a city that named itself after Pittsburgh in Pennsylvania, an original steel town, only without the "h."

Another SPMJ participant and myself interviewed the supposed rioters, people on the street, police officers, other officials. At least one building was burned to the ground. The town had a full-blown steel mill, workers' housing, poverty, gangs, and all the drama of a working-class area. I recalled how cool and cloudy the Bay Area was, but as soon as we crossed a tunnel into Contra Costa County, everything got hotter, brighter, harder.

The photos and stories I turned in were full of quotes, facts, and a little bit of insight. I interviewed one young man who was half black, half Mexican, and felt caught in the middle.

"I can't fight myself," he said. True that.

Two days out of the week in the program were devoted to lectures, analyses, newsroom decorum. The rest of the time *Deadline* editors, mostly writers and editors from actual newsrooms, assigned us articles. Two in particular, Austin Scott and Steve Montiel, were helpful in my development. Once in a while we generated our own stories. We were also taught how to take pictures, telling the news through striking images instead of just facts and narrative.

Several times a couple of us from the program drove over to San Francisco, across the Bay Bridge, with clouds alongside the parapets, and took photos of people on the streets. I drifted around the Mission District on weekend nights when lowriders from all over the Bay came together in a slow parade of colorfully painted and airbrushed cars with gleaming chrome or magnesium rims and with Chicanas, mostly in party dress, hanging out side windows or through sun roofs. *Vatos locos* from barrios all over Northern California congregated on various corners in their best *cholo* attire. It was the summer of 1980.

From one block to another, teenagers, although also kids as young as six, were break dancing, a phenomenon from the East Coast I also witnessed on Hollywood and East L.A. streets. With Funkadelic's "Atomic Dog" and some music called rap, people displayed the electric boogie, popping and locking, as well as full on breaking with body and head spins on hard ground.

We returned to Berkeley with shots of lowrider cars, handsome crowds, dancing gymnastics, and even a stabbing as rival gangs went after each other. Crime and violence were high on our list of stories to cover. So were soup lines in the Tenderloin District and female weight lifters. I profiled artists and covered street protests—the Bay Area had tons of these—as well as boring government meetings (the trick was to find anything interesting to expand on).

On our time off, I partied, mostly in San Francisco, "the City," including venues in the Mission, North Beach, Haight-Ashbury, the Embarcadero, the Tenderloin. Berkeley was interesting, of course. Telegraph Avenue still harbored hippies, homeless, and homies. I hung out at dusty bookstores, coffee shops, and rare-record shops that had been there since the free-speech era. I once went to a swimming pool where women were welcome to go topless. For a street dude like me this was a treat, although I got the impression most people there didn't think twice about this.

The SPMJ classmates—fifteen of us—that summer became fast friends. We lived on one floor of coed dorms at UC Berkeley. This was interesting. Men and women took showers in the same shower area and even used bathroom stalls next to each other. But we got used to it, although we were from mostly conservative inner-city communities. It was all a learning experience.

There was a short weeklong break in the middle of the summer program. I flew back to L.A. and took three SPMJ participants (from East Coast cities) with me. They had never been to L.A. before. One dude, originally from Philly, complained about the long periods on freeways necessary to get anywhere. *Welcome to L.A., bro.*

I also visited with my children. By then Camila was living with a dude named Ernesto, a Chicano from Colorado. The plan was for me to surprise Ramiro and Andrea. Camila and Ernesto had just left. But just as I walked in I heard muffled yells from the kids' bedroom. I ran to the room and saw Andrea standing to the side, not knowing what to do, and Ramiro trying to deal with a bunk bed that had fallen on top of him, wedging him against the wall. He had been kicking the top bunk from the bottom bunk when it fell. I heaved the bed away. Ramiro must have thought I was Superman or something.

If I hadn't shown up he may have suffocated.

At the end of the SPMJ program, there was a graduation in a small room on the UC campus. The great honor for me was when my classmates voted me to give the valediction. We had a simple ceremony with speeches from Robert Maynard, Nancy Hicks, and others. They gave each of us an embossed certificate. Some of the alumni had their parents and other loved ones in attendance.

Nobody came for me, but I was okay with that.

When it was my turn to speak, I became emotional, educing a few tears from my peers. I explained how ten years before I was sitting in jail in downtown L.A. after being arrested in the anti–Vietnam War protests of East L.A. At the time I had no life, no future, no dream. And now here I was, preparing for a journalism career, something I never conceived of as a teenager, whereby I'd put my awareness and sense of justice into well-documented and moving pieces of writing.

As a youth I lost many friends. A few were best friends. I witnessed much destruction and pain. Yet most media outlets didn't care. These friends died anonymously, unimportant, as nobodies. The media rarely covered our stories, our battles, our heroes. And when they did they focused on the violence, the drugs, the worst in our communities.

I remember once, when I was around seventeen years old, at the funeral of a friend who had been killed by a rival gang, walking up to a radio reporter and telling him to tell "our side." He hemmed and hawed and said he had to leave. Soon more young men and women gathered, insisting their voices be heard. He gave in, removed a tape recorder from a bag, and set up the mike. I thought, *Cool, we'll give him an earful.* Good words were spoken that day. The kids were articulate and collected.

After about ten minutes I looked over and noticed that the reporter had failed to press the "record" button. I told everyone to stop. "He ain't hearing us. He doesn't plan to air any of this." I pointed to the button. The reporter's face turned red. Not because he forgot to press the button, but because he was found out. He leered at me before I walked away.

Now, as a reporter myself, I could help right the wrongs, accomplish something long lasting with what I was being given. Now truth and the full picture could bleed from a pen or a camera, not from a gun.

Chapter Ten

I was drunk, early Sunday morning, driving the V-dub on my way back to the dorm to prepare for my trip back to southern Califas. Most of the other SPMJ reporters had left. I stayed the weekend to visit friends in the City. I had been out all night, partying, blacking out, finding myself with booze in hand as the sun enveloped the sky.

Somehow I got myself on the Bay Bridge to Berkeley. Still, I passed out as soon as I hit city streets. Before I knew it the back end of a tractor-trailer came through the window and roof of the Bug as the rest of my car folded underneath. Glass, fluid, and metal everywhere. As with my other accidents, a couple of which worse than others, I was able to walk away from this one. Against rhyme or reason. The car was totaled. But I stood uninjured along the sidewalk, looky-loos stopping to see, a police car pulling up behind the mess.

Man, I almost made it through the whole summer without screwing up.

Almost.

Luckily nobody was hurt, but now I had no car. I spent two weeks at the home of a family I knew in San Francisco's Bernal Heights while I waited for the insurance money. Unfortunately, I was supposed to be at my new job. SPMJ had assigned me as a daily newspaper reporter for the *San Bernardino Sun*, some sixty miles east of Los Angeles. The Gannett newspaper chain, which owned *USA Today*, also owned the *Sun*. It was a rare opportunity, only I was possibly blowing this chance by not showing up on time.

After acquiring an older-model yellow Bug, I raced down to L.A. to collect a few things, again with all my possessions jam-packed into the vehicle. I drove across Interstate 10 to San Bernardino, a city on the edge of one of the country's major deserts: the Mojave. Amazingly, the editors accepted my reason for arriving two weeks late. But I had to make up for this with dogged reporting as well as good writing. The newspaper provided me a desk, a forty-channel radio scanner, and a computer that linked to the copy editor's computer. I had first learned to use computers at SPMJ. Before that I pecked on a typewriter or often had only pen and paper.

I became a crime and disaster reporter, what rookies are generally assigned to in daily publications. I must say in nearly two years I saw more dead people from murders, natural disasters, and accidents than anyone should ever have to see in any lifetime.

The desert was big for this. People from L.A. often dumped their killings, their trash, their pasts in the desert. There were many buried bodies, stories, songs. Charles Manson and his "family" staked out a ranch in the desert. The Hells Angels were born in this desert. Hollywood notables often held secret trysts and orgies there. A hundred years before, Mexican and Native American warriors had sought refuge in the desert. More recently, drug traffickers landed planes loaded with marijuana or cocaine on the desert's dry lakes.

Most interesting were the carloads of people on their way to L.A. from Arizona, Colorado, Texas, Louisiana, back east, or Mexico who ran out of money and ended up in bleak trailer parks, in motel rows, or in and around the various Native American rezes. Sure, most people lived and survived, and a few even thrived, in the desert. But many others made their last stands there.

A word about Berdoo (the nickname locals gave to San Bernardino): When I got there, the city had a hundred thousand people and the second-highest murder rate in the country. Most of these killings were on the west side of town, the black and brown ghetto, often involving gang wars. The west side housed Crip and Blood sets as well as the large Verdugo Chicano gang. More than half of the residents lived below the poverty level. It was, as one fellow reporter claimed, "a rootin', tootin' cowboy town."

My hours at the *Sun* were from four P.M. to twelve A.M. when most murders, domestic disputes, gang shootings, and accidents occurred. Working these hours barely gave me time to make the deadlines for the next day's papers. As soon as I sat at my desk, I had to make calls to various police stations, sheriff's offices, coroners, and hospitals across miles and miles of desert territory for new or updated information. If anything was going on from earlier in the day, I was the one who had to track down the latest facts. Once the information was gathered, with quotes in hand, I often had only minutes to write coherent copy for the last headlines. Too often I stayed an hour or two later to finish a piece. It was hard, precise, demanding.

I loved it.

One of my tasks was to listen carefully to the scanner as it screeched and scratched through dispatches from police, fire, paramedics, and other emergency outlets. A lot of the talk was in code and I had to memorize the key ones, such as "one-eight-seven" for murder or "two-one-one" for robbery or "four-one-nine" for a dead body. Another was code three, when police put on their sirens to rush to a scene. The more codes I learned the better I could decipher what was happening on the scanner.

I had a partner on the crime desk named Scott Maple, a young white dude who grew up in the area and had been at the *Sun* about a year already. Scott had the codes down. One day, I heard code seven on the scanner. I shot a glance toward Scott. He stood up and said this was the most important code, rarely used, and that I should get out there right away.

I dropped what I was doing and sprinted down the stairs to the parking lot. I drove like mad to the doughnut shop where the officers were to meet. That's when it hit me. Doughnut shop? Cliché, I know, but that's what code seven meant—a food break.

I smiled, oh so slightly, as everyone in the newsroom roared with laughter upon my return. It was that kind of place. Scott and I became friends and all this ribbing was just part of the job.

One day I was making my round of calls when I heard on the scanner about a naked woman lying on the ground next to an apartment complex. I drove out there in case it was a dead body. As it turned out, I beat the cops to the scene. Yes, a young Mexican woman was on her back in high grass without any clothes on and very much alive, although unable to get up. I put my coat over her and told her to stay still while we waited for the paramedics and police.

I looked up and through a window on the third floor, I saw a dude, half-dressed, looking over at us.

"What happened?" I asked.

He wasn't talking. The police later told me the story: The guy upstairs was a marine from out of town who picked up the woman at a local watering hole. They ended up in this apartment and were apparently having sex from one end of the place to the other. At some point they humped near the window and the woman fell backward. Luckily she survived, though her back would likely give her lifelong problems. I didn't have a big story, but I still had to do my best to inform the community what the fuss was about. That was a major part of my job. Even if it was a nonstory, people still needed to know what happened.

The first dead body I had the misfortune to see was perhaps the worst—a fifteen-year-old Chicano youth shot in the face at close range by a shotgun blast on Mount Vernon Avenue, the main drag on Berdoo's west side. As a teen, I had witnessed shootings and even held a couple of wounded homeboys in my arms, but this was something else. His head was torn up as if it were wet paper—brain matter and blood on a brick wall, pieces of skull and an eye on the sidewalk.

Because of my job, I got to know the coroner's people well, even relying on one dude who often called me when he learned of a death. It was important to also have contacts in hospitals and with the police, although the police were the hardest ones to depend on.

On slow days, after all my calls were done, I'd walk over to the nearby San Bernardino police station, and then to the San Bernardino County sheriff's office, which was a few blocks from the police station. They had the day's arrests on a log that I asked to see. Most watch commanders were businesslike, passing me the log and then saying "no comment" when I asked questions.

One watch commander at the police station, however, didn't like me. On hot days, of which there were many in Berdoo, I had my sleeves rolled up, revealing tattoos of a long-haired *india*, a *pachuco* cross, and Camila's name. I even had the barrio symbol of a cross with a rose, only instead of Las Lomas in the ribbons, which I originally planned to put there, I had inked "Ramiro" and "Andrea." Despite the fact that I wore jeans or slacks, regular shirts, and, on occasion, ties, to the police and deputies I looked like a gangbanger.

This particular watch commander often yelled at me for wanting the arrest log. I stood my ground. This was public record and as a reporter I had a right to look at these and ask questions (of course, the police had the right not to answer me). At the sheriff's station, the deputies made fun of me. My appearance clouded their judgment. But I didn't care. I had a job to do. I was polite, but I didn't back down. A good reporter is nothing if not persistent.

Due to the murder rate, the police printed T-shirts that said PRAY FOR ME — I LIVE IN SAN BERNARDINO. Many of the officers were getting burned out. They were limited in personnel and equipment compared to the scope of the problem. By the 1980s, the whole area was inundated with the drug trade from Mexico, armed gangs, unemployed families, crack and heroin addicts, child abuse cases, and horrendous accidents.

In time I began to get along with a couple of the homicide detectives. I could see the toll violence and deaths took on their minds and bodies, how hard it was to close most murders, to constantly deal with people at their worst. As a reporter I also got affected by all this, only I didn't know it at first. The police were traumatized and I was traumatized. I had one outlet — I ended up in bars.

Like cops.

In the winter of 1980 a wildfire struck San Bernardino. Santa Ana winds blew through dry brush in the nearby mountains. The winds swept a blaze that supposedly began with arson into the city at up to eighty miles per hour, and it struck homes and other structures. Scott and I, among other reporters, were sent out to get interviews, stories, anything to bring home the scope of the disaster, which later became known as the Panorama Fire.

Trying to do my job, I got caught in the middle of the desolation.

I had to wear a yellow rubberized raincoat and cap. With helicopters and planes dropping tons of fire retardant, reporters were often hit below. I interviewed fire personnel—many of whom worked twenty-four hours straight, no rest, and were just about delirious. I also talked with police officers and fleeing residents as well as those people who stayed to stop the fires from gobbling up their homes. I saw the colossal damage these fires caused. The casualties were among people who didn't realize how rapidly the rolling balls of flame covered ground.

At one point, I interviewed a man whose family was busy moving valuables from their home while others watered the roof. I looked down a slope at the inferno, which seemed far away. I figured, like them, we had time. I hadn't gotten but ten minutes' worth of quotes when the flames began licking at the windows. The dude and I ran out of the house as the fire overtook the place, which in no time became charred rubble.

This went on at home after home. Finally, the firefighters pushed us out of the area after they forsook their efforts to save the houses. The winds blew the water from their hoses away from the flames and knocked firefighters to the ground.

When firefighters finally controlled the blaze, it had killed 4 people, injured 72, consumed 23,800 acres of land, caused $41.5 million worth of damage, and destroyed 325 homes.

I got into the crime beat before TV shows like *Cops*, *Law and Order*, and *CSI* ever aired, when intricate police work was not in the public eye. Before even kids could view dead bodies on their computers and cell phones. Back in the day you had to be there, to personally witness what was dead but also the misery of those alive—and would then find yourself unable to talk about it.

I dabbled in the forensic sciences, studying the multitude of ways people expire, decompose: how guns, knives, and blunt force destroy tissue; how something like fire can sear through skin, muscles, organs, bone. I've been floored by the stench of bloated bodies. The way skin turns black, regardless of race, or how fluids drip from any orifice if bodies are left to decay. It was morbid and gut-wrenching, fascinating and compelling.

Sometimes it was just too much.

Car accidents, for example—more people were killed on I-10 between San Bernardino and Los Angeles than on any other stretch of road. Local officials called this "the killer highway."

There was the young African-American male who had been sitting in the back of a pickup truck on I-10 when it rolled over. After the coroner's people moved him onto his side, I saw that his skin had been peeled off when it scraped across the asphalt, revealing pink meat and bone. Or the white motorcyclist who changed lanes and failed to see the car in the other lane—the lady in the car said she noticed his last expression, as if he knew he'd seen his last day. When I got there I spotted a bloody jawbone on the freeway's shoulder. And one multivehicle accident resulted in fifteen people being killed, including several members of a Spanish-speaking church who had been in the back of a van on makeshift benches with no seat belts.

On another occasion, I went to a call about a man burned to a crisp in a run-in with a drunk driver a block from his home. When they removed him from the vehicle his blackened hands were still clenched as if he were holding the steering wheel.

A dazed young woman in handcuffs sat on the curb nearby.

There was the double murder in the parking lot of a motorcycle club—some dude found out his old lady was making it with his best friend. There were the reeking remains of a suicide whose body had been left for weeks in an old weathered house. Also the dismembered body of a young woman found in an open field. I was talking with police when Scott stumbled upon the torso. Once I watched the removal of a family from a car that had been speeding down the mountains. The father apparently lost control and the car landed in a wooded ravine. Rescuers brought up two boys, seven and nine, in a stretcher, looking as if they were asleep.

They weren't.

And one day I arrived at the scene of the murder of a twelve-year-old girl who had been pulverized with a baseball bat by her mother's sadistic bench-pressing boyfriend. He had put her inside an army-issued duffel bag and swung at it at various intervals for several hours while the mother sat frozen with fear in the corner of the kitchen.

Yet despite all these tragedies, I'll never forget the afternoon I rushed out to a dispatch call for a six-year-old Mexican kid who had been run over by a car. When I got there the boy was lying on the ground, barely breathing. Paramedics arrived and began resuscitation efforts. Nearby a woman consoled a frenzied mother who was yelling in between Spanish curses.

The paramedics moved quickly with oxygen and other instruments, doing everything they could to keep the boy alive, all of us waiting, hoping, praying. I slowly wrote in my notepad, recording "color," as we called it—the sounds, the voices, the scene. A teardrop fell to the paper, smearing the pencil lines. The child went in and out of consciousness, crying then not crying. We all stood still, as if in a bubble, when the boy took his last breath, one or more of us sobbing louder. The mother was in stunned disbelief for a terrible second, then an unbearable scream surged from her.

I later found out the boy, hesitant to run across the street, did so after his mother on the other side told him to run quickly, that nothing would happen to him.

For a couple of months, one of the African-American reporters and I worked days manning a small bureau on the west side. I wanted to cover more than just murders and melodramas, to also feature positive outcomes from the barrio and ghetto. It seemed the only times Spanish-surnamed people or others of color appeared in print was for crimes and violence.

Some of the stories I did included profiles on local leaders. I interviewed them at the Mitla Café, a renowned Mexican eatery on Mount Vernon. One story was about a lowrider bike club where youngsters were taught how to paint and reshape their bikes in the style of this longtime Chicano art form. And I got to visit with one of the world's handball champions, Mexico's Naty Alvarado, who often practiced at California State University, San Bernardino. There were plenty of heroic stories to be told on the west side.

Yet this didn't last long. Our editor—a conservative Republican named Dean Grant—didn't care about this. The bureau was eventually closed and the reporter and I were reassigned to the main office.

As crime reporters, we were allowed to go on SWAT raids—with bullets flying past our heads. The SWAT team didn't like reporters hanging around. They confronted our editor about this. He may have been right-wing, but he was a good defender of a reporter's responsibility to get the news, even in wartime, regardless of the risks. He pointed out to the head of the SWAT team that more reporters had been killed around the world gathering news than police officers dealing with crime. He promised the reporters would be unobtrusive and responsible for their own actions—as well as their lives.

One time I accompanied sheriff's deputies on heroin drug raids around San Bernardino County. They targeted drug houses in the Inland Empire. The deputies often had operatives dressed as gangsters providing information on who to drop. When they went on raids, the operative was handcuffed in the backseat while he indicated which houses to hit and who to arrest. The deputies wanted the operative to keep working cases so they acted as if he were also in their custody.

Most of the raids were on houses rented by local Chicano street gang members. When the gangsters saw me, they looked around and asked each other, "Who's that *vato?*" thinking I was one of them. The homes were sparse as well as holy messes—trash everywhere. Piles of dirty dishes. Rigs and spoons on tables. One couple had a baby in diapers. I knew because the shitty diapers were scattered around the house.

One midnight raid struck a whole family. Little kids as young as four were jostled out of bed. With their parents in handcuffs, the kids were taken into custody by County Children and Family Services officials. The whole scenario saddened me. Drugs hurt. They can kill. But it was also a great waste to raid families, traumatize kids, and put away their parents, who for the most part needed help. Organized crime thrived because there were no adequate resources for these people.

Camila and Ernesto got married. They planned to move to Denver. Camila and I worked out an arrangement where I took care of Ramiro and Andrea for a few weeks while Camila and her husband readied their new home. This was during the time I worked days on the westside bureau. The kids were now six and four.

By then I had moved into a house that was part of an experimental solar-powered community. Another *Sun* reporter owned the place. I had a Mexican woman take care of the kids while I was at the job. In the evening, the kids and I watched TV together, shared dinner, enjoyed a father-children relationship. This was great for the short time it lasted.

Around that time, while visiting L.A., Ramiro and two other boys burned down a family shed near an apricot tree. Somehow they had gotten hold of matches. The smoke and flames curled into the sky, into the crevices and swirls of his brain, something that would stay imprinted for a long time. He got whipped, scolded, humiliated. But none of this would burn into his psyche like that fire.

To make rent in Berdoo, I had to consider a roommate. A young white woman, twenty-eight years old, came by with two kids of her own, older than my kids but also male and female. They looked at the place and liked it. Her name was Aileen. Although her stepfather was Mexican, she was all the way German-Irish. Her kids were also white. Apparently their father was in prison with ties to a white supremacy gang.

I thought they would be okay to room with. Aileen moved in the following weekend. She had a new refrigerator, new couches, new TV. It didn't take me long to figure out she was on welfare and food stamps. She also had a string of boyfriends buy her things she couldn't get with government checks. She was quite the hustler.

The day came when I had to take my kids to Denver. Hortencia, one of her sons, and a couple of her daughters—and their kids—decided to go with me. We had two carloads of folks for the trip. We all met at Hortencia's place in East L.A. We had packed so the next day we could leave. But that night, I decided to party with friends. I left Ramiro and Andrea with Hortencia.

At bedtime, Hortencia put Ramiro on a top bunk while one of her younger sons slept in a bottom bunk. In the middle of the night, Ramiro somehow fell off the bunk, smashing his face against a metal toolbox. The impact knocked several teeth out and pushed a few others into his gums. Hortencia had no way to reach me. When I finally returned that morning, the rest of the family told me what happened and I rushed Ramiro to the general hospital's emergency ward.

Chingao . . . Ramiro was a mess. His lips and gums were swollen, cut, and bleeding. Many teeth were missing or bunched up in his mouth. I felt terrible. He was in such pain. Then I thought about how Camila would react. I was sure she'd want to kill me. I stood by Ramiro for several hours—this was the "poor people's hospital" and there were many others with wounds from gunshots, bar fights, and car accidents to be seen before anyone attended to Ramiro.

A couple of days later we finally gathered everyone and caravanned the thousand miles or so through lowlands and then some of the highest peaks in the country—the Rocky Mountains. As for my son, he was loaded up with antibiotics and painkillers, and the impacted teeth had been removed. In time, he healed and looked well. The teeth he lost were baby teeth.

Hortencia often stopped to pick off-road cactus as well as other plants and foliage for eating and medicine. At one point she took a machete and slashed up a section of a high bush so she could sit down and rest beneath some shade. Then my VW broke down, but Hortencia's son and I tinkered with the engine and got it going.

On one stretch of highway through the dense Rockies, I got so sleepy I began to hallucinate—images of bears, rabbits, even people I hadn't seen in years floated in front of the windshield. I couldn't go any farther and pulled over. The other car did the same and I suggested we all rest there until we were fully awake again. I pushed my seat back and got Andrea into my arms. I slept there with Andrea's small arms around my neck.

We kept driving past the Rockies until we found a recreational space to let the kids stretch their legs. Despite his accident, Ramiro played with the rest of the children. But for the longest time Andrea complained about her stomach, although she didn't seem too disturbed. Yet when I put her down to run and play, I saw she had soiled her pants— the poor girl had diarrhea. We stopped for Kaopectate, bananas, and 7-Up.

By then my yellow Bug was on its last legs. It kept chugging along, but the engine could barely make it. I kept it running as best I could, adjusting the gas inlet and butterfly valve every few miles. It finally died just as we were getting ready to park in front of Camila's new house.

Chapter Eleven

Soon after I returned from Denver, I was driving home from the newspaper in the used 1976 Dodge Dart I had bought to replace the yellow Bug. It was past midnight. Tired, I opened the door, dropped my stuff on a tattered couch, and proceeded to the refrigerator for a beer. Aileen was behind the kitchen counter and requested I sit down and take off my shoes—she had a special mixed drink to share with me. Okay. I was down for that.

When Aileen ambled toward me, I saw she had no pants or underwear on. Now up to this point, we had never delved into the intimate possibilities of being roommates. Not that I wasn't attracted. Aileen was a long-legged, shapely woman with lengthy blond hair. Although her face had some wear and tear, she was a looker. She often walked around in "Daisy Duke" jean shorts with a good portion of butt cheek popping out. I thought this was fine, but I also felt I shouldn't make a move.

Aileen coming out half-naked from behind the kitchen counter changed that.

A Chicano gang member confronted a young undocumented couple to rob them in a dark westside street. Unfortunately, many Chicano, African-American, and white gangs preyed on the recent migrants, who often had no bank accounts and no legal basis to be protected, and were the least likely to go to the cops.

This particular confrontation involved a fifteen-year-old girl and her sixteen-year-old boyfriend, indigenous teens from the majority-indige-nous state of Oaxaca. After the gang youth took whatever money they had, he shot them both as they sat petrified in their car.

The girl died. The boy became paralyzed from the neck down.

After the initial news account, I visited the injured youth in the hospital. His name was Osvaldo Aquino, a Mixteco native who barely spoke Spanish, let alone English. I also talked to his family; obtained more information from police; showed up at a memorial for the girl, whose body had to be shipped to Oaxaca for burial; and followed up on the young man's struggle to stay alive.

Already deportation proceedings had begun against Osvaldo despite his irreversible condition. Because Osvaldo was quadriplegic, shot through the spine between the fifth and seventh vertebrae, he would have died if authorities dropped him off at the border, as they planned to do. Mexico didn't have facilities or resources for the kind of care Osvaldo needed, including help with breathing as well as bowel and urinary functions. Unless he had money.

Osvaldo's family lived in a dirt-floor shack. One doctor said he wouldn't last very long without proper equipment as well as the con-stant physical and psychological therapy required. I wrote several stories that received a good amount of newsprint, with photos of therapists try-ing to keep Osvaldo's muscles stimulated and prevent deadly bedsores.

When I first talked to Osvaldo he appeared upbeat. He insisted that God had plans and whatever they were he would accept them. But I kept returning, listening, gaining his trust. In fact, Osvaldo was deeply depressed, as anyone can imagine, with the sudden loss of a loved one and now his inability to control his body. And with a possible deporta-tion hanging over his head, he told me in a low voice, "I wish I would die."

To think, to plan, to pray, and not be able to make anything happen, nothing responding, carrying around dead limbs, toes, genitals. It was being partially human, partially ghost. What good was it to have a brain, a will, to love, to feel? I didn't know what this was like, and I knew no language could approximate it, but in Osvaldo's plea, in that moment when he transcended the distance, the unknowing realms, and uttered those words, I felt the torment, the unimaginable. I didn't know what it was like to be paralyzed, but I knew what it was like to want to die.

Osvaldo needed help with U.S. officials but also with the constant medical attention he would require if he stayed in the United States. His family had only one legal resident, his brother, who sought a lawyer to keep Osvaldo in the country. A number of organizations stepped up to offer assistance and long-term care. One in particular was a Christian charity that offered their services for as long as needed.

The battle was now in the immigration courts.

The increased media attention, highlighting Osvaldo's courage to keep struggling despite his profound grief and the terrible fate he faced if he were deported, helped turn things around. Public outcry to save Osvaldo eventually led to an immigration court ruling in favor of the young man, placing him in the care of the faith-based organization, allowing him to stay in the country. Other family members arrived, and many worked on their citizenship requirements so they could be available to him. A ray of hope emerged that perhaps he'd have an electric wheelchair and breathing apparatus to keep him alive, but also eventually allow him a level of independence.

When I last visited Osvaldo, after several months of talking with him, he appeared capable of meeting the difficult challenges ahead. I wished him well as family and community members transferred him to a facility for the next phase in his lifelong care.

I also attended the court proceedings for the seventeen-year-old who shot Osvaldo and killed his girlfriend. He looked like I used to look, with a cold demeanor and nonchalant attitude. I understood all this, including why he couldn't show remorse—from a developmental inability, but also from whatever he'd done to cut off parts of his humanity to survive. He had a terrible home life of painful abuse and poverty, surrounded by limitations at every turn.

When you mention these kinds of issues people say they are "excuses." I say this is knowledge that can help us understand why, in fact, there is no such thing as "senseless" violence. All violence has roots, impulses, motives, whether we like to admit this or not. By not truly comprehending the inhumanity of people like this teen, we fail to fathom the layers of our own inhumane practices, our detached decisions and indecisions, our public cruelties.

My friends in the *Nation* magazine—I had published a couple of pieces with them—invited me to participate in a gathering of progressive writers at the Roosevelt Hotel in New York City during October of 1981. They dubbed this the American Writers Congress after the writers' gatherings that *New Masses* magazine helped bring together in the 1930s.

Forty-six years later the Nation Institute did the same—bringing in the likes of Toni Morrison, Meridel Le Sueur, James Baldwin, Amiri Baraka, Noam Chomsky, Denise Levertov, E. L. Doctorow, Allen Ginsberg, Norman Mailer, and June Jordan.

The AWC turned out to be a head-turning and language-energized event—so many writers and not enough time to talk to all of them. In my presentations I focused on the lack of Latinos in newsrooms and in book publishing, an absence due not to a lack of stories, or even talent, on our part, but to the huge blocks most media and book publishers set up to keep out people of color, and especially people with new and progressive ideas.

The plenary sessions were feisty, as groups of writers tend to be—arguments, counterarguments, proposals and counterproposals. In the end a strong unity was established.

The Latino writers from around the country had their own meetings to discuss issues. A few listened to what I had to say. But a top Latino publisher took issue with this. He was the leading figure in this field and for some reason he felt threatened. My thought was there was plenty of room for all of us.

One day I strolled down a walkway when from the side this publisher and a big Puerto Rican poet coaxed me into a room. I thought nothing of it. But as soon as I stepped in, the publisher had the nerve to push me up against the wall. He tried to intimidate me, saying the big poet was going to kick my ass. He claimed I had no right to be a leader among Latino writers.

Okay, he must have thought I was some academic nonstreet snot-nosed kid. I kind of looked the part—I wore suit jackets or sweaters and black-rimmed glasses, and I was attentive to people and details. His mistake was in misreading me.

I shot that dude a killer stare, square in the eye, and told him he'd better remove his finger from my chest or I was going to break it off and shove it down his throat. Here was the test—was he real or jive? Well, he turned out to be jive. Fear streamed out of his eyes. Even the giant poet backed off. What the hell were they thinking? They became agreeable, full of apologies. They were just kidding, they explained. I told him that where I came from this was not kidding.

As a result, however, they supported me during the plenary sessions when I raised a resolution about writers of color. The Puerto Rican poet got up right after me to second my motion. Cool. Other issues addressed included censorship, economic injustices, libel insurance from publishers, and the detriment of consolidating the publishing industry.

Overall the AWC was outstanding. An outcome of this gathering was the creation of the National Writers Union, which I ended up joining and taking part in for a few years.

The "official" story from the police department in one of the far-flung desert towns was that an indigent white male stuffed a bag of marijuana down his throat after being confronted by officers, causing him to choke, lose oxygen, slip into a coma.

I called the hospital serving that area, where a doctor told me the man had no marijuana bag lodged in his throat, although he refused to say why the dude was in a coma. I called my police contacts, but they didn't return my calls.

I smelled fish in high waters.

The break came when I met with a young Chicano couple who insisted on talking to me about the article I wrote on this case. The first thing the woman said was, "We need to trust you."

The couple seemed nice, newlyweds, expecting a baby. But they were worried—police had apparently been watching their home, following them around, making threatening phone calls.

"Why would they do that?" I asked.

"We witnessed the choking of that homeless guy on D Street," the woman explained. They were talking about the very story I was working on.

"What do you mean 'choking'? The guy swallowed a bag of marijuana, right?"

"No, that's what the police stated," the husband claimed. "But it's wrong. We saw what happened. A police officer put a chokehold on the guy and kept it on until way after the guy passed out. Then they waited a long time to get paramedics to the scene. When we read what the police were saying, we made the mistake of filing a complaint with the department. Now we're under surveillance. Threats are being called in to our house—our house! They want us to back off. To say we didn't see anything."

"But as scared as we are of the police, we feel we have to tell the truth," the woman interjected. "The cops choked that man—that's what happened."

True to form, I submitted another article the next day that included the declarations from this couple. They felt if the news went out it would protect them. I told them to keep me posted on any developments. If the threats were true, I didn't think the police would stoop so low as to carry them out. I'd forgotten what police were capable of.

For some time, Dean Grant and I butted heads, although I did well on the crime and disaster beats. The short-lived westside bureau had been a great idea, but it was Mr. Grant who found a way to get rid of it. And apparently he wasn't too keen on the Osvaldo Aquino pieces.

Since those articles appeared, I had apparently become part of Grant's hit list. Because Mr. Grant had final say on special features he often turned down my ideas. It wasn't so bad, this back-and-forth between us, until I got the notion that Mr. Grant planned to get rid of me.

There was a guy named Harvey who inputted data for the weather and traffic reports. Basic stuff. He wasn't a trained journalist, although this was a good way to start. He was also funny and personable. People liked him. A large dude. Hefty in the waistline. Suddenly, he wanted to be my pal.

Harvey asked to talk, spend time. Because he had a good personality, I went along. Once we sat in a bar in deep conversation. What put red flags in my head was his questioning. He acted as if he were left-wing. But it didn't seem genuine. He'd say things like, "You know, sometimes I think the Soviet Union ain't so bad. I mean, they beat the U.S. in the space race, right? People get free health care. Their cities are clean. Look at how fucked-up our country can be."

I wouldn't respond—this thing with the Soviets was a misdirected notion on Harvey's part. I had no problem conversing with anyone about politics, even with right-wingers. But my politics were about the liberty and equality that the United States had been improving on and broadening since its founding (with much blood and many losses), moving toward an all-embracing, cooperative, and abundant society. This was homebred social transformation, not exported from any other place. I could see how simpleminded some people could be about the nuances and complexities.

When Harvey couldn't get much information from me, he stopped his buddy act. I felt Dean Grant was trying to close in on me.

After the piece appeared about what the young couple witnessed in that nearby town, the shit hit the proverbial fan. While the copy editor liked my work and made sure my pieces were in print, Mr. Grant called me into his office. He insisted on seeing the notebooks where I had scribbled quotes and facts. He wanted to know if I had proof beyond what the couple stated that the police choked the homeless guy.

I did have the words of a doctor who, the first night, said he saw no marijuana bag. And I was looking into other witnesses. Mr. Grant uttered that he wouldn't allow any more articles on this case unless I had more proof. Of course, the couple's statement was a legitimate lead for a story. But Mr. Grant wanted this out of the *Sun's* pages at any cost. I found out later that Mr. Grant and the police chief from that desert city played golf most weekends.

Then the phone calls started coming in. Not threats. These were more puzzling. A police officer from where the incident occurred, or at least a man who claimed to be, reached me at the newsroom.

"I have proof that the police have killed, beaten, and set up people in this city," he proceeded to tell me. "I can't give you my name. But if you want to know more, I can get you case numbers and verification. What you wrote about the police choking that dude . . . that's what really happened."

But, with some experience under my belt, I couldn't just go along with what this caller claimed. I insisted he give me his name, which I'd never reveal in the newspaper, to the police, even in court. I'd go to jail before I'd do that. But he wouldn't give this up. Instead he gave me information that I had to research on my own.

I decided to follow up on his leads.

The "cop" told me that police once set up a local gang member, including putting a gun in his hand after they shot him dead. I got the name and date and went through police records to confirm the claim. It looked like this may have happened, even though the police gave a different account on their paperwork.

"Give me more," I told the police informant. "I can't just go willy-nilly looking for information. I need to know more."

The caller then dropped information that high-level gangsters were bribing the captain of the vice division, including protecting the main prison gang shot caller, who often sat on his front porch, untouchable. He said others, mostly black and brown, were being targeted by police and, where possible, set up.

Each case I independently researched. I found much that suggested the cop's statements were true. But without knowing my source, I could not use what he gave me. I insisted the caller and I meet face-to-face. His identity was safe with me. I even named a restaurant where we could hook up. But he hemmed and hawed. Then the cop suggested I talk to the police chief himself. Throw some of these facts out to him. See how he reacted. I arranged an appointment.

The police chief was Donald Martin. When I met with Mr. Martin, I questioned him on the choking incident. The chief insisted there was a bag of marijuana in the dude's throat. When I told him what the doctor said, he told me to talk to the doctor again. Then I asked him about the gang member who was set up, about the infiltrated vice squad, about other cases the police were allegedly covering up.

That's when I suspected, by intuition mostly, that Mr. Martin might be in on this.

The police chief appeared perplexed that I knew some of this stuff. He had no comment on any of it but seemed to indicate I was onto something. This all seemed wrong. Then it hit me—that police informant was baiting me with information. He wanted me to write about one or more of these stories, stories that could be torn apart or proven wrong. This in turn would discredit my voice, my skills, my reporting.

That's why the "cop" didn't want me to meet him. He didn't care about whether I'd protect his identity. I believed he was setting me up. Of course, I had no proof of this—or of Mr. Martin's possible involvement. My deductions were based on gut feeling, which often helped me maneuver through the intricate layers of lies and distortions that "official" versions disseminated. But as a reporter, without actual proof, actual people willing to stand up, I had nothing to go on.

Several things began to unravel with this story. For one thing, the indigent man in a coma eventually passed away. I talked to his heartbroken mother. This was now murder. The man was about thirty years old. He was mentally ill but harmless. His mother believed the police killed him.

"They were always messing with him," she declared.

Then the young couple who witnessed the incident wanted to get out of the story. They felt more in danger. The surveillance and calls got worse after my article appeared with their claims. They planned to leave the area. I tried to convince them to see this story through. But I couldn't force them to do this. They were starting a young family. The homeless man was dead. There wasn't any more they could do.

They packed their things and moved out in the quiet of night.

Next, and this was the kicker, the doctor recanted what he told me about the marijuana bag. He called me one day to say that my quotes attributed to him in the newspaper were wrong. I told him, no, I wrote down exactly what he said. The doctor maintained he didn't say that. He now claimed there *was* a marijuana bag.

"Where is it?" I asked.

"The police have it as evidence," he retorted.

Of course, I had already seen the evidence—no marijuana bag was included.

Somehow the police got to the doctor.

The fix was in. I was being discredited on all sides. And now with no witnesses or the doctor's original statement, I was left to twirl in the wind. I had to drop the story. Mr. Grant looked pleased with himself. The cop informant stopped calling.

That was the last straw. One day, after much pondering, I entered Mr. Grant's office and handed him my resignation. In my letter I cited the reasons why I couldn't work for that newspaper and said that as a journalist for the *Sun*, my integrity in seeking the truth was compromised.

Mr. Grant took the resignation with a smile.

I made plans to return to Los Angeles. I sent my clippings to various L.A.-area newspapers such as the *Los Angeles Times, Herald Examiner, L.A. Daily News, Long Beach Press-Telegram*, and *Pasadena Star-News*.

The initial responses were encouraging—these daily newspapers were looking for qualified writers of color. I had my time at the *Sun*. I had won an award for a freelance piece in *L.A. Weekly*. Editors said they just had to check my references. I felt vindicated, back on track. I thought my biggest problem would be deciding which newspaper to go for, the *Los Angeles Times* or *Herald Examiner* being my preferences.

But the calls never came. When I inquired, when I finally reached somebody with authority, I got comments like "We're not looking for people right now." One after another, editors balked. They had lame excuses or no excuses. I never got hired.

For a short time, I ended up homeless in San Bernardino. I had to leave the house and Aileen—she was disappointed. She couldn't handle the rent by herself, so she found a place in working-class Fontana. She even asked me to come with her, but I said no. This relationship was good while it lasted, but it didn't feel like my life.

I helped Aileen and her kids pack up their things. With their final boxes stuffed into the back of a friend's truck, Aileen turned around, as if I might change my mind. I walked back into the house without a word.

In the next week or so I patched up the holes in the walls and fixed the roof and plumbing. I even found another family to rent the place. This was the least I could do for the *Sun* reporter who owned the house.

I put my things in storage—now mostly books, which I had been accumulating for years. I slept in my Dodge Dart, sometimes in the *Sun* parking lot. Other times I slept on the living room sofas of a few reporters. They were gracious to help me, and I was grateful. But some of them had families and it wasn't right for me to stay at anyone's home for too long. I needed to get back to L.A. with or without a newspaper job.

I also uncovered why the L.A.-area newspaper editors never got back to me. One organization I went to work for had the guts to tell me—the American Federation of State, County, and Municipal Employees in California. They also followed up on my references, including Dean Grant. They told me outright that Mr. Grant said I was "an advocate" and should *not* be hired. I thought Mr. Grant would be professional and recommend me based on my reporting and writing.

Instead he blacklisted me based on politics.

Chapter Twelve

In the summer of 1982, Manazar Gamboa and the L.A. Latino Writers Association came to the rescue—they offered me a position as director that included being editor of *ChismeArte* magazine. They received a small grant to cover my salary. I decided to take it despite the low pay. It helped me get back to "El Lay."

My offices were at the Self Help Graphics and Art studios in East L.A., back in the barrio, in a small cluttered storefront on the former Brooklyn Avenue (now Cesar Chavez Avenue). Self Help Graphics was located in an old two-story building owned by the archdiocese. I befriended Sister Karen Boccalero, a Franciscan nun who founded Self-Help Graphics in the early 1970s. For a time it was the only art studio, gallery, and printmaker for Chicanos—after the demise of spaces like Mechicano Art Gallery and Goez Art Gallery, among others, that had surfaced during the heady days of the *movimiento*.

I also found a barely-there space next door to Manazar's apartment in Echo Park. It was a room and a toilet. I removed my boxes out of storage and piled them high wherever I could. The rent was negligible. At least it was a roof over my head.

Manazar had big dreams, big ideas, which I liked. He self-published his poetry, using the talents of artists and makers of handmade books. He wrote short stories and plays. He continued to do workshops in prisons and juvenile lockups.

One of my favorite things was the salonlike gatherings we organized, usually on the spur of the moment, at Manazar's apartment. He and others brought out guitars and sang Mexican *corridos* and *nueva can-ción*. We read poems. We discussed politics, arts, the ways and byways of life.

Manazar also had another project: He wanted to create his own art gallery and performance space. This came about when Manazar located a small warehouse to lease on East Sunset. I took part in the founding meeting of what would become Galería Ocaso (*ocaso* means "sunset" in Spanish). I became the poetry curator, bringing in poets and performance artists from all over L.A.

We had visual artists fill the long walls with framed art pieces (Chicano artist Gronk painted right on the walls—the *Titanic* sinking with images of people trying to stay afloat). We had bands, none of which would be signed by major labels, but they were as skilled as any at the Hollywood Sunset Strip clubs.

We were creating a scene, a space, a multiarts extravaganza in Echo Park. Eventually, I obtained offices downtown at the old Eastern Columbia building. There was a floor for arts organizations and our space went for $60 a month. I ended up putting my boxes there and even sleeping on blankets across the floor. I used the restrooms down the hall to clean up—it was better than that place next to Manazar's.

The phone call came from Ernesto's sister, Alexis, who lived in Southeast L.A. Ernesto, Camila's husband, had apparently beaten her up. Camila managed to get into her car, with Ramiro and Andrea and a few belongings, and drive all the way from Denver to Los Angeles.

When Alexis called, Camila was at Alexis's house. I told Alexis I'd come over to be with the kids. Camila would have to deal with Ernesto. My concern was for Ramiro and Andrea.

Alexis lived in an industrial part of town with workers' housing in squat two-story apartments and small homes. I drove over there and parked near a row of worn-out buildings. When I knocked on Alexis's door, it was Ramiro, now seven, who opened it. He jumped up to hug me, this wonderful boy, whom I had not seen since I left him and his sister in Denver about a year before.

Five-year-old Andrea rushed up to me as well—she had the appearance of a china doll. Camila was in the kitchen, eyes red, looking away from me, perhaps in shame. We sat down at the dining table.

Although it was Alexis's brother we were talking about, Alexis appeared to be on Camila's side. Ernesto was an okay person until he drank. He was tall for a Mexican, built, handsome, with a decent personality. We got along for the most part. But Ernesto became belligerent once he hit the bottle. I assured Camila that she did not have to take his nonsense.

Although I communicated often with Camila and the kids while they were in Denver, they had failed to inform me about the beatings. Camila once called me in Berdoo to ask for money. I inquired about the babies—Camila said everything was fine, the kids were fine, she was fine. I later found out Camila had called from a battered women's shelter. The children also finally divulged they were largely latchkey kids, often left alone in their home. It annoyed me that I couldn't get a straight story from Camila, even though I understood she was embarrassed.

At the dinner table, Camila came clean. Ernesto had been hitting her for some time. Apparently he didn't hit the kids, but he once threw a shoe at her and it struck Ramiro on the head. Again, Camila felt Ramiro was okay . . . I was getting angrier by the minute. None of this was okay. I suggested she leave the dude, for the kids' sake as well as her own. When I was with Camila she never accepted abusive behavior— and well she shouldn't have. Now she seemed helpless, vulnerable, susceptible.

I stayed with the kids that night in a back room that Alexis prepared. I slept on blankets next to their bed like I used to do. Sometime in the early hours, Ernesto showed up at Alexis's house. He had driven from Denver to L.A. to find Camila.

And he was wasted.

I woke up to yelling from the living room, Ernesto's yelling. Camila's voice was softer, scared—I never thought she'd get this intimidated. I got up, put on my pants and shirt. Barefoot, I opened the door and walked into the living room. Ernesto was standing there. He looked over at me and went nuts.

"What the hell is he doing here?" Ernesto yelled at Camila.

"You don't have to ask her, I'm standing here in front of you. Ask me," I said, stern but not threatening. Ernesto glared at me, unsure of what to do. Now he was confronting someone who wouldn't back down. Who wasn't frightened of his yelling. Who could possibly kick his ass.

"I'm here for my kids. Not for Camila, not for you. You understand—you ain't going to cause a ruckus in front of Ramiro and Andrea as long as I'm here."

That's when Ernesto pulled out an enormous hunter's knife. Camila stepped back into another room. I didn't budge. I had to be a rock, an unmovable force, something he had to kill or he'd pay for it.

"Go ahead, stab me. But you don't want to do this," I stated, knowing I had to stand up to him, but in a measured way. Although drunk, he could still slice a good piece off my flesh. "It ain't worth it, Ernesto. None of this. Look at Camila—she's afraid of you. Is this what you want? Why hurt the ones you love? This is the wrong way of dealing with anything. Believe me, you don't want to do this."

"She's still in love with you, man," he declared. "Look—she's got you here. She's got you under the same roof. Fuck, man. Why the fuck did she *call you*?"

"She didn't call me," I responded. "Your sister did. Anyway, it's my kids I care about. There's no more Camila and I. That's long gone. It's Camila and Ernesto. But you're blowing it, man. You're not going to get any love from a woman who's terrified. That's not love, Ernesto."

"Fuck this, I'm going to cut you, man. I know what she's doing. She's trying to get back into your life—"

Camila and Alexis tried to interject, but he turned to them and yelled. I looked at Camila and with my eyes told her to move away, not to say anything.

"Ernesto, look at me," I said. "It's me you're mad at. It's me—here in front of you."

Ernesto held the knife in front of him as he continued with accusations. I looked for a moment, an opening, perhaps when he turned briefly, where I could jump him for the knife. I didn't think my words could stave off Ernesto for long.

But before I could do anything, little Ramiro walked into the living room from the back.

"What's going on, Daddy?" he muttered, in pajamas, wiping his eyes.

Upon seeing the boy, Ernesto suddenly fell back into the sofa. He dropped the knife and started to cry—from whatever fatherless place men lose their courage, their sense of being, their integrality.

After a long pause I said, "You don't want to hurt anyone here . . . Ernesto, go ahead and cry. Now I can sit down with you as brother, as *carnal*, as fellow beaten father, husband, man. We've all been there."

I picked up the knife near his feet. Ernesto didn't move. I carried the weapon to the kitchen and threw it into the sink. I went to Ramiro, squatted down, and held him.

"Don't worry, little man. Mama and Papa—and Ernesto—we'll be fine."

And we were. That night. That time.

At the urging of a former reporter from the *Sun*, I attended a party in the Baldwin Hills section of South Los Angeles. There was a mix of professionals, people of color, mostly African-Americans, talking, drinking, dancing. I stood in a corner with drink in hand, somewhat shy, a condition that struck me when I least expected it, checking out who was coming and going. One woman stood out—she had a cute face, a well-toned body. My reporter friend introduced us.

Her name was Deborah, and she was originally from the state of New York. East Long Island, to be precise. She had studied journalism but was also into acting, one of the main reasons she ended up in the City of Angels. Deborah had a college degree and was well versed in books, drama, the arts—something about her grasp of weighty brainy stuff appealed to me.

I had been with mostly working-class women, often streetwise. Nothing wrong with them. They were decent and good people, but not as schooled as I would have liked. Now that I was a "professional," with just a smattering of schooling, I thought I could overreach and maybe date a real educated person.

Later that night I walked Deborah to her car and asked for her phone number, some of the shyness falling off. She smiled—an amazing smile actually—and gave me the number.

Deborah and I went out after that. We had dinners—good food, fine wine. We went to the movies. We saw theater.

Deborah's family was one of the few African-American families in the more exclusive sections of Long Island at the time. Her father had turned a housecleaning service into a profitable business. For a long time African-Americans were mostly servants and cleaners in the complex of mansions belonging to the well-to-do. In time an African-American middle class emerged.

One night after a nice dinner, Deborah and I paused at her apartment door to say good-bye. I didn't want to leave. I turned to her. She smiled, knowing what was going to happen. I leaned in and kissed her—my heart raced, my brain in a sweet fog.

After the kiss, Deborah opened the door and left space for me to enter.

By the fall of that year the LALWA director's job ended. The grant was done and no more funds were available. I still needed money for child support, gas, and rent for a better place—the same *pinche rollo*.

The good thing was my kids were back in L.A. I could see them more often. And I had Deborah in my life.

Around that time I applied for the AFSCME job. The union was going after sixty thousand University of California employees—clericals, blue-collar, and some professional units. They needed a writer for the *AFSCME California* newspaper. I met with Vernon Watkins, the UC campaign director and a leading African-American labor leader. My newspaper experience helped—whatever Dean Grant told them about me was of little consequence. I ended up getting hired as an international public affairs associate.

For a union election to occur, UC employees had to sign election cards, join in significant numbers, and force the system to set up a vote. If the majority vote was for the union, contract negotiations followed. Other unions also contended for these cards. And we had to address the strong antiunion efforts.

We had quite a job here.

I maneuvered a place to stay. By then my brother and his wife owned a house on Fourth Street near State Street in Boyle Heights. It was a two-story Victorian. There was a basement studio apartment. Although it was musty, I moved in, again with boxes of books in all corners.

I hit the ground running. Vernon Watkins hired top organizers from the African-American and Chicano communities—and also from the white left. He knew what he was doing: They were the most consistent and veteran organizers.

The campaign had a number of issues and strategies to consider. There was the large number of women in the clerical positions—they were the key to winning. Many needed on-site day care, decent wages, pay equity (women were getting paid far less for the same work than men), maternity leave, and better health care.

The blue-collar workers—mostly maintenance, landscape, construction, and some industrial—had their own concerns. Professional units, particularly in the large hospitals, included researchers and nurses. These groups didn't always see eye to eye, let alone grasp anything that could unite them into a union.

With organizers on the ground, my job was to convince them with words. I created high-end newsletters, brochures, leaflets, and radio spots. It was the kind of challenge I liked.

The campaign cost millions of dollars and took several months. I worked long hours on written materials. I organized press conferences and media interviews. Once during the campaign I was quoted on the front page of the *New York Times* regarding pay equity for women (also known as "comparable pay"), an issue AFSCME strongly advocated.

I visited most UC campuses, scattered across the state of California, working with women trying to create their own newsletters and propaganda or organizers on their campaign speeches and publications. There were AFSCME locals we had to assist—although not part of the campaign, most had been around for years and still needed to be attended to.

On the job I wore a suit and tie and learned to keep my hair trimmed and my shoes shined. Overall it was exciting, lip-biting, tense work.

In the middle of everything I asked Deborah to be my wife. We'd only been together a few months. But it seemed right. She became active in Hollywood stage productions and some commercials. She even had a few lines in soap operas. Deborah had the combination of smarts and artistry I admired. She was also a nice person.

We married in a civil ceremony in a downtown L.A. courthouse with my youngest sister as bridesmaid and Deborah's brother Del as best man. My kids were there as well. It was one of those "line up to get married" situations. Each couple had a few minutes in front of a judge. One couple had on a groom's tux and bride's white dress. Deborah and I just came in with the best clothes from our closets, me with my dreaded suit and tie. Our photos were taken on the steps of the courthouse, a huge contrast from my first wedding with all the bells and whistles.

I was now twenty-eight years old.

We moved into an apartment complex in Angelino Heights known for housing Hollywood actors and writers since the 1920s. This was the neighborhood famous for its large Victorian and Queen Anne structures, most from the 1800s, which were kept in top shape and visited by busloads of tourists.

I bought my first computer—a Kaypro—so I could continue writing poems, stories, and literary things outside of the AFSCME writing. This kept me from totally losing my connection to words as a creative outlet.

For our honeymoon, we went to Deborah's family house on Long Island's seashore. We were there with snow on the ground. Her parents were gracious. We had an elaborate reception at a fancy hall to commemorate our marriage. A table full of wedding presents greeted hundreds of guests. Deborah's family was well known in the area. Everyone was glad to meet me. Deborah, who was two years younger than me, never married before, without any children, appeared delighted.

The union representation campaign heated up. I spent many hours away from home, from Deborah, from my kids. This worsened after AFSCME obtained enough cards for an election. We had organizers at all the campuses. We had other locals contributing people and resources. We had the media inundated with publicity. When the voting began, I informed the various media outlets about how things were going.

Finally, with all the votes tallied, the election results were announced—AFSCME had won most of the clerical, blue-collar, and professional units. We won the largest union representation election in history. The victory party at a large hall exploded with applause, whistles, popping champagne bottles, the usual victory outbursts.

I was worn out.

My anger rose again without warning. Deborah never gave it good reason to. Still, she was the target of my indignation. I'd find something I didn't like—a pair of pants she wore, a new hairdo, something she said. Most of the time, I was fine. We talked and laughed often. She was a devout Christian, which, of course, I accepted. I was an atheist, which to her credit she was willing to live with. We were an interesting couple that I'm convinced could have worked out fine but for my combustions and imbalances.

When I drank it was different. I relaxed. I laughed. I was the happy drunk. But Deborah and I didn't drink that much. She wasn't raised this way. Not having an escape valve, I often took my issues out on Deborah.

She didn't deserve this. Deborah was good with my kids. Ramiro and Andrea loved her attention, her games, her considerations. It wasn't that I didn't love her. I missed her during my late hours at the AFSCME offices or on the road. And we made love often.

My mother also took a liking to Deborah. Deborah came with me to the San Gabriel house to meet my parents. Dad, as usual, didn't have much to say. My mother, on the other hand, in Spanish only, tried to relate. Deborah struggled to respond in English. They missed most of what they said to one another, but they managed. Once Deborah got sick, a severe flu. My mother offered to take care of her. She gave

Deborah the *yerba buena* teas, the chicken *caldos*, I don't know what else. After two weeks in Mama's care, Deborah was back on her feet.

The one time I had problems with family concerning Deborah involved in-laws of my sisters and their friends during a boxing match between two world champions, the Nicaraguan Alexis Argüello and the African-American Aaron Pryor. It was a great fight, which Pryor won.

Most people at the party rooted for Argüello. At one point, when Deborah was in the kitchen, one of the in-laws called Pryor the "N-word." Among this crowd were Mexicans who were prejudiced when it came to black people.

"Hey, don't say that word around here," I snapped. "My wife is in the kitchen. This is offensive to her and to me."

That should have been the end of it, but a couple of the dudes stood up to defy me. I was ready to throw blows when my sisters and the other women tried to calm everybody down. I went to the kitchen, pulled Deborah away, grabbed our things, and walked out.

Another time, Deborah and I were in Beverly Hills sitting on a park bench with her brother Del. Beverly Hills, the rich enclave famous for high-end shopping on Rodeo Drive, was notorious at the time for keeping black and brown people out. We had gone there for some reason or other and decided to just hang.

As we talked, patrol cars parked on the two streets to either side of us. I looked over and saw officers step out of their cars and stroll toward us. Because of the troubles I had with police as a teenager, some of the old memories sharpened my stance, filled my veins with adrenaline, got me ready. But for the sake of all of us, I held this in check. Sure enough, the officers approached me.

"What are you doing here?" an officer asked.

"What are we doing? We're just enjoying ourselves in this park," I declared, trying hard not to get mad and have the cops turn on any one of us.

"We got a call that a Mexican with tattoos fitting your description just robbed a gas station nearby," another officer said. I didn't believe them. It was too convenient for me to fit a description like this. I knew they were rousting. Luckily, we were congenial, relaxed. They couldn't get a rise out of us. The cops searched me, finding nothing. They eventually decided to let us be and returned to their patrol cars.

I took part in the founding meeting of a new AFSCME affiliate—Local 10—made up of statewide UC employees. Congratulations went around, photos were taken, and a new era in statewide union growth opened up. AFSCME was now a major player in California labor politics.

I had to deal with Local 10's public affairs as well as those of other locals in the L.A. area. In addition, as an international union representative, I was sent to various cities around the country to troubleshoot publicity snafus in other campaigns. I ended up in Salem, Oregon; San Diego; Austin, Texas; Portland, Oregon; Oakland; and Denver, and often had strategy meetings in Washington, D.C.

The unfortunate thing was that many organizers in the campaign were being walked out the door. This seemed to come from higher-ups at International headquarters—as if these organizers were welcome to help win elections, gain new members, and build the union, but when the hard day-to-day work was over, they were pushed out. We lost many strong people. Locals that appreciated their skills and politics hired a few. The state office tried to hang on to as many as they could. But too many good labor organizers were simply let go.

Soon, too soon, Deborah and I were having big troubles. I became more abrasive. I challenged Deborah on politics and religion, things that had no bearing on whether we loved each other or not. It was an ideological response to my own unwarranted irritations. I found fault with Deborah when there was none. Deborah had her own insecurities. She questioned my love, even my love for my children.

I get that I could be mean and aloof. I could do this even when I loved someone. But my behavior didn't feel or act like love. This I didn't get.

Chapter Thirteen

In the spring of 1983, I was invited to visit Nicaragua with a group of independent journalists. The Sandinista government launched these trips to garner worldwide attention to their progress. This government, a result of Sandinista rebels winning a civil war in 1979, was under intensifying attacks by right-wing contra groups, supported materially by the Reagan administration—although at the time the U.S. government denied any involvement.

I asked Manazar to go with me. Manazar was a leading Chicano writer and activist the Nicaraguans needed to know. Many Chicanos fought alongside the Sandinistas. One friend of mine got wounded in Nicaragua and for almost three decades brought clothes and medicine to the countryside after the civil war. Other Chicanos contributed support work in the United States, helping pressure the U.S. government not to back the Somoza regime, which they saw as violent, torture-ridden, and exploitative.

The trip involved two weeks of visiting most of the country, including the departments (what we call states) of Managua, Leon, Granada, Esteli, Chinandega, Masaya, and Chontales. We talked to government officials as well as Sandinista rank-and-file. We were allowed to enter prisons holding former Somoza National Guard members as well as a facility on the Mosquito Coast that housed rebel Miskito Indians. We went to the community of Bluefields, where the descendants of mostly English-speaking escaped or shipwrecked African slaves lived and worked.

And we looked down the mouth of a sulfur-cloud-spouting volcano after climbing several yards of rust-eaten stairs and handrails.

I met Sandinista leaders such as Daniel Ortega, Humberto Ortega (Daniel's brother), Tomás Borge, Sergio Ramírez, Rosario Murillo (Daniel's wife), and others. We attended study sessions of Jesuit priests, farm workers' collectives, meetings of former Sandinista fighters, youth gatherings, womens' circles, and more.

We had dialogues with indigenous tribes, which held great interest for Manazar and me. We attended writing classes on the islands of Solentiname, where poet-priest Ernesto Cardenal created a legacy of revolutionary arts expression. And Manazar and I read poetry in a couple of Sandinista barrios—this was, after all, the "Land of Poets."

Most of the time Manazar and I stayed in Managua, which still had ruins from the 1972 earthquake, a catastrophe that killed ten thousand people and destroyed 90 percent of the city (Puerto Rican baseball great Roberto Clemente died in a plane crash trying to bring supplies to the earthquake victims).

We visited toppled churches, government buildings, and homes that remained as a testament to the poverty of this country and the incalculable help it needed (the Somoza regime had embezzled much of the international aid that should have been used to rebuild the city).

We once walked into the Hotel Inter-Continental, a pyramid-like structure that housed many of the foreign correspondents. I was dismayed at the mainstream U.S. journalists who stayed there, hardly venturing out, drinking and partying, and often using official State Department reports as their main sources.

Since Manazar and I spoke Spanish we broke out into the streets, alleys, and dirt roads, interviewing mothers, children, workingmen, the unemployed, war amputees, and vendors. We had tape recorders and cameras. We imbibed Flor de Caña rum. Even though we also attended "official" Sandinista events, tours, and speeches, Manazar and I went off on our own.

The truth of what was happening in Nicaragua lay somewhere between what the U.S. government was putting out and what the Sandinistas were sharing. I knew any "official" statements failed to provide the whole picture.

What I learned was that the Sandinistas were trying to create a new social model: The cadre studied Marx and the Bible. They tried to establish a politically pluralistic society with combined socialist and capitalist economic features. They were carrying out a literacy campaign for a country that had an extremely low literacy rate. There was still low-scale commerce, mainly in the crowded and colorful marketplaces, and individual farm fields. But large-scale collective farms and state-run industries were also in the works.

They had inherited, however, an extremely poor and class-divided society following the fall of the Somoza regime (the Somoza family had been running Nicaragua since the mid-1930s). The war took fifty thousand lives, created a hundred and fifty thousand refugees, and left much of the country in disarray.

We found strong support for the Sandinistas among the youth, among the poor, among the *campesinos* and working people. Most of the opposition came from the relatively well-off areas, privileged students, and former National Guard members.

But with the grinding poverty—change was churning too slowly for most people—would-be supporters began opposing the Sandinistas, including indigenous groups and former fighters. Some Sandinistas took part in corruption and a few lived high on the public trust. And the Sandinistas got taken off track by internal bickering—and then overpowered by external attacks.

The contra opposition carried out terrorist acts—such as planting underwater mines to disrupt shipping—and conducted guerrilla warfare. "Contras" stood for "*contrarrevolucionarios*," or counterrevolutionaries. President Reagan opposed the Sandinistas, including their widely recognized fair elections, and imposed a trade embargo on the country while providing funds and arms to the contras.

However, Reagan denied he supported the contras, especially in 1983 when the U.S. Congress prohibited this. The administration then orchestrated the infamous Iran-Contra Affair by selling arms to Iran and using the proceeds to assist the contras. There were also allegations linking the United States to the international drug trade, such as that they had introduced crack cocaine to poor African-American and Latino communities in South Central L.A. so they could divert drug-related finances to the fight against the Sandinistas.

During this trip, I thought seriously about Deborah. How wrong I'd been. How I needed to be patient, kind, loving. I questioned my sanity, why I persistently destroyed good things. Why I wanted to love and be loved, and yet when I had love, I would tear it apart. I'm sure this was tied to my addictions, my youth, to the violence I saw but also contributed to. I'm sure it was linked to my sense of failure.

This was not what I wanted. I wanted to prevail. To apply myself in love and relationships the way I did in work and politics. I had to consider my children as well—to be there for them. I had my kids on most weekends, but I rarely knew their school life, their teachers, their friends, their thoughts.

Deborah's Christianity wasn't the problem—unless I made it a problem. My intractable political concepts were getting in the way. It was ego caught up in a great cause and my thinking, for some peculiar reason, that this made me better than others. I had no right to go there.

If my worldview clashed with being balanced, with connecting, with organic and real love, with relationships, especially the fundamental ones like with my children and Deborah, I needed to evaluate this and grow up. There had to be a way to have my politics *and* my life. I needed to find out how. I resolved to dedicate time and effort in this direction. I resolved to love Deborah and my kids the way they deserved to be loved.

The Contra War was escalating, especially along the Nicaraguan/Honduran border. Most of the contras were encamped above the Río Coco in Honduras. Manazar and I knew we were in the middle of a war and could not stand on the sidelines.

We decided to do a risky thing—to cross over into Honduras and find out more about the contras. We went over in a jeep with a couple of unarmed Sandinistas. This was extremely dangerous, but if I could prove the United States was arming the contras it could be a journalistic coup.

We stopped in a wooded area where we glimpsed guerrilla camps through bushes. We spotted tents, rows and rows, a few people in and around them. But we couldn't see if there was a cache of firearms. Then the firing began—high-powered weapons that could cut a tree in half. We scrambled to the jeep and jumped on, the driver taking off like a monkey in flames. In seconds the jeep reverberated with the explosion of a bomb that missed but threw enough debris to scare the holy crap out of us.

We joggled inside the jeep as its tires rammed over crevices, cracks, and holes in the ground. We swerved around thick tree branches, going as fast as possible to the other side, to Nicaragua.

Then we saw it, in slow motion, a bomb falling right in front of the jeep, a whistling sound accompanying its descent. The driver braked, who knows why. The rest of us bent down and put our arms over our heads as if this could shelter us from the blast. There was no shelter. We were goners. Our lives detonated in an instant. Finally dead.

But nothing happened.

Slowly we removed our arms from on top of our heads. The air was still. Sounds stopped. We stayed in our seats for prolonged seconds. Nobody said anything. Then the driver got out and peeked at something in front of the jeep. I stood up to see what he was staring at. The other Sandinista got out as well. Manazar and I joined them.

A few feet in front of the jeep was a wing-tailed device, about the size of a pineapple, embedded in the dirt. We got closer and realized the bomb was real but had failed to explode when it hit the ground. A dud. We also saw markings that indicated this was U.S.-issued ordnance. Here was proof. We had to take it back with us.

One of the Sandinistas went to the jeep and found a towel. He lugged the bomb out with the towel, little by little—with the rest of us standing at a distance. Then, with the bomb cradled in his arms, he placed it carefully in the back of the jeep. With hardly any words we all drove, much slower, the few yards to the border.

I'm sure retrieving that bomb was a dim-witted idea—it could have gone off. But now we had our evidence. The Sandinistas held on to the device. Manazar and I took photos. I felt I had a big story.

———

I made phone calls to various publications to see who'd be interested—newspapers and magazines. Nobody wanted it. At the time it was a hot potato. There was also an ongoing issue—a reporter of color was rarely seen as "unbiased" enough or "expert" enough for these kinds of stories. In the end only a couple of progressive publications honored our work. It was frustrating.

Next I had most of my photos and journals confiscated by some entity at the Miami airport. I had a box with materials from the Sandinistas on a new movie they were promoting. The box also had a good portion of my writings and rolls of film. This box failed to appear at the baggage claim. I filled out all the forms and talked to all the bureaucrats. Nobody knew what happened. No official claimed my things were being appropriated. The box was simply "lost."

Weeks later I received the box, with no note, no explanation. It had been opened and then hastily taped up. The movie's promotional materials were still there. The journals and film were gone.

I learned a valuable lesson—always carry this stuff with you.

I had stayed on in Nicaragua longer than I had planned. I let Deborah know, but after a time I couldn't reach her. She wasn't answering the phone, which I thought unusual but didn't worry about. I also called AFSCME and they seemed okay with my delay but urged me to return. After the problems at the Miami airport, I got back to LAX and took a cab home.

I opened the door to the apartment, expecting Deborah to be there, although I was unable to reach her from the airport. I thought she was busy with theater work. I walked in and put my bags down. Something was wrong. I felt it before I saw what it was—the place was almost empty.

I strolled into the kitchen, the bedroom, my office, with my Kaypro computer on a small wooden desk—thank God that was still there. Deborah was missing and so were many of her things. Sometime during the end of my trip, Deborah had moved out.

Regardless of the reason, or even the fact she was justified, or that I missed her badly, or that this was probably my fault, I became raving mad. The betrayal. Giving up. Moving out when I wasn't there to do anything about it. The punishment that seemed implicit in this. I yelled, banged a wall, threw a coffeepot.

I loved Deborah, but I was too disconcerted to think straight.

Deborah and I met at a restaurant. My pain surprised her. For some reason she didn't realize how this would affect me. But moving out like that destroyed the little bit of caring I tried to build on. We were only some six months married. There was a point we could have crossed to work out our issues and stay together. Perhaps have children. Be a life-long couple. But now I felt only the wrath.

Days later Deborah approached me: She wanted us to come back to-gether. I said no. I felt she would do this again. What guarantee was there that she wouldn't leave like this in the future? Of course, she couldn't guarantee it. Nobody could. Still, I didn't want to go through this again.

Del talked to me—we always related well. I told him I wasn't ready to move back. I was deeply hurt. He didn't argue with me. He had to know this was a silly and immature thing for Deborah to do.

Soon after, Deborah's parents came to Los Angeles from Long Is-land. We got together at a restaurant with Deborah sitting next to them. I liked her parents. I remembered how considerate they were during Christmas, when they treated me like one of their own. This whole upheaval was terribly heartbreaking. I didn't want to be away from their kindness, but I also couldn't see beyond the hurt.

At one point Deborah's dad said he would do anything for her hap-piness and he wouldn't stand for her to suffer. His message was clear. But I had to tell him calmly, respectfully, that I was not ready to take Deborah back. This situation was too raw—I didn't know if I could see past it. That was the last time I ever talked to these good people.

One of the things I had to do was tell Ramiro and Andrea that Deborah and I were no longer together. I thought this would be an easy enough talk, but Andrea began to cry. I didn't know what to do. This lit-tle girl, like her brother, in her short years, had experienced many losses.

It was a miserable situation all around.

———

One day, Sarita contacted me. We had not seen each other for some time. Although I had partied with her in the past, she dated other men, including friends of mine. But she was now alone, still in Echo Park, and wanted me to come over.

I drove to her place, situated in a hilly foliage-ridden area. There was a long set of stairs to climb to get up the hill to her basement apartment. When I reached the top I was huffing and puffing. I knocked on her door. No answer. I knocked again. She wasn't there. I began to laggardly step down those damn stairs. Then I heard a voice from below— it was Sarita, rushing to catch up.

"Louie, Louie, hold on . . . don't go," she yelled.

I walked up again and waited in front of her place. Sarita somehow ran up the stairs and was soon in front of me. For some reason we crossed a line we had about how far we'd go together. She kissed me. I kissed her. It stopped being a friendly kiss and soon became a full-on spit-and-tongue spectacle.

I always liked Sarita but kept this to myself since she seemed to be more about booze and letting loose. She opened her door and I sat on the couch. Sarita sat on my lap, kissing me some more. Before I knew it, I had her blouse unbuttoned and my face in between her breasts. Soon we were both naked. Soon we were licking each other. Then we made love.

With Sarita my drinking started up again. That's what we were— drinking partners. Making love didn't change that. But it did change things with Deborah. I was now emboldened to let this marriage go, something I was not entirely sure about until then. My anger became revenge. The drinking gave me a new incentive. I became cold and shallow.

Deborah still tried to find ways to get together. One night she came to the apartment at the wrong time—she should have called. Deborah stopped by to work things out. Instead, I figuratively shut the door in her face. Oh, I let her into the apartment all right. But Sarita was in the living room with dance music emanating from the stereo. Deborah had no idea what was going on. She stood by the doorway, her hands trembling, perhaps trying to deny what was in front of her—her estranged husband cavorting with another woman. She left without a word.

Sarita and I danced, kissed, kept drinking. She took off her clothes to a disco beat. Later we made love in the bed Deborah and I once shared.

This was a heartless display of how resentment can turn into something ugly. How the depth of pain can become malice. The fact was our expectations as people were out of sync: I wanted to travel and work more, to be a writer, to live in struggle. Deborah wanted a home, a settled life, maybe a family.

Nothing wrong with any of these—we could've had it all. But I didn't handle this in a dignified manner. That last incident destroyed everything between Deborah and me. She was now furious. She wanted the Toyota we had bought before I went to Nicaragua, all the wedding presents and appliances, her name back, and her self-respect.

I gave her everything but the Kaypro.

I got word about a fellow activist, originally from Bolivia, although she grew up Chicana in the Southeast L.A. area. Her name was Yolanda, and she was a little more than a year older than me. She was one of the most beautiful women I ever met, voluptuous with cascades of black wavy hair down her back. She had a flawless face and was endowed with brains and talent. She was someone I never thought would want to be with me.

There were rumors she was interested.

One concern was that Yolanda was still married to an old friend from the Chicano movement. They had a four-year-old daughter named Tania. They were, however, separated. Yolanda lived alone with Tania in a house they bought in Huntington Park.

I didn't know how to take this rumor. I was hesitant to follow up in case it was false, yet the thought of Yolanda and I getting together was appealing. Over the years, whenever I saw Yolanda, she was sociable. She also played guitar, sang brilliantly, and once took part in a mariachi group with her husband.

One day Yolanda turned up at a community meeting in Huntington Park. I had no way of knowing for sure if she wanted to go out with me. I tried to be cool but couldn't concentrate. My thoughts turned to Yolanda. I was getting hot under my shirt, perspiration on my forehead. It was the nervousness that came with the way certain women affected me. Only with Yolanda it was particularly strong. My heart told me she was my last best hope for love.

After the meeting, I stood next to Yolanda and said, *"Hola."*

She turned around and smiled. We managed small talk. Her Bolivian features were arresting—mocha skin on a clear, naturally beautiful face (she never used makeup and didn't need it). I then asked her to join me for a taco. She said yes, still smiling, as I fell into her eyes, deep, gone, in another time, another place, like inside that Nicaraguan volcano.

At a taco stand nearby, I told Yolanda my predicament—Deborah and I were breaking up for sure. She told me her marriage to my old friend was through. Although neither one of us was divorced yet, she was a quality woman. Somehow I had attributes she liked.

A week later, Yolanda and I went out. We each put our best foot forward. I wanted so much for this to work. She seemed to feel the same. Later that night we sat in her living room. I didn't want to blow it so I didn't try anything. I held back so I wouldn't confirm how eager I was to linger in her arms. But I did blow it. She walked me to the door and we said our good-byes. Before I knew it I was back home.

What the fuck happened?

It was just rehearsal. The next night I knocked on Yolanda's door and she let me in. We talked again. She was nice, attentive. Finally it was time to leave. I felt awkward, afraid, but thank God she wasn't. Yolanda kissed me—the most scrumptious feeling of lips on mine I ever had. She put ardor and a long string of dreams into that kiss. She grasped my arm and walked me to her bedroom, where I'm sure she spent many lonely nights. We didn't just make love. She directed my hand, my mouth, my sex—she wanted this a certain way and I was her puppet, her plaything.

I didn't even have time to actually leave Deborah behind. In Yolanda's gaze every woman disappeared. I fell hard. More than I had ever fallen for a woman until then.

Some friends of mine decided to cross the Mexican border to party. They invited me but I had other commitments. This was their first time. Four people crammed into a *carucha*—an old beat-up and smoky car—and sped down to Tijuana. They thought they were embarking on the revelry of a lifetime.

One of them was Sarita. She went out with these *vatos* she barely knew, looking for a good time again. Sarita was okay people despite the fact that she seemed to find action when she least wanted it—and often missed it when she did want it.

Like all newcomers, these young people were wide-eyed and stupid about Tijuana. At one point another beat-up and smoky car pulled up next to them. The driver revved the engine, luring my friends into a race.

Did I mention they were stupid?

My friends sped up, smoking weed and laughing all the way as they pushed a hundred miles per hour down a bumpy dirt road, too fast for any decent car, let alone a *carucha*. But the party was over before it started. The other car turned out to be an unmarked Tijuana police vehicle. The sirens came on as the guns popped out.

As they say, it was *un desmadre*.

Now, this is something you don't want to do in Tijuana. You've heard the stories: the open-air jail cells, the rapes and murders, the overcrowded holding tanks with excrement and blood on the walls. My four friends, including Sarita, were soon forced to give up everything they had—the car, any money, booze, and weed—while they were transported to one of the local jailhouses.

I received a desperate phone call late at night from Sarita's sister.

"Louie, we need your help," she said. "You're the only one we can turn to. They have no money and no lawyers. The police will take them to the federal prison called La Mesa if we don't do something fast. You know if they end up there it will probably be two years before we can get them out."

For decades, La Mesa was considered the most notorious lockup in the hemisphere. More than a hundred years old, in 1956 La Mesa had held six hundred prisoners. By the time the Mexican government in 2002 brought in fifteen hundred armed federal agents to raze the semicity that grew inside its walls, close to seven thousand people lived there, including drug lords, prostitutes, vendors, gun dealers (some prisoners allegedly had Uzis), and children who were born and raised in

La Mesa. Reportedly some of the adults had lived in La Mesa all their lives—they had nowhere to go and pleaded to stay.

Anyway, when I received the news from Sarita's sister, I got upset. Whatever I was doing—I don't remember now—was going to have to be put off while I figured out a way to get to Tijuana. I threatened to leave my friends there so they'd learn not to be so dumb, but early the next day I took off for the border in a pickup truck I had just bought.

I came with some money for *la grasa*—the "grease" required to get my friends released. The entire adventure took me several days, and more money than I had planned, but I managed to get them home.

What happened was that I went to the police station and tried to negotiate a deal with the officers. As expected, they gave me the runaround. They claimed my friends weren't in their jail, or they had been let go, or they were there but were being detained for drug dealing, which meant I had to prepare for more serious rounds of negotiating. The more elaborate the obstacles, the more money I had to put down. The police weren't making this easy. I ended up having to find a sleazy, roach-infested hotel to crash at while I spent the days pestering the cops.

The old exhortation on the border, *ni tu, ni yo*—"neither you nor I," meaning unless a bargain is struck we both lose—was given new meaning. I had visited Tijuana many times over the years. I knew its culture, admittedly from its dark side.

In my teens one of my heroin connections there was a police officer. I also once fell for an Afro-Mexican prostitute when I was seventeen and she was fifteen. And years later I closed down strip clubs and whorehouses. However, in more recent years, as a family man, I had visited Tijuana and Rosarito Beach to bargain down items like rugs, furniture, and replicas of Aztec sculptures.

Ni tu, ni yo.

But this was another matter altogether. The more I troubled the police, the more obstinate they got. I knew they would go for the money, but I figured they wanted to hold out for as much a possible. These were L.A. guys they'd caged. The officers must have thought, *They gotta have more money.*

During a lull in the talks, I walked out of the small office and snuck around to the back of the jail. I was able to talk to my friends through a windowless barred opening. They kept the men in one holding tank and the women in another. The tanks faced each other across a small courtyard. There were no toilets, sinks, or beds. The detainees had to sleep on the cold and wet floors. There was a hole in the middle of the holding tanks for pissing and shitting. The women had to do their thing in front of the men and vice versa. I talked to my friends, letting them know what I was doing. But it was Sarita's pleas that gave me the greater urgency.

"The police are trying to get into my pants," she told me. "Every night, when it gets cold, they come by and offer blankets to any of the women who will go with them. One woman here lasted two nights, but she finally gave in. I'm trying not to but I'm freezing in here, Louie. If you don't do something fast, I'm going to have to get me a blanket— and you know what I will have to do to get it!"

I got it.

But the police weren't going for the price. I finally offered them $100 per person. They refused—they didn't want to hand over Sarita until I went higher. I knew that every night my friends were in jail, their chances of going to La Mesa were greater (and this would involve a much higher cost in time and money). But, more importantly, every freezing desert night meant increasing danger for Sarita.

By the fifth day, I became frantic.

I decided to break them out. I know this sounds crazy. It seems like something from a movie, but believe me when I tell you that barrio life is stranger than the movies.

The police were watching me, so I strolled a few blocks away from the jail. Then I headed back, keeping a careful lookout. When I reached the back of the jail, I noticed an old wooden ladder lying next to another building. I propped it up against a wall and climbed to the roof. I went over to the window where the holding tanks were located. I saw that the cinder blocks were losing mortar along the seams. I began to look for reinforcing metal bars inside the blocks. Without these, the walls would be easier to knock down.

I surveyed inside the building and saw my three friends and Sarita. They saw me and yelled, waving and throwing up hand signs.

"Sshhhh," I whispered. *"Thrucha*—I'm trying to get you guys out of here. I think I can tie a rope to these bars and pull this wall down with the pickup truck. But I have to do it at night. When I blow the horn, you'll have to run out like mad, get onto the back of the truck, and then we'll take off. You all with it?"

Not surprisingly, they were. Desperate fools, all of us.

I didn't get far with the plan. I didn't stop to think that even if I tore the walls down, I would still have to get to the individual tanks, which had their own bars to get through. But none of this mattered. After I climbed down the ladder, a couple of brawny in-your-face Tijuana cowboys pressed some pretty big guns—.44 Magnums, maybe—into my face.

"Oh shit!" I said.

"¡Como que 'sheet,' *pendejo!"* one of the officers replied.

"You want to get into the jail so bad, we'll help you," the other said in Spanish.

My goose was cooked. Now five of us were being prepared to go to La Mesa. All I kept thinking about was Sarita and the blanket and all those guards. The problem now: Who was going to get *me* out?

To shorten a long story, getting caught red-handed only meant I had to go even higher on the price. The TJ cops really didn't care about sending us all to the federal penitentiary. A waste of paperwork and gas money, I supposed. But pressed with my own incarceration—and Sarita's potential fate—I ended up going to $250 per person, including myself: 1,250 big ones.

The police finally yielded. It turned out that one of the guys in the cell had a mother who owned a Mexican restaurant in Southern California. I almost canned his ass when I found out—why didn't he tell us sooner? We made a phone call and then the money got wired. Unexpectedly, we all left with our hides.

After my breakup with Deborah, I stayed with friends for a couple of weeks until I found a small duplex to rent in Echo Park. By then

Yolanda and I were an item. She helped me move and put things away, especially the new kitchen stuff I bought.

Yolanda had a master's in social work and was employed at a women's health center in South Central L.A.—again, a woman far more accomplished than myself. She was a genetic counselor. Poor women of color had little or no access to information about possible defects in their unborn children such as spina bifida and anencephaly. Yolanda checked for these and helped counsel mothers whose fetuses tested positive.

I still worked for AFSCME. Although based in L.A., I was now spread out around the country. I didn't like working in other jurisdictions or at International headquarters. Vernon Watkins was my friend and teacher, but now I had to answer to others who were nowhere near as skilled or knowledgeable as my former boss. And the excitement of the UC campaign had waned. Nonetheless I continued to work for the union—I needed the pay and benefits.

I had barely spent a month in my new place when Yolanda threw me for a loop: She wanted to know if I'd move in with her.

I wish I could say I thought about this for a long time, that I considered the new place I just rented as well as the hassles of moving again. The fact is I told Yolanda yes, right away, *por supuesto*. I wanted to be as close to Yolanda as I could. Having to move again? This was a secondary consideration.

Yolanda lived in a modest house, two bedrooms with a backyard and an unused work shed. She had a small basement, where I piled most of my boxes and unpacked things, including my new dining table and kitchenware. I kept my computer and small items in her room.

Her daughter Tania was another matter. She didn't like my intrusion. She had her mother full-time until I stepped into the picture. Tania often woke up in the middle of the night to invade our bedroom, disrupting our cozying up. Most mornings she made a scene, crying, screaming, banging things. In time I would ingratiate myself with her. For now it was torture.

I fixed up Yolanda's house—cutting grass, edging, trimming bushes, watering. I cleared up a jungle of grass and weeds in the backyard. I also found plaster walls, stones, wire, and other junk back there. I piled it all onto the bed of my pickup truck and made several jaunts to the local landfill.

One neighbor told me, "I've never seen Yolanda so happy—you're good for her."

One day, I received another assignment from AFSCME: I was to help a union representation election in Florida, an antiunion right-to-work state. They were organizing Miami's large Jackson Memorial Hospital and other Dade County offices. I didn't want to go since Yolanda and I were barely starting out. I understood AFSCME expected me to stay there for a while. I asked to be on a trial period.

I left Yolanda and Tania with trepidation. I had found the love I wanted since my teens. I didn't intend for anything to undermine this. Yolanda didn't get upset. It was a gentle good-bye. This was work. I was off to Miami.

It was March 1984. Miami was mostly a conservative Republican city—the majority of Latinos there were Cubans, refugees and their children from Cuba's 1959 revolution and beyond. Still, by the time I moved there, other Latinos had moved in. Puerto Ricans had longtime strongholds in the city and their population was growing. There were increasing numbers of Colombians, Panamanians, Ecuadorians, and Peruvians, and a few Mexicans (but nothing like in the Southwest).

I noticed tensions between the Latinos based on race—darker-skinned Afro-Latinos or indigenous Latinos did not fare well with the lighter-skinned, better-educated, and moneyed Cubans. There was also a class divide—Latinos in Miami were the most well-off of any U.S. Latino population. But many new Latino migrants were poor and struggling. Of course, Cubans of color also existed, but their numbers didn't become significant until the Marielitos Boatlift in 1980 that brought about 125,000 Cubans, mostly of darker hues, from the Cuban port of Mariel.

The Miami Latinos were a mixture I was not used to in Los Angeles since Mexicans and generations of Chicanos were the primary Latino group for more than a hundred years (refugees from civil wars and poverty in El Salvador, Guatemala, Nicaragua, and Honduras altered this in the 1980s).

In Miami I lived in a corporate hotel overlooking a bridge and the river. AFSCME brought in a crew of organizers after a union organizer was allegedly thrown off the balcony at Jackson Memorial Hospital for trying to get employees to sign union cards. Right-to-work states, mostly in the U.S. South, use strong-arm tactics to stop unions from organizing. I was in the South now, another culture with another set of rules.

AFSCME International also took over one of the Dade County locals—a receivership, they called it—due to large-scale corruption. The president and his officers were all removed and the International now managed operations until new elections could be held. I was allowed to work out of their offices.

The former local president had an extravagant wood-and-mirror-paneled office with an expensive polished wood desk and shelving and up-to-date mimeograph and copying equipment. I created my leaflets and flyers for our campaigns on this equipment. I sat on a plush leather seat just to know how it felt.

The intrigue required to get around antiunion goon squads was important. Companies, even government agencies, paid roughnecks to scare off organizers. I had to be careful whom I talked to, what I said. I was told not to go anywhere alone in case I'd be attacked.

One of the organizers was Carl Hutchins. He claimed to be a former singer with the Five Satins, who scored a hit in 1956 with "In the Still of the Night." I couldn't say this was true, but he often parlayed this tidbit into singing most nights at the hotel's bar downstairs. We became good friends.

On weekends, I made my way to Calle Ocho—Eighth Street—and the heart of Little Havana. I found the food enjoyable—*arroz con pollo*, *moros y cristianos*, fried *platanos* and yucca. There were tropical fruit stands next to shops selling hand-rolled cigars. At Maximo Gomez Park, oldsters sat around playing domino games for hours, talking of old times in old Havana and other topics in that guttural chopped Spanish of theirs.

And the salsa music poured from most stands and appliance stores—this was just what I loved. The culture helped mediate the politics.

I also arrived during the largest and most varied annual Latino festival in the country, the Calle Ocho Festival. There must have been tens of thousands of people. *La gente* paraded in the streets in costumes, drums and salsa music clashed at every turn, food stands from most Latin American countries abounded, and floats cruised by with scantily clad *rumberas*. I walked for blocks alongside one float where a beautiful *chica* danced and danced, capturing me with the sway and bounce of her hips.

During the day, I cranked out leaflets and newsletters, which organizers took to all the major sites, including the volatile Jackson Memorial Hospital. The large-scale effort began to pay off. We made inroads among the disaffected employees.

In the evenings, I settled down at the hotel bar with Carl. We drank, told stories, and ended most nights with Carl onstage crooning doo-wop songs. If he wasn't one of the Five Satins, he sure sounded like it.

I also called Yolanda as much as I could. I missed her. She was charming on the phone. I closed every call with "I love you," and she answered back, "I love you, too." For me this was everything.

After about a month's time, I'd had enough of Miami. Not with the people or the culture but with the strangling political environment: It was old and stuffy, southern-bred and outdated. Blacks were treated especially bad, leading to a number of riots in the 1980s, including in the ghettos of Liberty City and Overtown. I went out one evening during a battle between police and residents that led to the burning of cars and buildings, many arrests, and little sympathy outside of the black community.

And the antiunion goons came around with their threats. One night Carl and I were chasing beers with rum, sitting at a table we often occupied at the bar, when two large slick-suited men, one African-American, the other Cuban, walked up to us. They asked if we were AFSCME organizers.

"Who wants to know?" Carl snarled.

The dudes opened up their coats to reveal firearms in their waistbands.

"Leave town—you have a week," the African-American gunslinger told us.

Carl and I didn't say anything. We gave them "fuck you" looks. The goons turned on their heels and walked away.

We related this to AFSCME. The International wanted Carl and me to stay in Miami for at least a year. We were both cut from tough material, ghetto and barrio, unlikely to be intimidated. And we weren't. The threats made me want to stay.

One idea we took to various local union leaders and staff involved halting business in the city until AFSCME received its proper recognition. We were talking about a general strike. AFSCME represented the drawbridge operators, who, if they were inclined, could paralyze the city by refusing to lower the bridges.

But the top echelon of the union nixed all this. A general strike would have to involve other unions, a big strategy and a major commitment of funds and resources. Carl and I felt we should go for broke— why piddle around with this? People were already losing their lives. We were already facing death threats.

After we were told to back off from any talk of a general strike, I lost my commitment to stay. If we were going to possibly lose life and limb for this work, we needed to go all the way. Beyond that we were wasting our time. I also thought about Yolanda—I would lose her if I had to be in Miami that long.

Again, I was hardly one to back off from a fight. But then I had to make sure this was *the* fight not to back off from. I decided to pull out. AFSCME respected our decisions. Soon I was on a plane to Los Angeles.

Something happened to Yolanda while I was gone. I didn't know what because Yolanda had one troubling aspect to her personality: She didn't explain herself most of the time. And she wouldn't directly take me on, although I'm sure she wanted to.

Like when I worked around the house, fixing small things, Yolanda bought a DIY book on household repairs, hid it away (although I found it), and then started to give me advice—she didn't want to feel less than me, which was her issue, not mine.

If Yolanda did get mad, she didn't always express it. She found ways to hurt me, sideways or from left field. She held in her feelings then hit me later with some nonsense or other. Like when I returned from Miami, Yolanda may have been upset, maybe because I left, which we agreed I had to do. Still, she probably wanted me to turn the Miami assignment down. Who knows?

What I felt from Yolanda was distance. She wasn't as passionate as she had been before I left. We made love, yes, but I instigated this every time. She also paid more attention to Tania. When the girl entered our room, even if we were on the verge of getting close, Yolanda would take Tania to her room and stay there.

My response was immediate. I asked Yolanda to sit down so we could talk. She never found time. We simply didn't communicate well.

One time Yolanda wanted me to help with dinner. Fine. My idea of cooking, however, was "ghetto goulash" or "spread"—any edible stuff in the refrigerator put into a pan and baked. I asked her advice on a potato casserole. She said I could figure it out. So I began to chop up the potatoes, obviously wrong. Yolanda stepped in to say that wasn't how this was done. I responded, no, this is how it's going to be done since I asked for her help and she very casually said it was up to me. I had no problem taking her on.

Finally, after other tense moments, Yolanda took me aside to say she didn't want us to be together anymore. Tania needed her, she explained, and she couldn't be my girlfriend *and* her mom. I was flabbergasted, confused, irritated. My emotions tended to bunch up like that. I tried to salvage what I could, arguing against this concept that love couldn't be divided. But it didn't go over well. Yolanda suggested I could stay with them, like a roommate. She would move in with Tania and I'd have the main bedroom to myself. I'm sure this helped with the monthly house note.

I slipped into a depression. Again a restless current passed through me, a haze over my mind, my feelings, my workday. When I came home the next day Yolanda had moved her things into Tania's room—she even put up a new shelf to hold some of these. I went to the king-sized bed and lay down in the middle with blankets up to my neck, feeling belittled.

That night I couldn't sleep. It was dark outside. I stepped quietly into the living room and parked myself on the couch, the stillness my enemy, the minutes painfully slow. After excruciating hours, I finally heard the first chirps of the morning birds, calling out to the sun, the dew, the dawn's rays. This only reminded me how pathetic I was. It was not a good thing. This went on for a few nights.

I wanted Yolanda. Tania might have been in the middle, but it wasn't her fault. She was a child. It was Yolanda, a grown woman, who still played games with life and love.

At work I had to figure out what to do. I planned to move out of Yolanda's house. Find myself another apartment. Stop falling in love with fantastic women who showed any desire toward me. Take my time with everything. I was addicted to drugs, booze, excitement, love . . . and apparently any display of affection.

To add to my dilemma, to undermine my resolve, to drive a stake into these brave and reasonable plans, Yolanda called to have lunch. I was beginning to figure a way out of the jam, but once I saw her—with long hair across her shoulders and arms, natural skin of Pachamama, those magma eyes—I melted in my seat.

"I was wrong in what I did," Yolanda confessed. "And while this is hard to do, I want you to come back to me, to share my bed."

A part of me, a sturdy and clearheaded part, wanted to tell her "No way." That this was flattering but I had moved on. Thanks but no thanks.

Instead I sat there speechless. Unborn. No mouth. Witless.

"I'd love that," I finally blurted out, back in her clutches, in the layered folds of her hair, nothing but burning flesh in the reflection of her eyes.

That night Yolanda slowly opened the bedroom door and jumped onto the bed. Tania was asleep in the other room. My heart beat in my ears. Tentative at first, we finally reached an ardent rhythm, making love like we were bodies free-falling from the highest ledge in the rockiest peaks of the Andes.

Chapter Fourteen

I traveled to Mexico in 1983 and 1984 to investigate a number of peasant and indigenous uprisings. These were the other side of my Tijuana stories.

This research began in L.A. when I attended the meetings and fund-raisers of social clubs created by Mexican migrants from their various states—prominent were the Michoacan, Zacatecas, and Oaxaca clubs. These clubs sent money and other assistance to their families and *pueblos* in Mexico, establishing a parallel economy, which, among other things, carried out street repairs and school construction in the face of government neglect.

Mexico always had a tumultuous history of poor against rich, the powerless against the powerful, indigenous against nonindigenous. By the 1980s, the political kettle in the country had reached the boiling point. The economy plummeted in 1982 after oil prices fell. The country accumulated $85 million of foreign debt, borrowed largely to exploit its oil reserves—46 percent from U.S.-based lending institutions. Consequently the price of food and staple products increased 75 percent in 1983. The unemployment/underemployment rate became 60 percent. This contributed to a mass exodus that in thirty years amounted to the largest migration of people to the United States.

The Mexican people also fought back. Stories of insurrections filled national headlines. Thousands upon thousands, mostly poor and displaced, marched into Mexico City in protest. Thousands more built concentric rings of shantytowns around the capital, creating new municipalities overnight and swelling the population of one of the largest cities in the world. At the time, Mexico was both unstable and revolutionary.

One of the most volatile regions in Mexico was the narrow waistband of the Isthmus of Tehuantepec in Oaxaca. A center of unrest was the coastal city of Juchitan, led by a cultural and political coalition—integrated with the Zapoteca indigenous communities—called the Coalición Obrera Campesina Estudiantil del Istmo (Worker-Peasant-Student Coalition of the Isthmus): the COCEI.

When I arrived there in November 1983, the coalition was becoming a political alternative in the region to the governing Institutional Revolutionary Party (PRI)—and in the eyes of its leadership, a threat to foreign investment. COCEI had already spent ten years organizing for land rights, public works projects, wage increases, and the defense of the Zapoteca language and culture in an area where multinational giants such as Coca-Cola, Pepsi, Sears, John Deere, and Massey Ferguson had set up shop.

Events came to a head in 1980 when the coalition elected a mayor as well as federal and state representatives in Juchitan, by then Oaxaca's second-largest city with a population of 120,000. State officials nullified the elections. Another election, in March 1981, however, produced the same results. The people elected as mayor the young and charismatic COCEI leader Leopoldo "Polin" de Gyves.

COCEI established a "People's Municipal Government of Juchitan" alongside the PRI's phony municipal government. This "unofficial" government built health facilities, a sewage system, roads. For once, court cases and broadcasts, through the COCEI-run Radio Ayuntamiento Popular, were conducted in the Zapoteca language as well as in Spanish.

I reached Oaxaca city by plane to meet COCEI leaders. After my arrival we gathered in safe houses to avoid the eyes and ears of political police and informers. Then we drove six hours through La Ventosa, a horrendous trek rife with bandits, chicken buses, and vertical cliff drops.

We were warned to stay in a caravan to curtail bandits. But scarier to me was the actual road. We passed through a mountain range known for high winds that supposedly toppled big rigs, thus the name La Ventosa. The road became narrower and unpaved. All the vehicles moved at speeds that, in my opinion, were too fast for the winding turns. I could see remnants of other buses, trucks, and cars strewn across the steep sides of the mountain as we negotiated the curves, sometimes with the outside tires literally over the embankment.

Finally in Juchitan, with an appetizing Oaxaca-style meal in my gut, I prepared to receive updates from the uprising leaders.

"With our victories, the PRI realized they had to stop this at a given point," COCEI spokesperson Oscar Cruz Lopez told me. "They could not permit this political opening in which Juchitan would achieve levels of popular support not tied to the government's control. They had to crush this dream, this hope, the possibility of the first popular government in the country."

The government-sponsored terror, however, was classic: brutal and swift.

PRI thugs murdered a councilman, a local woman merchant, and a police officer linked to the COCEI. Two peasants were killed and seven wounded during a machine-gun attack on a new medical center being inaugurated by Mayor de Gyves. In another incident, a child was wounded during a gunfire attack on schoolchildren. The homes of de Gyves and his brother were also machine-gunned.

The "legal" response was also dramatic.

In July 1983, the state government issued a warrant for de Gyves's arrest, accusing him of assault, plunder, illegal behavior, bearing arms—and responsibility for all the violence in the Isthmus of Tehuantepec that had been directed at him and COCEI.

By the end of that month, Oaxaca's governor declared a state of emergency. A thousand federal troops and about three hundred state police were dispatched to Juchitan. That's when several hundred Zapoteca men and women occupied the *palacio municipal*, the equivalent of a city hall. They defended their positions with piles of rocks and whittled sticks wielded by barefoot sentries at the building's main entrances and top floors.

Protests throughout Mexico against the PRI's actions led to the establishment of new municipal elections, slated for November 20, 1983, on the seventy-third anniversary of the 1910 Mexican Revolution.

Journalists, government officials, tourists, and spies swarmed Juchitan. Green-helmeted soldiers rolled past in armored vehicles, automatic weaponry cradled in their arms.

Juchitan's town center was shaped like most Spanish-built colonial towns on the continent. A public square was its heartbeat. The *palacio municipal*, a Greek-pillared edifice, overlooked the square. Next to the building was a noisy and well-tended marketplace, run by Zapoteca women, known in these parts as Tehuanas. The marketplace displayed meats, fruits, vegetables, cookware, brooms, handmade jewelry, and many other items, laid out in row upon colorful row.

Baskets of live iguanas, their mouths shut with bands, lined the entrances. The women's hearty laughs burst forth from their round faces. One young woman poked out a brown breast to feed a sleepy child nesting in her arms.

Alongside the square, peddlers set up food stands. There was a line of stands along the walkway with several large steer heads, their eyes bulging, flies swarming. I ordered a taco. The proprietor grabbed a machete and scraped the meat off the animal's face, then threw it onto a blazing grill.

I turned toward the public square filled with running children, men gathered around tables conversing, elderly sharing white-painted metal benches. The Tehuanas wore embroidered cotton blouses known as *huipiles* and multicolored floor-length flowing skirts called *enaguas* over wide hips. This place, this experience, began to take on a magical quality. I connected in a spiritual and emotional way with the people: their faces, their eyes, their gentle manner.

I was drawn to the trees, where small black birds called *zanates* carried on their dialogues. This banter rose in the afternoon as people rolled in. I cut a path through the dampness, the children's laughter, the singing of blackbirds. I wanted to keep hearing their song, which had something peculiar about it. The birds flew across the dense foliage above me. Then my eyes wandered down to the people and I felt as if they, too, were speaking in the *zanates'* tongue.

The Zapoteca language, called *didxa*, has a singsong quality, like most idioms of the original peoples of the continent. This is because modulations in tone, pitch, and inflection determined meaning. I stood there for a long time, captivated by what I thought was a conversation between the people and the birds.

In the square, benches filled with young lovers and the sleepy-eyed. Harried merchants called to one another, women related the news, and drunks brawled over obscure points. A thick-haired girl ran past me with a T-shirt that read JUCHITAN: CAPITAL DEL MUNDO ("Juchitan: Capital of the World").

Later that day, I attended a PRI-sponsored press conference. No COCEI journalists were allowed to attend. The journalists assembled there were almost all Mexican. I saw a non-Mexican face or two, but somehow the U.S. media didn't seem to be interested in what was going on in the isthmus region.

I talked to one *gringo* photographer, a long-haired young man who looked more like an adventure seeker than a newshound. After the initial presentation by the PRI representatives, the floor was opened for questions. I did my journalist thing. I asked questions, but clearly not the kind the PRI people had expected.

"What is being done with respect to the accusations that the PRI is preparing to stuff the ballots?"

"Can someone tell me how long the armed troops are expected to stay in Juchitan?"

"What assurances are there that these elections will be free and democratic?"

These were the kind of questions that could get someone in trouble, because they asked for a modicum of truth. And, as in most responses to such questions, there was no commitment to facts, context, the full story. There was posturing. There was evasion. There was doublespeak. I'd seen enough of this in the United States to spot the subterfuge.

I struck a nerve. As I left the conference, I noted glares from PRI goons standing by the doorway. I strolled toward the main square and turned a corner. That's when an eight-year-old boy approached me.

"Come with me, sir," the boy commanded in Spanish. "I'll take you where you have to go."

"But I was going back to the public square," I answered.

"Listen," he said in a low but firm tone. "You are being followed. As soon as you enter an alley or empty street, they'll attack you. Your friends have asked me to escort you to where they're at."

I grasped the urgency and gestured to the boy to lead the way, not looking back, although I now felt the presence of others not far behind. The boy meandered through crowded areas, past vendor stands, down a couple of dusty streets, and then into a small storefront restaurant with its name barely visible in peeling paint over the doorway.

There I was led beyond a few diners toward a dirt courtyard in the back, where various rooms looked toward two trees that had a well-worn hammock strung up between them. COCEI organizers briefed me on the quandary I faced being tied to them in any fashion.

After their takeover of the *palacio municipal*, the Zapotecas held twenty-four-hour vigils. The entrance was guarded by fairly old men with sticks and rocks. COCEI did not display any firepower in their campaign—mainly to maintain a moral edge on the public's perception of their struggle. An armed struggle—right or wrong—would only invite even more repression, COCEI leaders told me.

An old cast-iron bell was situated near an open window on the second floor of the baroque structure, another large heap of stones nearby.

"This is to call the people to our defense in case we are attacked by the Mexican forces," explained an ancient, wrinkled man. He said "Mexican forces" as if they were a foreign invading army, which in this part of the country they were.

In the months before the 1983 elections, rallies in support of COCEI were held in Juchitan and throughout the isthmus, drawing more than twenty thousand people from throughout Mexico. The new COCEI mayoral candidate, Daniel Lopez Nelio, had become the focus of a growing popular movement.

The PRI mobilized before election day. Hundreds of outsiders were trucked in as "voters" (mainly migrant workers coerced with threats of losing their jobs). Millions of *pesos* were poured into Juchitan to provide temporary jobs for unemployed *Juchitecos* (which lasted only until after the elections). And thousands of sandals for the barefoot and hundreds of work implements for peasants were distributed by the truckload.

I slept nights in the hammock behind the restaurant and in the one-room homes of COCEI leaders. Other nights I slept on metal benches in the square. People stood around there almost all night long. I liked to linger among them, asking permission to record their sweet language.

One night, two girls stayed next to me, talking away in their native tongue. I didn't know what they were saying, although I got the impression much of it was at my expense. I didn't care. The timbre of their voices was so soothing and musical that I could have listened to them for hours.

During my stay, I hung around Lopez Nelio, who had a sharp wit and a mellow approach to life, in the manner of the Za—the Zapoteca people. A reporter once asked him to describe the *Juchitecos*, to which he replied: "The *Juchitecos*, they are a bunch of no-good bums, rabble-rousers, and drunkards . . . and I am their leader."

But he was also serious and tough, a master strategist and powerful speaker.

Lopez Nelio showed me the thatch-roofed huts where many of the people lived, lacking anything close to modern amenities, including water, electricity, or sewers. The ribs of their beasts of burden protruded under sagging skin. He showed me the factories and the toxin-infested lake waters nearby, which contributed to various, often deadly diseases affecting children and other residents.

Several COCEI-sponsored marches and talks were held right up to election day. The biggest one, which occurred the night before the balloting, began with a march through the various *colonias* and deprived huts in and about the town. Pigs waddled beside us as the people chanted and played drums, displaying placards and banners.

We were joined by thousands of people, winding through dirt roads toward the *palacio municipal*. There the bell rang out and tapes of *nueva canción* songs by artists such as Victor Jara, Mercedes Sosa, Silvio Rodriguez, Amparo Ochoa, and Gabino Palomares blared out of large speakers. Several of us were allowed to enter the building as COCEI leaders stood on a worn balcony to address the people in Spanish and Zapoteca.

Along the perimeter, behind where the people had gathered, uniformed soldiers stood their ground, their faces stoic and cold.

At one point, I left the city hall to check out the PRI gathering. The PRI held a solemn party with mariachis, balloons, giveaways, and dry political speeches in the middle-class section of town, protected by armed state police who numbered as many as the participants. The differences between the events were striking.

It appeared that COCEI would win the elections hands down.

The next day, voting day, the battle was on. Skirmishes between PRI and COCEI members erupted at voting sites. An international team of election observers examined the ballot boxes. Much was at stake, and it appeared that all of Mexico was holding its breath.

By the middle of the day, reports were rampant that people were not on registration lists although they held voting credentials. Others couldn't obtain voting credentials although they were on the lists (a bag of credentials was later found in a lake with the names of COCEI supporters who had been denied credentials).

Some people were seen voting again and again at different booths— in some instances up to seven times. And PRI henchmen jumped on at least two Mexican photographers while they were taking photos during the balloting.

Uniformed police and soldiers were everywhere in Juchitan and in the twelve other isthmus municipalities where COCEI was taking on the PRI.

Incredibly, the PRI won in Juchitan with 56 percent of the vote. In the other municipalities where COCEI actually beat out the PRI, the elections were invalidated. The independent observers, however, including Mexican as well as foreign journalists and students, reported widespread fraud by the PRI. The state moved quickly to recognize the new PRI municipal government as soon as the results were tabulated, fraudulent or not.

The following evening, an angry crowd of some six thousand people gathered at the *palacio municipal*, still occupied by the townspeople, to hear their COCEI leaders denounce the electoral fraud.

"Mexico has tried to show the world that it is a democratic country," Lopez Nelio declared. "But it is nothing more than a brightly lit house on the outside, while totally dark on the inside."

COCEI leaders, including Lopez Nelio, went on hunger strikes. Isthmus-wide mobilizations ignited in the various municipalities where COCEI had been cheated out of victory. More city halls were occupied.

I stuck around after the elections to see if the army would attack the occupiers of Juchitan's city hall. The troops made several threatening gestures, encircling the square and moving toward the building, then backing off. At one point, COCEI leaders removed everyone who was not a COCEI organizer from the building. They let me stay one night and I slept near the rock piles. I didn't want to leave with an assault imminent—I was prepared to help defend against it.

I stayed in Juchitan as long as I could but eventually had to return to Los Angeles. I walked out of a small hut at three A.M., strode several blocks, and took a taxi to the bus center. Then I jumped on a bus to Oaxaca city and later a flight to Mexico City. I clung to the bag that held my journals, tape recorder, and film for fear they would be confiscated. They weren't. Soon I arrived back home.

The only threatening incident occurred near the taxi area in Juchitan when a man walked up to me and said, "I'm going to kill you." For a second, I thought he was a member of a PRI goon squad. But he was drunk. I glared at him. He turned away. It's the threats you don't hear that are the most dangerous.

At home, I wrote my stories and tried to solicit interest in the pieces, which except for small publications in the United States did not pan out. Then on December 12, 1983—on the day of La Virgen de Guadalupe—I heard that Oaxaca state police, supported by Mexican federal troops, had assaulted the occupied city halls throughout the isthmus cities, wounding some defenders and detaining scores of COCEI men and women. That same day, some fifteen hundred people held a sit-in in front of the state government building in Oaxaca city. After being denied an audience with the state governor, they were forcibly removed.

In the early hours of the next day, some three hundred state police surrounded Juchitan's city hall. The bell was rung, alerting the people and pulling in around two thousand unarmed Zapotecas, mostly women, to stand between the police and the defenders. With assistance from the soldiers, the police attacked. They killed three people, injured many more, and arrested three hundred and fifty—many of them women and their children. One of those reportedly detained was a three-month-old infant.

The roads were muddy and filled with deep crevices in the Valley of San Quintin in Baja California Sur, Mexico. On either side bamboo fences encircled corrugated tin-roofed and tar-paper shanties as well as slightly better-constructed stucco dwellings.

I arrived there in October 1984 after I heard of about eighty thousand *Mixteco* Indians being partially enslaved in miles of hidden tomato fields owned by wealthy landlords, a couple alleged to be from the United States. That day I made my way through one of the many migrant labor camps scattered throughout the area. I eventually found rows and rows of plastic and carton shacks where hundreds of families made their homes. The people slept on the ground with sticks to hold up the plastic, using cardboard sheets for "beds." Single abodes housed several families. These debris-constructed homes were scattered among cactus groves and prickly bushes, over dry earth, in the heart of dust.

One of my guides talked in Mixteco to a group of migrant women cleaning their clothes in a mud creek, their babies wrapped in shawls on their back or beside them under torn blankets or ripped umbrellas. He told them about the need to organize.

At two of the camps, which the natives called Yamas and Papalote, workers complained of working up to ten hours a day without overtime pay. They had no medical insurance or social security benefits. If a woman gave birth, the family paid for it.

Migrants built most of the camps themselves. The camps also lacked running water. Yet in the middle of one camp, a large motor pumped water from a well to irrigate the tomato fields nearby. A single faucet was available for the *campesinos* to get water, but only when the fields were being irrigated.

A thirteen-year-old girl was killed when her hair got entangled in the motor's gears. Following the accident, the *campesinos* hammered jagged pieces of wood as safety guards around the motor's moving parts. The owners did nothing.

Nearby was an open-air school for the Mixteco Indian children. The teachers were bilingual instructors paid for by the federal government. But they had no money for learning materials or for a building. Raindrops pattered down, but the "classroom" didn't stop its activity.

I continued to climb the red dirt of the Baja hills along rain-drenched paths and waded through a field of waist-high grass, stopping at a clearing where a rainbow of piled stones, colored sticks, and flowers shared communion with the ground of the living to the ground of the dead.

Dozens of baby graves filled the hillsides—little ones who passed away during the harvest period. Their tiny bodies were in shoebox-sized coffins adorned with painted rocks, seashells, and wooden crosses, sprinkled with dry leaves.

A meeting of *golondrinos*—this is derived from the Spanish for "swallows" and refers to migrant workers—was being held just before midnight in total darkness. There was no electricity. The cover of darkness also kept the camp owners and their hired overseers from finding out about the clandestine gatherings. The migrants knew they would be severely punished or fired if their activities were detected.

The San Quintin Valley was a tourist's paradise, boasting some of the most scenic beaches in all of Baja. Most visitors were unaware that not far from their beach flats and resorts, migrant farm workers were struggling against poverty and inhumane working conditions. The near-enslavement of Indians—although long a practice in these parts—was a well-kept secret.

With me was Associated Press photographer Glenn Capers. We

became friends at the *San Bernardino Sun* when we both worked there. We were there to cover the activities of the Central Independiente de Obreros Agrícolas y Campesinos (CIOAC), an independent union of farm workers and peasants. The union was trying to organize natives from the southern and central Mexican states of Oaxaca, Guerrero, and Puebla to demand better pay, vacation benefits, transportation pay, and seniority rights during layoffs, and address other concerns.

The natives were brought in yearly to this part of Baja—men, women, including pregnant ones, and children as young as ten. They received an average daily pay equal to the price of a sack of flour.

I got to the area a few weeks before the harvest ended. The majority of the *campesinos* would then leave to work fields in the state of Sinaloa. Others would return to their native lands in the Oaxacan rain forests. Many ended up in Guatemala or Belize. And a few crossed into the United States to find work. CIOAC knew if they didn't get the migrants organized, it would be nearly impossible to do so after they'd gone.

CIOAC organizer Benito, thirty years old, spoke to the families gathered for the midnight session about their struggle for improved pay and dignity. He encouraged them to sign up more union members and to keep on organizing wherever they might go for work.

"You must be solid in the struggle," Benito told them in Spanish, every word then translated into a Mixteco dialect. "Let the world know, we will not be abused any longer."

Benito listened intently to the migrants while also suggesting to them what they should do. In the distance, fires burned bright in the residential section of the camps, warming the families huddled in the autumn cold.

"Hundreds have been killed, kidnapped, or jailed in our fight," Benito explained to me. "Gangs have tried to attack us. They have stopped our van, taken the keys, and threatened us. The police have refused to hold them."

Benito was a veteran of these struggles. Despite his youth, he and other members of his family had participated in countless union strikes, walkouts, and organizing drives, spending many nights in jail. Across his young face were numerous scars. Benito said that over the years he had been kidnapped and tortured. In 1978–79, there was a great repression by government forces against CIOAC, and Benito was targeted as an agitator and beaten by municipal police.

Benito related how he was once taken to a "very ugly place" known as El Espinazo del Diablo (the Devil's Spine). He was hanged there by his arms and fired at with guns. His torturers left him for dead. After several days he was found and taken to a safe place to recuperate. Despite this, Benito continued to organize.

After visiting the migrant camps, taking photos, and recording interviews, Glenn and I drove up the main road in my pickup truck toward the U.S. border, primarily to arrange talks with state officials and to conduct more research.

Somehow the word must have gone out about the two "North Americans" (even if they were of African and Mexican descent) leaving the migrant camps in an area that was off limits to anyone.

At one point, I flew past a group of armed military men on the road. Glenn told me they were trying to flag me down, but I didn't notice. In a matter of seconds the soldiers threw a spike strip across my path. I stepped on the truck's brakes with a loud screech just before the tires hit the spikes.

The soldiers rushed up to the vehicle, pointing machine guns at us. They ordered Glenn and me out of the truck and pushed us to the ground. Soldiers searched the vehicle while slamming us with questions. We offered up our press credentials and other U.S. identification cards to prove we were journalists on a legitimate story.

"What story?" a soldier demanded in Spanish. "Don't you know we were going to blast you with our machine guns just before you stopped?"

I realized the risk at which I had placed my friend and myself. But we also knew we couldn't tell them about the migrant camps—for all intents and purposes, the camps didn't exist. But by keeping our mouths shut, we invited more problems.

One soldier claimed he found residue of marijuana in the back of the truck—they seriously thought about accusing Glenn and me of smuggling drugs. Glenn had experience with international assignments, including in Peru. His air of professionalism and his insistence on our benign intentions seemed to go over well. The soldiers transported us to the state's main offices in Mexicali, where we were allowed to cross over to Calexico on the California side.

This saved us from having our butts thoroughly kicked.

Chapter Fifteen

After my return home, I missed Mexico, especially the indigenous communities, especially Juchitan.

For a moment—forgetting about my kids, my community work, my job—I mulled over the idea of staying in Oaxaca, a state rich with history, languages, customs, songs, ingenuity. It's considered the birthplace of maize, a staple grain that over the past five hundred years has kept much of the world fed (including animals that in turn feed humans). Monte Alban, the most renowned preinvasion ruins in the state, was one of Mesoamerica's best-preserved historical sites.

I hungered to connect to the Mexico I lost when I was born, which my parents had removed me from. Even my participation in the Chicano movement stemmed from this reaching back, this clamor for birthright, for undeniable and profound heredity.

I had raised this issue with my COCEI friends while standing near them in the occupied *palacio municipal*, prepared to fight with sticks and stones for their freedom. Many of them agreed—stay in Juchitan, they told me, with the Tehuana warrior women; with the COCEI leaders who battled mostly with weapons of words, tapping into living mythologies and ancient but lasting values; with the sun-baked children who laughed and played without concern, fully embraced.

It was a young Zapoteca, Analisa, a conscious fighter and organizer, who set me straight.

"It would be good if you stayed with us—you are most welcome," Analisa said. "But your place is somewhere else, to the north, within the power structures of the world's mightiest military, its mightiest capitalist class. You were born in the United States . . . native, yes, Chicano, *como no*, and for reasons rooted in who you are, you must go back. You must take our stories, our struggles, and also our victories, and convince the American people to finally end their empire, their political maneuverings, to let Mexico belong to Mexicans again."

This stopped me cold. Yet it was insightful. I needed to be in places like Los Angeles, beside the corridors of power and privilege, and fully express the unglossed reality and resolve of people like Analisa, like the members of COCEI, the Zapotecas, the poor and powerless everywhere. Analisa's words compelled me to reconnect with the organizing efforts in L.A., to begin teaching and orienting new activists for the intensifying conflicts of *my* country, the United States of America, rent with class and racial divides, but with immense potential for human rights and universal equity.

This meant I had to understand what the United States and its people were going through. Robotics had brought labor-replacing devices into industry, leading to increased layoffs—marking the 1980s as the greatest period of job loss since the Great Depression. Low-paid, and largely unorganized, service jobs became more prominent in formerly industrial communities—many people simply couldn't work again.

The "rust belt" became the name used to describe the string of these communities in Michigan, Illinois, Indiana, Pennsylvania, and Ohio that witnessed factories, mills, and mines being shuttered and dumped. Most people didn't consider the Los Angeles/Long Beach area as part of the rust belt, but it was the country's largest manufacturing center and boasted the most active commercial port. The plants I once labored in—St. Regis, National Lead, and even Bethlehem Steel, among others in autos, textiles, tires, canning, shipyards, meatpacking, and aerospace—were closing forever.

I was with AFSCME when I got word that the Bethlehem Steel mill had shut down. The leadership of the United Steelworkers Local 1845 did something noteworthy: They created a food bank at the hall, becoming the largest food pantry in the country, feeding four thousand to six thousand families a week—partially funded by Bruce Springsteen during his Born in the USA tour. And they hired Susan Franklin Tanner (from my days with Manazar and the prison writers) to do theater and poetry workshops with the unemployed steel-men and -women.

Bruce was there at one of the workshops, along with a *Los Angeles Times* reporter, when I read my poem "Bethlehem No More." Bruce gave me one of the best statements on the personal imprint one places on a poem, song, or piece of art: "Only you could have written this."

Local 1845 received national attention when Susan organized the Theatre Workers Project, which included a tour of an original performance piece called *Lady Beth* with the words and stories performed by the former steelworkers themselves. The troupe traveled to devastated communities across the country, bringing laughter and tears—as well as calls to action—to audiences suffering from plant closures.

I continued to live with Yolanda and her daughter, Tania. Soon we planned to buy a house together in the hills of Highland Park.

I painted her Huntington Park place and her wrought iron décor on the windows, and helped get her roof fixed. We redid the bathroom completely with new tub, toilet, and quality Mexican tile on the walls. In no time we found a buyer.

The move to Avenue 57 in Highland Park required a long-ass rental truck. I couldn't believe how much stuff Yolanda and I had between us. Many friends and family helped carry our things—which seemed to go on forever, box after box, furniture piece after furniture piece—into the new house.

The house had long glass windows on the back and sides of the living room as walls. It also had a built-in swimming pool (I kept it clean and properly alkalized, having done this at well-off people's homes as a teenager). In the garage was shelving—for the first time in many years I unboxed my books, dusted them, and carefully placed them on the shelves. It was a relief to finally provide them a home.

Camila had by then broken up with Ernesto—he returned to Denver and years later became sober. I visited Ramiro and Andrea as much as I could, bringing them to the new house. They loved the swimming pool and that summer they were often there.

Tania and I also became at ease with each other. The hostilities washed away after Tania caught chicken pox and I took several days off work to take care of her. She seemed to appreciate the little things I did to make her feel better.

For most of that summer and fall, Yolanda and I enjoyed our new place, the first house I ever owned, although it was really Yolanda's since we bought it with the equity from her previous home.

I recall looking out into the hillsides of Highland Park, a community in the vast Mexican Eastside. But now parts of Highland Park were becoming gentrified with new money and new residents, mostly young and mostly white. Still, I had reached a secure point in my life, although I felt somewhat isolated. It was quiet in the hills, perhaps too quiet. But Yolanda seemed happy and that mattered most of all.

Sometime that winter, both our divorces came through—mine from Deborah and Yolanda's from her husband. We were now free, even though we were already living like husband and wife. I got the notion to ask Yolanda to marry me. I treasured the times we were together. Yet she was also standoffish, barely acknowledging me when I came home from my trips.

And I got the impression Yolanda wanted Tania and me to be more like dad and daughter. But Tania and I had a different relationship, able to talk, but not in each other's faces. I didn't want to be Tania's dad. I had my own kids and she had her own father. I liked that we no longer annoyed each other. She was now five years old.

Maybe Yolanda wished things were different, but talking to her about this didn't help. She shunned deep discussions. I was constantly badgering Yolanda about this and that, but I could see this was only pushing her away.

Still, I loved her. I loved thinking of her. I loved being next to her. And behind closed doors, after I initiated intimacy, she became game, an artful devotee of the sensual life.

Marrying Yolanda made sense.

The problems with AFSCME had been developing for some time. I didn't mind the task of representing and assisting workers in the public

sector. They were tough and courageous. AFSCME also had great organizers and caring personnel. But like many institutions, the big unions
often became ossified, stuck in old forms and protocols, sometimes
thinking only of their own growth and dues collection. I began to feel I
was wedged in that old trade union stuff instead of the new dynamic that
younger workers, women, and immigrants were bringing to the table, to
truly challenge unfair labor practices, to bring forth new ideas and new
methods. And when the workers needed a real fight, they required a
union leadership that pulled out all the stops. In far too many cases, the
large unions talked tough but then capitulated to the corporations.

Of course, nothing was worse than a nonunion environment. The
eight-hour day, decent working conditions, and health and other benefits were results of a hundred years of union organizing. AFSCME
also played a heroic role in various municipal battles, highlighted by
the 1968 Memphis sanitation strike that, unfortunately, included the
murder of a key supporter, Martin Luther King, Jr.

But by the early 1980s, in too many instances, the union honchos
were more militant about getting rid of the militants than about taking on the corporations or public-sector entities. Their politics were
mostly tied to the Democratic Party, even to their detriment, instead of
being fiercely independent so that the interests of the workers never got
lost in the political arena. Once I was called upon to chauffeur a U.S.
presidential candidate during one of the national elections. Drive him
around and do his bidding? Not what I signed up for.

By spring of 1985 I'd had enough. AFSCME assigned me to the Bay
Area to do public relations for a local battle. The main guy I reported
to was mostly inaccessible, partying in some fancy San Francisco hotel.
He also had it in for me—he'd be unreasonably critical of my work and
then make outrageous demands on my time. As soon as this assignment
was done, I left AFSCME and never turned back.

Manazar and I accomplished many things in East L.A. and Echo Park.
But due to my extensive union work and travels, I let go the work with
LALWA, including putting out *ChismeArte* as well as organizing read-
ings and workshops.

One day I asked Manazar how things were going. He said he had turned everything over to some young people who seemed eager to take all this on but were unable to follow through. Soon it all disintegrated, which I felt awful about. I didn't want to be part of any dissolution of LALWA's publications and cultural work. But without strong new leadership, new blood, there was no engine to keep things going.

Galería Ocaso was one of the casualties—due to higher rents and low income. I knew this was hard for Manazar to let go.

Then, out of the blue, Manazar began to argue with me, refusing to return my calls. I knew Manazar had a hard side. Once, when I first came around, he looked at my writing and said I shouldn't be a writer, I had no talent for it. I could have fallen apart—his opinion meant much to me. Later, of course, we became allies and I forgot about this statement. But now he was back to turning me away. I was stronger and wasn't going to let it get to me. I stopped meeting with Manazar.

Let me explain: Manazar will always be a key mentor of my writing life. His contributions to Chicano letters, his writing workshops in prisons and juvenile facilities, and his legacy of reaching out to disaffected and neglected communities will live on. It was Manazar who first brought me to prisons to do talks and workshops, which I've now done for more than thirty years. So whatever personal issues ate at him, I didn't let it get to me—I loved and respected Manazar.

Ten years later, when I went to Los Angeles to visit from Chicago, I saw my old friend. He showed me some of his plays and other writings. By then my book *Always Running: La Vida Loca; Gang Days in L.A.* had been published. I believed he was proud of me and wanted to let me know there were no hard feelings.

I didn't hear from Manazar again until the year 2000, when he was in the hospital, in his final hours, trying to make an appointment for me to see him before he left this world. Regrettably, he passed early on the very day I was scheduled to visit. He was a harsh teacher, but he was also my *camarada*, fellow poet, and inspired community leader.

Alrato, carnal.

———

Yolanda turned down my marriage proposal. She said she liked the living arrangement. But I felt strangely alienated from her. She wasn't forthcoming with love or ways to come together. Even though Tania and I were now relating better, Yolanda hinted we still weren't close enough.

There were days I sat in that nice house on the hill, above the urban malaise, in almost total silence and felt disjointed. Yolanda liked the solitude. I didn't. It became apparent that as much as I loved Yolanda and would have tolerated most anything from her, she didn't appear to have the same feelings for me.

A few things began to happen, small things. For example, Yolanda had a dog, a Chihuahua, that was already old when we got together — it had been with her since she was a teenager. However, she had the animal in the house, even when it was unable to manage its bowel movements. So our cream-colored carpets had dog poop here and there.

I insisted she put the dog outside. I built a doghouse near the pool. Yolanda hated this, but I just couldn't have the house smelling bad all the time and me walking across the living room as if it were laden with land mines.

It was just my luck the Chihuahua had a heart attack one day and keeled over near the pool. Yolanda lost it, blaming me for the dog's death. It was the dog's time, but I saw how easily Yolanda turned against me.

Then Yolanda suddenly announced she was giving one of the three bedrooms to her younger sister, who brought along a boyfriend, some guy from Spain she met while vacationing there. I didn't think this was a good idea, but instead of seeing me as a partner to consult on such things, Yolanda decided on her own to go ahead.

Soon her sister and a dude I didn't know were living under the same roof with us.

Eventually the dude left and the sister stayed. I had no issue with the sister, and with her being family I'm sure I would have agreed. But apparently my opinion on this subject was not valuable enough to solicit.

The kicker was the way I perceived Yolanda treating my kids, in particular Andrea. She was gruff with them. Both kids played with Tania when they could, but they felt Tania was given most anything she wanted, and my kids weren't considered in the same way. Ramiro was nine and Andrea was seven.

One Saturday afternoon I took a nap, leaving Andrea (for some reason Ramiro didn't come along that time) with Tania and Yolanda. I woke up and walked into the living room. I noticed Andrea was distressed. When I asked her why she said she hadn't eaten yet. I thought this odd—it was past suppertime. I asked Yolanda why Tania and Andrea hadn't been fed. It turned out Tania did eat, and so did Yolanda. They just didn't give any food to Andrea.

I grabbed my jacket, put Andrea's sweater on her, and we drove to York Boulevard to find a place to eat.

Soon after I sat Yolanda down and asked her to decide—she had to be closer, more active in the relationship, more loving toward me, and at least respectful to my kids, or I would leave. She didn't know what to say. I didn't want to leave, but I felt Yolanda was tired of me and wouldn't say so. Sure enough, after a long period of my talking, and her silence, it came out—she didn't want me around anymore. I asked her more than once to make sure (she had gone back and forth before). Yolanda finally insisted—she didn't love me.

I was devastated. Who knows how long Yolanda felt this way? It was the hardest move of my life. I truly felt Yolanda was the "one," the last chance at love, the best of the best. Emotionally I was spent.

I had those books on the shelf that I had to take down, one by one, and rebox. I had to remove a hollow door I used as a long desk. I had placed my computer, papers, reference works, and files on it so I could write my stories, poems, essays, and work-for-hire press releases, newsletters, brochures. I had this house with my name on the mortgage papers.

I think Yolanda worried I was going to stiff her for big bucks. But I wasn't about doing that. I only asked for the money I invested to fix her other house and make it ready to sell. Pleased I didn't want more, she quickly agreed, and I signed the quit deed.

I moved back to my brother's house on Fourth Street in Boyle

Heights. He had fixed it up so I now had a room, kitchen, and bath to myself, not the beaten-down basement room I once stayed in.

Things looked bleak—no job, no mentor, no woman.

The worst troubles that year began much earlier. When I was still with Yolanda, I received a call that police officers had brought my father home one evening. The officers said my father was trying to molest little girls in a park. They arrested him but because of his age felt it was best to bring him home. They insisted that my mother get my father therapy or another incident would put him behind bars. My dad refused treatment. My mother then made him a virtual prisoner in the house.

We knew my dad was in a bad way for some time. He suffered from dementia, but years earlier we found out something else about him. In the late 1970s, my father, the closed-minded, emotionally shut-down Republican, committed the most despicable act: He was caught trying to molest my daughter and a niece, both in diapers at the time.

One of my sisters found them in the garage. A storm erupted in her, remembrances that my dad may have molested her as well. This tore up the whole family. Part of the family turned against her for talking about this. Another part shut down. My mother took a strange position—accusing my sister of making all this up, but locking my father in his room for hours at a time and refusing to let him out whenever the grandchildren came around.

I went morose, then hard, then crazy. I wanted to kill my dad. That he would attempt to do this to Andrea, my precious baby, the worst of all betrayals, turned me inside out. I already had strong resentments toward him for how he failed to connect with my brother and me, an issue we carried since we were children. Our dad never threw baseballs or footballs with us. He never showed us how to ride bikes or how to work on cars (these we learned by ourselves). He was never there when we had curiosities and questions. My dad apparently liked little girls, not boys. He never touched my brother or me. My teenage rage had a different source.

Unfortunately, when I was in the streets as a drug user and gangster,

I failed to be at home to protect my younger sisters—something I didn't think about at the time.

And this wasn't just about my father.

Once my youngest sister told me that when she was twelve and I was sixteen, my mother pulled her by the hair and beat her all the way home after my sis ran up to me on a street corner to embrace me. I had just been released from jail. Since I wasn't living at home, my mom and I weren't talking, and my sister suffered for this.

My dad was cold and, as we found out, a molester. On the other hand, my mother, a most able and intelligent person otherwise, could be physically and verbally abusive. She beat all of us. My brother and I learned to take it, eventually forcing her to give up. I didn't get that she hit my younger sisters as much, except for incidents like the above. But Mom knew how to demean, belittle, degrade. I suspect this is why both of my sisters ended up pregnant and eager to leave home, separately, at seventeen.

Decades later, I reconciled with my mother after she was diagnosed with lymphoma and the first stages of Alzheimer's. We understood by then she had hormonal problems that remained undiagnosed for years (she eventually had her thyroid removed). When my mother died in late 2008 of complications from a gall bladder surgery, my last poignant memory of her was of her blowing kisses with her hand, smearing her lipstick on her mouth, to family members and those at the residential home. She had become kind at the end—as if she'd forgotten she used to be mean. I didn't have the same resentments toward her as I did with my dad.

Who knows how long my father had been messing with kids? My father must have led a double life for years, even decades. Or it's possible he finally acted on long-harbored feelings and impulses, all internal brakes gone. He was in his early seventies when the police brought him home that day, his sense of right and wrong askew.

Once I visited Dad's room when he wasn't there (my mom and dad had separate rooms). My mother wanted me to see how his mind had splintered. All around the room were mounds of papers, junk mail, coupons, unopened envelopes, much of these sticking out of drawers, in piles on the floor, in a shapeless heap in a corner. On a wooden bedpost was a ball made up of hundreds of rubber bands. Cereal boxes were thrown about, some half-full, most empty. There were writing tablets on top of a dresser, filled with numbers, numbers without pattern, over and over for pages on end. My father was obsessed with killing flies. The white curtains my mother had put up were spotted with blood specks.

Dad's dementia was probably why his pedophilia was now pitilessly revealed. And none of us was prepared for the damage, least of all me. For the incident with the police, Yolanda was most helpful. Part of her preparation as a genetic counselor included personal therapy. She tried to get me to understand that I was not to blame, that I could not be the "savior" by destroying what was wrong with the family, the world, our sad and defeated existence.

Yolanda also had intense traumas in her life—her own family suffered through abuse. And one of Yolanda's boyfriends when she was younger, physically abused her and once put a shotgun to her face. The more we talked the more my rage peeled away to reveal deep grief. Inside I felt fragmented, but with Yolanda's help I began to skim the edges of being a whole person.

I stopped wanting to waste my father, although my hatred toward him lasted for years. This part of my life has been the most painful to recount. I can't speak for any family members, since they have their own ways of dealing with this. Yet I'm sure many of them would prefer this story never be shared, that the facts be buried, the incidents forgotten, the horror of living with pedophilia and other abuse pushed aside.

But this is the chronicle of too many families, too many communities, particularly in our Chicano and Mexicano households, where people keep their mouths shut, the devastation bottled up, and consequently, healing cannot occur. To come out stronger from this I had to go through these wounds.

My father passed away in 1992 from a quickly spreading stomach cancer. He was in his early eighties. I was in Chicago at the time. I told my mother, although not anyone else in the family, why I wouldn't come to his funeral. She seemed to understand.

At one point before my father succumbed to the disease, I called Mom. My dad was at home, unable to speak, breathing his last. My mother requested that I say something to him, even if he couldn't respond. I didn't know what to say, although I heard his shallow breathing.

All my life I wanted another father. Yet, as I recall, he brought books home for me to read, even books I didn't care about. He showed me how to play chess—another obsession of his. And despite spending long hours away, he came home (most of my young friends had no fathers). This was the only father I knew, the one given to me by forces vaster and more mysterious than I could ever comprehend. So I told him something he never told me: "I love you, Dad."

My mother said he had a reaction, ever so slight, to my words. The next day he was gone.

Chapter Sixteen

After moving away from Yolanda, I worked out in my Boyle Heights room with the same barbells and weights I hauled from one part of the state to another—to the Bay Area, to Berdoo, and back to L.A. I ate sparingly, losing the pounds I'd gained. Then most evenings, while it was dark outside, I jogged around Hollenbeck Park.

When I mentioned this to people they gasped. Hollenbeck Park was at the time the preying ground of La Tercera gang, mostly from Mexico, unapologetically at war with the older and larger Chicano gangs. I never had any encounters with them, although once I ran while a lowered Impala glided behind me, its occupants probably wondering if they should inquire, "*¿De dónde eres?*" ("Where are you from?") After following me for several yards, the Impala took off.

Around this time, Nelson Peery, on a visit from Chicago, asked if I'd come to the Windy City, to the center of the revolutionary work in the country, as editor of the *People's Tribune*. Without AFSCME or Yolanda, I couldn't think of any compelling reason to stay in Los Angeles. The timing seemed perfect.

But I did have two major reasons: my boy and girl, Ramiro and Andrea, who were unable to weigh in about my leaving.

Things between Camila and me weren't going well. I would've spent more time with my children, devoted more time to their schooling, their concerns, their health, but Camila made this a war of nerves. I should not have let this get to me—let Camila set up stumbling blocks to my fatherhood, stop me from enjoying my time with Ramiro and

Andrea. But I will admit I eventually let this drive me off, make me find excuses not to show up. That was on me. This was a big mistake, one I'd pay for in due time.

I also missed Yolanda. I missed the time Yolanda and I lay naked in the backyard late at night alongside the lit chlorine blue of the swimming pool. Or the simple joys of watching her get dressed in the morning, trying on a blouse or skirt, perhaps a belt, taking them off again to examine another piece of clothing. I missed her fabulously endless hair, her uncanny loveliness.

For what it's worth, I missed Tania, too—a tiny voice with a demanding personality.

But the prospect of going to Chicago, of leaving behind this desert city of vast distances and multiple heartaches, loomed larger than I ever thought possible. I told Nelson I'd go, that I'd bring whatever expertise I had gained in journalism and my travels to the *People's Tribune*, a new and exciting challenge.

Sarita and I had one last night together. I'm sure she eyed me now for a long-range partnership after seeing me fail at my previous personal dealings. But my love for Yolanda colored this and other possible entanglements. Nothing relieved the loneliness, not even Sarita.

I continued to drink too much, alone in my room, with the TV on, surrounded by paper plates of half-eaten burritos. I tried to write. I tried to get back into the swing of things but found myself with a pull in my gut, an emotional drainpipe that seemed to suck everything down.

Sarita and I, after an awkward night on the town, ended with a big blowout. I yelled at her, but this time the indignation was stronger than ever before. I don't recall what the disagreement was about. Sarita grabbed her things, along with a jazz cassette tape I had given her earlier, and stormed out of my pickup truck. We never called each other again.

It took a while to make all the arrangements to leave, to make sure I left with nothing owed, nothing that anybody could hold against me. My family was still unraveling from Dad's deterioration, but when I left things were beginning to stabilize, even if most of this involved every-one closing down.

Then a community organizer, who I suspected had feelings for me, invited me to stay at her home while I got everything ready for departure. I'm not sure why, but I went along with this, taking my boxes, furniture, toolbox, weights, and clothing to her place and piling them into an empty basement room.

I slept upstairs, exercising most days, including running up and down wooden stairs next to her two-level house that spiraled four or five stories to a street below.

This friend and I toyed with the possibility of making it together. But the one night when this could have happened—with wine bottles, soft music, and dimmed lights—I hesitated, perhaps knowing that if I started something while I prepared to leave, I would be too emotionally knotted to make a clean getaway. She seemed disappointed, and so was I. Although she was good-looking and personable, I knew the snare I'd be caught in if I took this any farther.

By May 1985, I had packed my belongings into the back of the pickup, including those wretched boxes. I rented a small U-Haul trailer for the rest of my stuff that I hitched behind the truck. Before heading out, I said good-bye to my boy and girl, not aware how shocked they were that I was actually going—they didn't say anything. We hugged and kissed. Camila was pleasant that day.

I also took time to see my mother. I had a blue plastic tarp covering my things stacked on the truck's bed. My mother looked at this, at the haphazard way I roped things up, and began to take everything apart. I told her I needed to leave and I'd be fine, but she insisted on repacking the boxes, then retying the tarp over everything. I was glad she did. The tarp was now taut and evenly laid across a tighter-packed haul.

I managed one last thing before making my way out of town: I went to a free concert at Lincoln Park to see Los Lobos, the quintessential East L.A. band of the time. Thousands of people were prone across blankets with food and drink. Children of all ages ran up and down the green slopes, past the lake with foot-pedaled boats, in and out of the

Plaza de la Raza cultural center, or fooling around on the monkey bars and swings. Vendors of *paletas* and *elotes* rang bicycle bells on wheeled carts. Tattooed *cholos* with wraparound shades, many with no shirts on, strutted among the throng.

Then a fight erupted at the park's edge. For some reason the LAPD saw this as their signal to halt everything instead of isolating the brawlers and making sure the rest of the well-behaved audience could enjoy the concert. The police on horses rushed through the crowd, forcing people to jump up and run, grabbing little ones, as the horses trampled through blankets and coolers.

The band stopped playing. Megaphone pronouncements urged people to leave. Helicopters whirled overhead.

I loved driving long distances. I often drove from L.A. to Chicago. I'd gone on routes through El Paso or Denver. I also pushed the miles through the New York City-to-Chicago corridor. And more than once I navigated the L.A.-to-San Francisco highways and back, including a relaxing excursion with Yolanda.

On this trip, at first, I took my time, visiting with friends along the way. I made a quick stop in Fontana to see Aileen. She ran out of a neighbor's house, shrieking like a little girl—she was glad to see me. Her kids, older now, were also friendly. I felt bad about Aileen. But this was now behind me.

On the road, whenever I stopped for food and fuel, I ran a few laps in the desert, passing saguaro cacti like sentinels guarding the sparse earth and lizards squiggling along the caked dirt. I revisited the old Rockies, humongous galloping steeds of stone and pine trees, snow-capped manes, and deep ravines in brown-green hide. In Denver, I walked along copper-colored buildings, taking in the thin air with gulps.

But as I left the Mile-High City, I did something I had never done before on a road trip. I drove for fourteen hours straight, stopping only for necessities. I became kind of road crazy.

In the middle of the country, I weathered intense thunderstorms, rain like marbles against my windshield. At one point, I pulled over beneath an overpass when the downpour blocked visibility. After the skies cleared, I got out to check on the tarp and found my things were holding up. My mother's rigging was awesome, everything in its place, despite fifty- to seventy-mile-per-hour winds and the most wretched rain I'd ever witnessed.

Praise to moms.

In Nebraska I passed cornfields and the occasional silo, barn, farm-house. One evening, as dusk rolled in, I drove slightly too fast over a pair of train tracks, forcing my pickup to jump a few feet and break the hitching ball, leaving the U-Haul trailer marooned on the thorough-fare. I thought for sure I'd done irreparable damage, stuck in the middle of a cornfield nightmare.

But I glanced over and not far from the tracks was a rail yard mainte-nance shop. I drove over, sans trailer, and explained to the two mechan-ics still working there about my dilemma. I thought they'd just hand me a phone to call U-Haul and I'd have to wait another day or so to get U-Haul's people out there.

Instead these dudes proved to be angels.

One guy went to pull the U-Haul over and the other put his welding gear on, and before I knew it they had reattached the hitching ball and connected the trailer to the pickup, and I was good to go. I offered them money and they said no, it was their pleasure. I couldn't believe I'd come across people like this, proving how decent most Americans could be.

I drove on, looking back toward the mechanic's shop in case it van-ished, like the miracle it seemed to be.

Most of my thoughts on the trip were of Yolanda, her face and voice still haunting me. I lip-synched songs to her from the car radio. I called out her name. A couple of times I stopped to write letters I never sent. I didn't miss Yolanda the real person. I missed the illusion.

After several days crossing the country—taking my time or driving as if there were no tomorrow, days filled with backtracking, excitement, and fear—the jagged Chicago skyline appeared on the horizon one humid afternoon.

Chicago. Now there's a city. The skyscrapers were taller than any I had ever seen—Chicago had the tallest building in the world at the time. The housing was largely multistory red brick, old gray stone, or lathe and plaster with wood frames in varying architectural shapes. The poorer abandoned buildings had soot on the walls and trash in the yards. There were people everywhere, on stoops and corners, thawing out from the winter freeze that had ended several weeks before. Fire hydrants with rubber tires wrapped around the openings blasted wet relief to kids darkening under the scorching sun. The city thrived. The city smirked. The city played hopscotch and "bones."

The pickup truck, dusty and dented, lurched along the potholed surface of Damen Avenue, with rats scurrying across the way, to an address on the Near Northwest Side. In a few miles, I went from Mexican neighborhoods to African-American to Italian to Polish to Puerto Rican.

I was thirty years old. My kids were back in L.A. All my romances and jobs, rampages and drinking partners, bloodshot nights and fistfights, had been left behind for a new start, a new time. A new city.

I ended up in the back room of a Humboldt Park flat, where I placed books, clothes, music tapes and albums, scattered writings, photos and clippings—still packed in their boxes—around a stained mattress on cinder blocks. I began work immediately as editor of a national publication with ties to the most active fronts of struggle in the country.

I met up with old activists from the much earlier work we did in Watts and other parts of L.A. and was introduced to new cadre from around the country. One particular person of interest was Trini. Yes, that Trini, whom I had known since my Pasadena days when Ramiro was one year old and Camila and I were a relatively happy couple. Trini was now editor of the Spanish-language *Tribuno del Pueblo*, sister newspaper to the *People's Tribune*.

Poet and journalist Michael Warr already lived in the front section of the one-bedroom apartment I stayed at. We got out of each other's way—he was busy in the poetry world and with magazine writing. Michael stayed in the living room while I ended up in a back room. The building creaked and groaned, reminding me of the generations it had existed on this block.

I also began a morning routine of running around Humboldt Park, a large city park space and lake surrounded by the largest population of Puerto Ricans on the mainland outside of New York City.

At the *People's Tribune*, we tried to have a variety of political stories, analysis, photos, headlines, and captions to create a thought-provoking and community-engaging weekly. We incorporated columns by actual grassroots writers/activists on labor, education, housing, and, eventually, on prisons and spiritual affairs. The newspaper was passed around at factory gates, homeless encampments, housing projects, marches, rallies, and sometimes door-to-door in major cities of the country.

During whatever time we had off, which didn't seem like much, everyone worked on maintenance and repair on the buildings that housed our offices as well as our staff. We helped with roofing, including sweeping heavy mops filled with tar on flat rooftops; carpentry (I built walls, doorways, and storage sheds); tuck-pointing around brickwork; plumbing; and painting.

To relax, we ended up in local bars, blues and jazz clubs (Chicago was famous for these), salsa joints, and *quebradita* dance halls (a new Mexican musical phenomenon), and we often enjoyed a block party or two.

When winter moved in, I stood up in the middle of a meeting as the first snowflakes fell. There was no snow in the winter in L.A. Although there was snow within a half hour's drive, I had rarely gone to see it. I rushed out to let the flakes fall on my face and hands. The other staff members must have thought I'd gone loony.

Trini and I first related as editors of the newspapers. Late one night, I invited her for a drink. Soon I asked her to catch a film.

She didn't seem like the old Trini I knew—she looked pale, depressed. She didn't dress up or put on makeup. She devoted almost everything to her editorial and design work. She didn't seem to have friends outside the office.

One of the reasons I didn't think we clicked in L.A. was her shyness. But when I saw her at meetings, she was well read and interesting. I began to see Trini as decent—no drugs or heavy drinking, carefully weighing outcomes and commitments, a person of substance who in a sense scared me.

Mostly, over the years, we had remained friends. I had even shown up to the reception for Trini's wedding to her first husband, a nice dude, a photographer, to wish them well. It struck me that they were not a good pair together. Her husband was a friend of mine and suitable—but somehow I felt Trini was rowing up the wrong river. I couldn't say a thing.

By the time Trini ended up in Chicago, about two years before I did, she was divorced, alone, although seemingly suspended with no moorings. I now looked at her and felt she was miserable, unlike the person I knew she was—the competent, intelligent beauty I recalled from L.A.

Interestingly I heard from people that Trini was available, open to someone like me. Even her ex-husband gave someone the message that now, going to Chicago, I would probably hook up with Trini. Others indicated to me she seemed ready for something new and good to happen.

But was I that person?

I still carried Yolanda around in the darkened recesses of my heart. But being in Chicago, putting out publications, with my writing in the midst of activist work, I matured again. For the first time, I actually turned down women I felt weren't what I wanted—in the past, I'd go for anyone who gave me the time of day. Even having sex, which I used to be game for without a relationship, needed negotiation, serious consideration, with two feet on the ground. I still had love inside me for someone special, someone for the long haul, someone of deeper significance.

Someone like Trini.

Trini invited me one evening to have Carson's ribs near Lake Michigan. I sat down with her in a grassy spot along the lakefront, framed by the tall, ritzy apartments of the Gold Coast glistening in the sun. Trini threw out a blanket then placed the ribs and some beer on top. Nice. I didn't realize, however, the real aim of this invitation.

"Louie, these past couple of weeks we've gotten close," Trini said in that hardly audible voice of hers. "Last weekend when we went out, we kissed. I really liked that. But I've been thinking a lot about this ever since. Is this what we really want? We may ruin a good friendship by trying to take this to another level. I value what we have. But to make more of this—I'm not sure I'm ready."

I knew what she was getting at—or at least I thought I did. It was the old heave-ho, the dreaded "let's be friends" talk. I felt like I was drowning, like I had to hang on to something, anything, even though up to this point I was prepared to take my time before making a move on Trini. But when I heard those words and that familiar refrain, I felt the ground pulled out from under me.

"Trini, I don't know about you, but I don't have time to waste anymore," I argued. "I have many friends—I'm not looking for more friends. I'm trying to find a lasting and wonderful relationship. I'm telling you upfront. I've been down that 'fuck my way to love' road. I've been down that 'I'll be your friend and hope it becomes something else' road. Both of these are paved with broken hearts and in the end I've walked out alone. I wasn't even sure where we were going with this thing when we began spending time together. But since you brought this up, here's my two cents: I'm interested in something meaningful, maybe a love of my life. I'm not afraid. I sense you are. What I hear from you is fear talking. 'Stop this before it goes too far' kind of thing. Well, Trini, I may be destroying this before it gets started, but I'm here for more than friendship. If this is all you want, I don't want to take up any more of your time."

This got Trini going. She countered that friendship was a foundation, the true underpinning of any relationship, that she'd seen sex and romance and overblown feelings get in the way. She wanted to make sure this wasn't the same old thing—she'd recently been through one fantasized relationship gone dry. She, too, was tired.

I re-countered. She added more. I responded. She re-responded. Years later, we realized we were saying the same thing but from different angles, with different words, crying up from different sources. Yet at the time we appeared to be at odds, of contrary mind-sets. The fact was, both Trini and I wanted to be serious about ourselves and our relationships.

After a long period of going back and forth, I conceded, although I probably didn't know what I was conceding to.

"Okay, Trini, we'll be friends. I'm not going to ask anymore. Nobody can really convince somebody about taking it to other levels anyway. It has to come from their heart. So okay, I agree. Let's be friends."

I resigned myself to the failure of this effort, to the fact that Trini and I weren't destined to be together. That I just had to stay true to myself—my work, my art, for love, even if I had to hold on to it for a while. I'd find somebody. I trusted in that. If it wasn't going to be Trini it would still happen. Part of me was saddened, but I was not the same person, perhaps transformed on that journey through the country, from L.A. to Chicago, toward a new life ahead of me—where anything was possible.

I went home that evening. Trini did so as well. We lived in the same two-building complex on one lot, each building three stories, on Mozart Street south of Augusta Avenue. Our apartments were separated by one floor and worn gray-painted wood landings.

In my room I curled up with a book, trying to keep my mind off what had just happened, able to take this in stride, which for me was an accomplishment. I was glad I didn't lose it. I held on to my demeanor and honor. And I was glad that Trini did the same. We were both steady, adamant, clear.

Later that night, Trini called.

"Louie, do you want to come over?" she requested, her voice different, daring, no doubts noted.

I didn't question her or try to reopen another line of defense.

"I'll be right there."

Trini and I began a serious love relationship, not even two months into my move to Chicago. Perhaps we both secretly wanted this, not knowing how or when, but when I made the move there, new roads opened up for both of us.

After Trini's call, we made love untiringly, insatiably, boldly. In the middle of our intimacy, still naked on the bed, Trini grabbed a Kinsey book on sexual behavior and read a few passages. Strange, but it was endearing. Almost any strange thing Trini did endeared me to her. In the following weeks, Trini began to dress up, wear perfume, get color in her cheeks. We made love in the office. On the beach. At her place. At mine. And in out-of-the-way places in between.

One of my efforts at the *People's Tribune* was to do more hands-on stories—in the noose, through the mud, among the most downtrodden. This was difficult since most of what I did was in the office, behind a computer, on the phone, and in tons of meetings. So I proposed spending a night in a large Chicago homeless shelter.

Unlike Los Angeles, Chicago had a long history of settlement houses for the poor as well as shelters for those without homes. They had sleeping accommodations (on a per-night basis) or day-only facilities. A few provided both. In day facilities there was often art, writing, reading, computers, and lots of Bible study.

Deindustrialization was creating a class of people who would never again find a job. Many didn't have homes either. There was also the closing down of psychiatric treatment centers—many mentally ill people roamed the streets. And there were parolees being let out of prisons with no families, resources, work, or adequate skills. A considerable number were Vietnam War vets.

I decided to go incognito. I took the name of Juan Acuña. It was in the winter of 1985. There was snow everywhere, temperatures below zero—with the windchill factor driving the numbers to minus fifty degrees or worse.

I'd had a few bouts of homelessness in my time—as a kid, as a teenager, and in my twenties. But the homelessness I saw in Chicago was deeper, longer, more devastating. I met people who had been homeless for years. There were heroin addicts who started out like me but never stopped. There were whole families living in cars or vans. Some tore down planks of unused industrial structures or apartments and slept there with no heat. Or they found shelters, which were often too overcrowded to take in all who needed them.

As Juan Acuña, I lined up at a Catholic-run facility southwest of downtown Chicago. There were around three hundred people allowed each night, and at least a hundred more were turned away. I signed up at the front desk, where I was told to grab a mattress from a pile and locate a spot to lay it down.

The building was a former warehouse, and the main hall was cavernous, with mattresses strewn about any available space. There were rows of pipes on the walls and tracks on the ceiling where an overhead crane used to roll. On one wall was an imposing statue of Jesus with outstretched arms and imploring eyes of painted plaster.

I found a spot in the middle of several other mattresses. There were only men allowed in the warehouse. Women with children were next door in a much smaller space.

The hall was alive with noise—talk, laughter, arguments, and coughs (some sounded so rancid I thought those guys had TB). I didn't say much of anything. I listened. There were gangs in there, bullying the weaker men. I looked hefty so nobody messed with me, despite my medium stature. Still, I had to be wary. There were homeless dudes stealing from homeless dudes.

Most of the guys were honest. Many were newly homeless after losing jobs and apartments. I had good conversations in English and Spanish. The majority were African-Americans but there were sizable numbers of Mexicans and Puerto Ricans as well.

At a given point lights were turned off. I lay back on my mattress, using my shoes as pillows and guarding my beanie cap and gloves. These were the first to go in places like this, and losing one's shoes, cap, and gloves was like murder in the winter. I held on to them for dear life.

Between the coughs and bedbugs—I scratched all night long—I barely slept.

Promptly at six A.M., the lights were turned on and shelter staff went around waking up the men. We had to gather our minimal stuff and then pick up the mattresses and repile them on the way out of the warehouse. My shoes were still there, my gloves stuffed inside, wrapped in the beanie cap.

Praise to shoes.

At a loading dock the shelter provided bad coffee and a granola bar. Then the staff opened the large metal entrances with loud creaking. I stepped out and lingered in the snow for a while, the wet cold slapping me across the face. Daily-newspaper vans were parked in front to gather homeless men to hawk papers on the main streets for twenty-five cents a paper, a portion of which went to the sellers. Some climbed into the vans, others walked to vacant lots to fire up metal trash cans until the day shelters opened up.

Holding on to a near-empty cup of coffee, I strolled into a heartless dawn.

I wanted to spend more nights at the shelter but realized I was taking up space for a real homeless person. I had what I needed for articles in the *People's Tribune* and a poem.

Eventually I returned to these shelters, donating my time to teach writing and poetry through organizations like the Chicago Coalition for the Homeless from the late 1980s to the late 1990s. I helped produce individual poetry chapbooks and anthologies of writings by the homeless. I worked in large shelters like Cooper's Place, with several hundred people, and smaller ones such as Irene's Place, a day shelter for women. At the latter, I was slated to do workshops for six weeks but ended up there for four years—the women and I just wouldn't let each other go.

I traveled to various cities in the United States to speak. Community leaders set up events in churches, in labor halls, in community centers, in homeless encampments, among people who occupied boarded-up buildings, in schools and universities.

I also wrote many pieces, including stories of a homeless union organizing campaign. Of industrial strikes, including the big meat-packing strike in Austin, Minnesota, where I interviewed key leaders and took photos. I spoke to police shooting victims and their families in New York City and New Jersey, including a young man at Bellevue Hospital recently injured by police. I covered undocumented migrant battles, such as the fight to bring justice to Mexicans drowning in the Rio Grande or being shot on the border, and their struggles for better wages and conditions on the job.

I went to Alabama's Black Belt region during elections of new leaders from the birthplace of the civil rights struggle. This also involved community canvassing and talking to poor black and white families in isolated "shotgun" shacks. I traveled to east Ohio coal country to hang with restless punk youths. I covered the beginnings of the low-powered micro-radio movement (so-called pirate radio) and the many fights against the censorship of alternative rock and hip-hop.

I ended up in Kansas City several times to take part in a Culture Under Fire free expression week. I read poetry and spoke at the University of Missouri–Kansas City but also at music halls like the Grand Emporium. Once I advised leaders and teachers there and it led to the founding of a new school in a high-dropout Mexican community. When I returned twenty years later this school had become an alternative institution called Alta Vista (Grand Vision) Academy. I met many wonderful people, including Katrina Coker, a Muskogee Creek activist who became a longtime friend.

In Philadelphia I got to know the members of the Kensington Welfare Rights Union, which fought for men, women, and children left behind by the economy. One of these was Cheri Honkala, who also became a leader in the Poor People's Economic Human Rights Campaign, which has since organized marches, building occupations, and tent cities to demand the government ensure the well-being of families and eradicate poverty.

One time I landed in the Appalachian coal country of West Virginia, home to countless generational union battles in dank and dangerous coal mines. I spoke at an isolated run-down school auditorium about the pressing issues of labor and capital. After my talk, a young African-American man stopped me and said that members of the Ku Klux Klan wanted to meet with me. They were intrigued by my talk and figured if an African-American conveyed the message I'd know they meant no harm.

I probably should have backed out of this one, but I decided to take a chance and talk to these KKKers. I followed someone in a car and drove for a long time to a "holler"—a forested ravine with scattered unpainted wood shacks, similar, in fact, to my old-time Las Lomas barrio.

In this one shack we went to, a train track lay but a few feet away, so that when a train rumbled by I felt as if it was going through the middle of the house. The KKK members were young white dudes, poor, with thick Appalachian accents.

"We heard what you said earlier today at the school," one of the ringleaders stated. "We got interested in this idea of organizing in our class interests and that race is used to divide the poor. We've never heard anyone talk like this before. Some of us are thinking this makes sense."

"The problem here," another dude explained, "is nobody talks to us at all. We're not working. We can't feed our families. We're white—and the only ones who come around to talk is the Klan."

"At first we didn't know what you were," the first guy added. "We thought you were Chinese until someone said you were Mexican. We ain't never seen no Mexicans in these parts."

"But when you started talking," a third person threw in, "we got your words, your message—that we're having the same problems as other people and that we have more in common with them than rich folk. We're interested—we want to know more."

I spent a couple of hours with these guys. At the end, I linked them to community organizers in the area—a mixed-race collective with homegrown ties.

These KKKers were curious and open. I'm sure a few still harbored racist thoughts, but I also felt they were tired of their circumstances and wanted something new and different. Hardly anyone had anything to do with the "holler"-dwelling or trailer-park whites, leaving them vulnerable to the most backward and racist ideas. This experience demonstrated the possibilities of poor white people taking up the revolutionary destiny they were meant to fulfill along with people of color.

Dating Trini was hot and cold, good and bad, some of the most loving moments along with some of the most exasperating. A problem was Trini's fears, her tendency to overthink things, often paralyzing herself from making a move. I was the opposite, moving on things, then afterward (perhaps) thinking about the fallout. But we pushed on, often breaking up after a flare-up, then coming across each other again and falling into each other's arms.

One night, at Quencher's Bar on the North Side, Trini and I were tossing back a couple of brews when I noticed she was introspective, not saying anything, looking around the club as if she were seeking someone. I asked her about this. She didn't want to talk, but, as always, I insisted. Finally she exclaimed that she didn't want to see me anymore. She was having a hard time getting over a lost love, and he was in the bar. She felt it was wrong for her to see me if her heart was still torn. She wanted to try, if possible, to work something out with him.

Just like that.

Well, I wasn't the old Louie. I could get irate, but these kinds of things stopped shredding me up. I walked away, leaving her beautiful face and body sitting alone at the back of the bar. I went to the counter and ordered another beer.

It turned out that dude had long gotten over Trini. I actually knew him and we talked. Trini had made more of this guy and their short romance. She carried that longer than she should have and found it hard to accept that things had changed. This guy even told me not to give up on Trini.

Nonetheless, in between our breakups, instigated each time by Trini, I tried to date other women. I had one-night stands and drunken moments with friends, and one time I connected with a Puerto Rican artist named Maydé. I used to spend time at Guild Books, a progressive bookstore in Lincoln Park run at the time by Richard Bray, a longtime friend of writers and thinkers. Following a poetry reading there I went to an artist's home nearby for drinks and dialogue.

Maydé was sitting on a couch, an outgoing, firmly built woman with an attractive face and curly black hair past her shoulders. Her eyes and lips were full and delectable—a great combination.

We talked that night, exchanged phone numbers, and then she became my focus as Trini and I went back and forth. The first date with Maydé, we made love in her clean, artistically decorated flat in Humboldt Park. We then saw each other as much as we could. Sometimes, without my calling, Maydé showed up at my place.

One time I was in the basement, washing clothes, when she popped up and leaned against the doorway. She looked sexy in a long gypsy skirt and tight blouse. She came up to me and we kissed. Then I put my hand beneath the skirt and realized she wasn't wearing underwear.

When Trini came around again, I let go of Maydé, which was agonizing to keep doing. Maydé called. She invited me to events. And I wouldn't be available. But as soon as Trini called things off again, I went back to knocking on Maydé's door.

It all came to a head when Trini and I had a serious talk in a back room where she was now staying. Trini was sad, afraid, and telling me how she failed me, how she destroyed a good thing, and that she'd now have to live without me. I listened. I thought about leaving and perhaps shutting the door on this relationship. But something kept me in the room. Something kept me fixated on making this work. After Trini's tears about defeat and the end of love, I told her I still loved her, it was not the end, and if she still wanted me, I wanted to keep trying.

Trini was bowled over. I just couldn't live without her. I didn't know at the time how considerably vital our connection was going to be, but I felt compelled to not let go, against some complicated internal turmoil. I was on new ground here. That was the last of our breakups.

But now I had to deal with Maydé.

I went to Maydé's house to tell her I was going to devote myself to Trini and that Maydé and I would have to end our sweet, but no longer workable, relationship. Maydé didn't take this very well. Even as she yelled at me, called me out, I remained steady. I apologized, but I didn't want this to go on. She told me to get out of her place.

Later, I had a window smashed in my pickup truck with a note from Maydé about what an asshole I was. And then she showed up one night with no clothes on except a long man's white shirt, her ample breasts visible through the fabric. I maintained self-control, told her I couldn't do this anymore, and she left, terribly shaken.

I thought for a second I was dealing with a *Fatal Attraction* kind of thing.

But after this Maydé stopped acting crazy. I actually liked her. But I loved Trini. And it was time to decide. For once I didn't want to play around. I had to fight for Trini, and once I did, I had to keep her. In time Maydé and I became friends, bumping into each other among the artists and organizers in the Puerto Rican and Mexican communities.

Once I came upon Maydé at a summer dance. She looked fine, in overalls, believe it or not—her face made up nice, her body smoking. When she saw me she cried. I had on a sleeveless T-shirt and she remarked how she loved my muscles. I told her I appreciated knowing her, being with her, but that Trini and I were serious. She was resigned to this, even as she wiped her tears and caressed my cheek.

Yolanda often invaded my mind, my dreams—not the real woman, but the diminishing image I still had of her. I was into Trini, but I had to confront Yolanda one way or another.

An opportunity opened up when I returned to L.A. for a week to visit my children. The kids and I had a good time. But I called Yolanda to see how she was doing. She wanted to see me, have lunch. I felt my nerves and blood cells open up, like an addict's, waiting for the next fix.

We got together at a Japanese joint we often went to when I worked with AFSCME. Yolanda looked as radiant as always, although her long hair now popped with a few frizzled gray ones. We talked about movies, books, things we used to share. I asked about Tania, who was doing well.

I thought to invite Yolanda to a film. My hope was to have the love rekindled. But an interesting thing happened. As Yolanda and I stood by the side of her car to leave, we locked lips. Before, this would have driven me through the asphalt. But nothing happened. No rush, no heightened blood levels, no racing heartbeat. Nothing. I was puzzled, unsure of what I felt. In spite of myself, my feelings had already shifted, even if my head had not caught up. Trini's kisses were now my joy, the fire starter, what woke up my senses.

Yolanda, her aura, was no longer sharing my heart.

Chapter Seventeen

Louie, guess what?"

"What?"

"I'm pregnant."

With those words my life made another turn. Leading up to this, Trini had moved into my place after about a year and a half of dating. Michael Warr moved from the flat to accommodate us. We then lived together for another year and a half before Trini made this announcement. She knew how to take her time before committing to anything, but once she did, she was definite.

And the pregnancy wasn't an accident, out of the blue, a "mistake." Trini wanted to have a baby with me. She'd waited thirty-five years of her life for this—and she was ready.

Trini and I decided to get married. The marriage was set for March 1988. To get around the long wait required by the state of Illinois for a marriage license due to a new HIV testing policy, we took our vows in front of a judge in Kenosha, Wisconsin, a fair-sized city on Lake Michigan, some fifty miles away.

The next weekend an intimate ceremony and reception were held at a home in Wicker Park. Our many friends, labor leaders, activists, artists, poets, their kids, and neighbors came by. Trini looked astonishing, her normally long native hair now curled and teased. Nelson Peery officiated, honoring us with some potent words.

"You both can still rescue love, can nurture and develop it, but you have to try," Nelson said, following his comments on the political-economic history of love, the best I ever heard. "Try against the drag of centuries, against the call of the wild, and you will find as others have that the effort is worth it . . . We love you and want you to succeed in this. You both know how much I love you. Should what is between you sometimes become weak and shaky, rely on what is between all of us for strength."

I was in a splendid state, very much in love, very much content.

Trini was three months pregnant with our child.

Soon after the wedding, I resigned from the *People's Tribune*. I had been there for three years, the last year without pay. Donations had fallen and all staff members had to find other jobs while volunteering extra hours to put out the paper. The sacrifices made by everyone, even those with children, were awe-inspiring.

For income, I learned computer typesetting and rotated jobs at various printing and public relations companies. Trini worked as a teacher, through the community college system, in the Mexican Pilsen barrio teaching English and citizenship classes to newly arrived migrants at Casa Aztlan Community Center.

In an ironic move, the archdiocese of Chicago hired me as a type-setter in their publications department, called Liturgy Training Publications, situated in a former convent next to St. Mary of the Angels Church in the Bucktown neighborhood.

On weekends, I was also a reporter/writer for WMAQ-AM, All News Radio ("Give us twenty minutes, we'll bring you the world"). On the graveyard shift, I drove in the dead of night to the monstrous Merchandise Mart building, where the station was located. My job was to get facts—gleaned from my own reporting as well as national and international wire services—and write twenty to thirty seconds of copy on each news item for the on-air anchors.

I entered the Chicago poetry scene through my friendship with Michael Warr. He introduced me to another emergent poet, a *Chicago Sun-Times* reporter named Patricia Smith.

We often walked in together to the various North Side bars and cafés that held weekly poetry events: the Get Me High, the Artful Dodger, Batteries Not Included, the Gallery Cabaret, Edge of the Looking Glass, the Bop Shop, Weeds, and others. I met more poets—Deborah Pintonelli, Tony Fitzpatrick, Marvin Tate, Lisa Buscani, Carlos Cumpian, Jean Howard, Cin Salach, C. J. Laity, and the ever-popular David Hernandez.

I signed up for the open mics, nervous as hell. I wanted to learn every move and moment, how to use an outstretched arm or severe gaze, how these wordsmiths sank a verse line like a great pitcher sinks a baseball—in the territory of the unexpected.

Some poets read in monotone. Others had bad timing. A few over-performed. But the performance poets of Chicago who rocked put all the elements together, containing an often-rowdy crowd with the most versatile and animated gestures, cadences, anecdotes.

For at least a year prior to this, I arrived at these spaces and sat in a booth or on a bar stool, alone, ordering drinks, with a folder of newly typed poems, revving myself up to read, but even soused, I didn't.

During this period, I met Marc Kelly Smith, the main creator in 1986 of slam poetry and fevered impresario of the Uptown Poetry Slam. Every Sunday night in front of three hundred people or so at the Green Mill Lounge, Marc matched the clinking of bottles and loud talk with heightened oratory and signature poems. Here poets were pitted against poets as they performed their best three-minute opuses. The audience—or a selected trio of poets for the night—would judge with numbers from one to ten who best owned the poem, controlled the mic, kept the audience amused, engaged, or in serious thought.

Finally, in early 1988, I got the nerve to read my verses, emboldened by seeing Patricia and Michael (both African-Americans) and people like Carlos and David (Chicano and Boricua, respectively) perform. Most of the open mic'ers and slammers were white, but Chicago was open to and enriched by poets of color.

I slammed a few times, because every poet of note seemed to. I wasn't good at it. Still, it was a great way to learn about bringing poetry back up from the throat, to the eyes, to the head, the arms, and the shifting of one's feet. Where the body becomes the poem. Where the poem is worn as jacket, as scuffed shoes, as hat. Poem and person were one. My participation helped me hone my confidence, my timing, the phrasing, knowing how to hold an audience at one's fingertips or with the twist of a phrase.

The real star became Patricia Smith, who once had poems sticking out of kitchen drawers for years until she took them to the mics and tore up the competition. Literally. She reigned as the Chicago Poetry Slam champion, four-time National Poetry Slam champion, and a Taos Poetry Circus bout winner. She also served as an international poetry slam idol when slams spread to more than eighty cities in the United States and several more in Canada, Europe, Australia, and other places.

In time all these poets became my teachers, my critics, my community.

My way of honoring the slam world, however, turned out to be as a publisher, not a slammer. In 1989 I produced my first poetry collection, thirteen poems. Out of hundreds I had stashed, these were the ones I deemed publishable. This was after getting rejected by publishers and magazines for a few years. I spent hundreds of dollars in fees and postage sending out my poems—writing letters, getting stamps and envelopes—to no avail.

With my typesetting skills down, I got permission from LTP's director to use the computers and photo-developing machines after work to put together my book. Part-Menominee native Jane Brunette, who was LTP's book designer and knew about publishing, designed the cover and inside pages. The Puerto Rican artist Gamaliel Ramirez donated the cover art. I sold the book, *Poems Across the Pavement*, out of the trunk of my car.

This effort also got me chosen as one of sixteen "next generation" writers for the fifty-fourth World Congress of PEN, held in Toronto and Montreal in December 1989. My old friend Richard Bray of Guild Books played a role in getting me nominated. I sat on panels and read poetry among renowned wordsmiths such as Jamaica's Mutabaruka, Argentina's Alicia Partnoy, Guatemala's Arturo Arias, and Canada's Ruby Slipperjack, among others. I now entered the global writers' community.

After my book appeared, a number of Chicago poets, including slam poets, approached me about publishing their works. I thought about this—why not? I again solicited the expertise of Jane, who has been our designer ever since. Over the years, I mustered a collective of editors—Reginald Gibbons, Michael Warr, Julie Parson-Nesbitt, Quraysh Ali Lansana, to name a few—to help with reading manuscripts and moving each book's production. We named the press Tía Chucha Press, venerating my brave and creative aunt from Mexico (considered crazy within the family) who played guitar, wrote poetry and songs, and even made her own line of perfumes and colognes—although they smelled really bad. Yet it was this spirit that eventually helped fire up my own creative furnaces.

Trini had a healthy pregnancy. She looked fabulous. She had cut her hair short and she had warm eyes, a ready smile, and color. Then the day came for the delivery. The baby was to be born at a nineteenth-century-era hospital near the lakefront, covered by my insurance. Despite its age, the hospital had a state-of-the-art birthing center. You could play your own music on built-in tape players. The rooms were nicely painted, the surroundings tranquil.

I drove Trini to the hospital soon after her water broke around six A.M. It was late September 1988. I parked in a nearby lot and helped Trini walk to the entrance, where a wheelchair awaited her.

I was allowed to stay in the labor room. I took that to mean I'd be there until the baby was born. However, Trini was forty-eight hours in labor. Yikes. That baby just didn't want to come out. Hour upon hour, we attempted conversation. She mostly rested. At one point, the nurses felt they had to induce labor so the baby wouldn't get stressed. Trini didn't yell or lose her composure.

At night I made myself comfortable next to Trini's bed, although I didn't get any sleep. This turned out to be a no-no. The morning nurses were startled to see me still in the room and told me to leave. I could return at eight A.M. and it was already five A.M. I questioned their logic but they insisted. I told Trini I'd be right back. She held my hand, whispered that this was fine, then dozed off.

I decided to sleep in the car for a while and wake up in time for visiting hours. I slept longer than I planned. I got up, sun high in the sky, and ran to the hospital. In the elevator I saw two of Trini's friends, who had come in such a rush that one of them spilled coffee on her blouse. I smiled and tried to say hello, but these women practically pushed me up against the wall.

"Where have you been?" one of them demanded. "Trini is having the baby and she called the house saying you were at a party."

What?

By the time we got to Trini she was racked with pain.

"Where have you been?" she managed to say in between contractions.

When we finally straightened things out about my sleeping in the car, and not whooping it up somewhere, we got down to business. Trini was taken to the delivery room. She was put up on stirrups with her body almost upright, her legs splayed. I never saw a birth like this. When the contractions intensified I tried to help her with breathing and getting into a natural rhythm. But that child must have found something in the womb to grab on to and wouldn't let go.

At one point, Trini's friends, a couple of nurses, and myself were in front of Trini like a cheerleading squad.

"You can do it . . . puuushhh, Trini!"

About an hour into this, I turned around and it appeared that half the hospital floor had joined in the cheering section, including what looked to be other expectant fathers, and perhaps even visitors from nearby rooms. Trini looked embarrassingly exposed up there. I glanced at the nurses to see if this concerned them. It didn't. I gave them a signal like a quarterback to clear the room, not wanting to panic Trini. One nurse got it.

"Okay, everybody, please leave now. Give her space. Only nurses and the father, please."

At one point, Trini felt a desperate urge to push but held back since the doctor hadn't arrived yet. Sometime that morning, he walked in. Originally from South Africa, an Afrikaner, he apparently cut women as part of his standard procedure in delivering babies, unbeknownst to us at the time. When the baby's head appeared, the good old doc got his clippers and slit Trini, blood pouring out of the wound. Shocked, I looked to the nurses for relief. None there.

Finally, the little guy pushed out of his mother, all the baby goop mixed with blood on his purple skin. He cried like he was raging at the world for removing him from Mama. A nurse cut the umbilical cord and placed him in a stainless steel tub to be washed. Trini put her head back, dead tired. I then snuck a look over to the baby and saw a young nurse, perhaps just starting out, open the clip that held the end of the baby's umbilical cord. Blood spurted out.

Without making Trini aware of this, I went up to the nurse and in a low voice asked, "What are you doing?" Flustered, the nurse put the clip back on, apologized profusely, and walked away.

I was horrified. I mentioned this to another nurse and she said removing the clip was dangerous—the baby could have bled out. I said, "Right, so please investigate this woman." I couldn't believe a staff person would make such a disastrous mistake.

Later, both mother and baby were finally safe at home. I told Trini about the incident with the umbilical cord and she got upset. But with the baby in our arms we both calmed down. He was a fine boy. We named him Rubén Joaquín.

When I moved to Chicago, and before Trini and I were married, Ramiro and Andrea came to visit in the summers. They were ten and eight years old that first year—and I continued to be extremely busy the first three years.

A couple of times I was late in picking them up from O'Hare Airport. Once the airline staff admonished me when I showed up after the kids had arrived and they had to wait in their offices. I felt out of control when it came to my time at the *People's Tribune*. Regardless, it was simply wrong and I had no one to blame but myself.

I enrolled the children in a settlement house day program for kids. I often found babysitters during other hours. I worked all day and late into the evening, with a short break for dinner. Even when Trini and I were living together, Ramiro and Andrea were largely watching TV or playing. Both Trini and I were on similar schedules.

To make up for this, Trini and I decided one summer to drive the kids to Canada in Trini's Toyota pickup with a camper shell. I first wanted to check out the Diego Rivera murals at the Detroit Institute of Arts, then continue on to Ontario. Driving up to Detroit, everything was fine—standing in front of the Rivera murals I felt I was in a Gothic cathedral, a Mayan temple, a sacred place.

On the Canada border we were told to pull over for a thorough check. Border officials treated us as if we were undocumented and/or drug dealers. After that we pushed on to Lake Erie, where we heard there were good campgrounds. The day was nice when we got there. We walked around a small, charming town. Then we entered a national park to track down a spot to pitch a tent. The lake water was lapping gently at the shore.

The first day was fun. The kids had their own pup tent while Trini and I stayed in the camper. But that night we got pounded with bullet-like rain. In the middle of the night, we heard screams. Trini and I peered out the camper to see the pup tent in a pool of water. The kids, soaked, stuck out their heads, terrified.

I jumped out into muddy ground and slipped trying to get ahold of the tent so I could pull the kids out. I finally got both of them under my arms and carefully transferred them to Trini inside the camper. I was surprised at how quickly the rain affected the lake, which overflowed its banks and flooded much of the grass area.

This torrent hit us all night. The next day, the rain stopped but we couldn't leave due to deep puddles on the way to the road. We had to wait until the water receded. Meantime, with four of us crammed into the small camper, we got on each other's nerves. Ramiro and Andrea, by then, tended to fight all the time. When they were smaller Ramiro was the protective older brother to his quiet and vulnerable sister. Now they were like cats and dogs.

Trini and I didn't do much better—we soon yelled at each other, complaining about this and that, about whose idea this was (mine?) and other aggravations.

Finally, by midday, we scuttled back to the road.

———

The year Rubén was born, Ramiro was having troubles with his mother.

About four years earlier, Camila had moved in with Lionel, a tall African-American city housing official. When I knew him he struck me as a nice guy. But the kids, years later, told me another story—he was obsessive and abusive. The kids had to keep their rooms spotless, everything in drawers and boxes. He forbade them to go into his office to get anything. He had everything in that office accounted for—he knew where every pen, paper, tape dispenser, and staple was located. Lionel emotionally terrorized Camila as well.

One day Lionel came home and found a pencil missing on his desk. Neither of the kids admitted to taking it. So Lionel beat both of them. Andrea cried, but Ramiro refused to. So Lionel had Ramiro pull down his pants while his mother, in tears, held him for the whupping. This was one of the horror stories I extracted from Camila and the kids about those years—only it was too late for me to do anything about this.

Later I heard that Ramiro tried to run away several times. The first time he asked Andrea to go with him, but she was too scared. When he was found and beaten, Andrea hid Ramiro's shoes so he wouldn't leave again. Other times Ramiro was found riding trains or sleeping on a neighbor's porch. The last time, when he was nine, police discovered him walking along a freeway. When asked where he was going, Ramiro replied he was on his way to Chicago to see his father.

Camila finally left Lionel. Still, incidents like these destroyed a level of trust that Ramiro and Andrea needed to have in their mother. She had let them down as a protector. Ramiro acted out—getting into fights in schools, turning against teachers, yelling back at his mother.

Around the time Ramiro turned thirteen, Camila called. She said that Ramiro had gotten so angry he threatened her with his fists. Camila apparently responded by picking up a board with nails in it. Now Camila wanted me to take him. She had reached her limit with the boy. It was my turn to be a parent.

This scared the hell out of me. I could handle being a weekend dad, or even one during the summers. But having Ramiro full-time, with a new baby in the house, a new life, made me feel disoriented and inadequate. I didn't disagree that this was necessary, though—he was my son. He needed his father more than ever, whether I was ready or not.

Ramiro was intelligent, although his behavior was atrocious. Still, I got him enrolled in a prestigious school in Hyde Park called Kenwood Academy. We had Ramiro stay in my old bedroom at the back of the flat. Trini and I slept in the living room with Rubén in his crib. At first things worked out. But Ramiro was terribly maladjusted. He used to pee in the corner of the room rather than go to the bathroom. He gave Trini such a hard time that I thought she'd leave.

Ramiro eventually got kicked out of Kenwood Academy. Ramiro hated authority. I tried to exert mine, but it felt like a sham. Ramiro's resentments were more than I anticipated. I'm sure he thought, *This dude has never been a dad to me—why should I listen to him now?*

The real problems surfaced when Ramiro attended the local high school, Roberto Clemente, which at the time had almost twenty street gangs in one of the most violent gang communities in the country.

Chapter Eighteen

The practice of medicine has two branches—the physical and the spiritual. Poetry is one of the spiritual healing arts. It helped to tune what Sir Francis Bacon called "the curious harp of man's body." When I think of that, I think of Jack Hirschman.

Jack was America's leading street poet. Born in New York City in 1933, and mostly raised there, Jack ended up in San Francisco—walking the North Beach streets, a regular at the cafés and bars, at City Lights Bookstore and Café Trieste. Jack gave up a prestigious academic career to be among the poor, the homeless, the forgotten.

I first saw Jack read when I was in L.A. He'd have both hands on the podium, leaning forward, blond locks over his ears and shoulders, missing teeth, and that booming voice, with a vigor that shook the rafters in buildings and within one's psyche. I learned much about poetry from Jack, mostly by watching, catching the thread, riding that voice. Jack's poems often explored hunger, derailed lives, and how poetry can lift up, fill in, transform, reshape, and orient.

It was Jack who introduced me to Alexander Taylor and Judith Doyle, the founders of Curbstone Press. This was one of the best progressive literary publishers, based in the former textile town of Willimantic, Connecticut. On Jack's recommendation, Alexander—known as Sandy—asked me for a poetry manuscript. I went through my worn-out papers and offered Curbstone a large variety of my best work. This became my second book, *The Concrete River*, which saw the light of day in 1991. It pushed me into a world of poetry outside of the Chicago scene.

———

Poetry became my thing. I gravitated toward words, releasing their power, their possibilities, their textures and tones, their music and flavors. Of course, my first poetic lines were badly written. But a poet isn't born with poetry. He or she is born with the latent love of language that, with reading, skill, and contact with other writers, compels words to be twisted and bent with the rhythms and sense that make up a poem.

Even in my journalistic endeavors, even with my pieces on the most disaffected and marginalized members of our society, I found time to write poems. I eventually had file cabinets and boxes full of journals and papers, including jottings, ideas, lines, and images in various stages of formation.

In Chicago, all this came together. This rough-hewn industrial town bled poets. I interacted with most of them during the height of the literary explosion in the 1980s and 1990s. I wrote critiques and reviews for *Letter eX*, Chicago's poetry newspaper. I performed poetrytheater with Club Lower Links, Blue Rider Theater, and other venues. With Gregorio Gomez and Juan Ramirez, and others, I put together a production called *Metaphoria—Chicago Poetry with a Twist* at the Firehouse Theater. And I helped organize the Chicago Latin American Book Fair as well as the Neutral Turf Poetry Festival. In the latter, we'd have around three thousand people at the lakefront to cheer on poets, including competitors in citywide slams whose winners would travel to Osaka, Japan, or Prague, the Czech Republic, or Accra, Ghana.

Along with Michael Warr, Richard Bray, and others, I helped establish the Guild Complex, once part of Guild Books until chain bookstores forced the independent bookstore to close. With Michael as visionary and director, the nonprofit literary arts center thrived, finding a home at the Chopin Theater (with full stage, café, and basement bar-like performance space) and organizing close to two hundred events a year. Eventually Tía Chucha Press became the publishing wing of the Guild Complex, tied to its extraordinary programming and reputation.

I now made my own way into this art, following a well-traveled road until I reached a pathless opening not trodden by anyone, without any outlines or markers, a road I'd have to make myself, where every mistake could turn out to be a new style, truly my own.

In late 1990, I was invited to Paris. This became my first European trip.

A number of Parisian intellectuals were interested in Chicano art, music, and literature. A young French couple set up two weeks of reading events at English-language venues like Shakespeare and Company and the Village Voice as well as the University of Paris. I asked Trini to join me. I had full houses at the readings, which surprised me. Local and expatriate writers invited me for coffee, including the renowned Ted Joans.

During our trip, Trini and I got embroiled in an argument about shopping. I hated shopping and this anxiety caused problems, since Trini had agreed to get things for friends. Feeling I was too controlling, Trini, in a huff, jumped on the metro back to the hotel but inadvertently took all the money and subway tickets. I was stranded.

I decided to meander around the city, catching every inch of its lively center, including a few of the immigrant streets on the outskirts, mostly North African communities, before somehow finding the hotel. I was so tired when I knocked on the door late that night, I couldn't stay mad at Trini.

At Shakespeare and Company bookstore, on the Left Bank across from Notre Dame Cathedral, the eccentric and beloved owner, George Whitman, invited Trini and me to stay in a room at the "Tumbleweed Hotel," the second floor of the bookstore where many English-speaking writers and students were allowed to stay without paying. George only asked that in return I spend a couple of hours daily in an afternoon tea talking with young writers and travelers. I loved these interactions and this saved us hotel costs. We stayed about ten nights.

The rooms and bookstore were filled to the ceiling with books. We had to climb over them on staircases and push them off tables, beds, dresser drawers. Many were valuable first editions. The pulp and cloth were meant for me. They brought back a time when I first held a book in my hand, a stammering boy of seven, in between languages and silences, finally discovering worlds that didn't hurt or dismiss me. In a book, the writer doesn't have the last word—the reader does.

During the day, Trini and I rode the subways, viewed the whole city from on top of what was then the world's highest Ferris wheel, climbed the Eiffel Tower, engrossed ourselves in the Louvre, checked out the Greek food stands.

One interesting talk was at an Arab-French women's center. This took four hours with translations from English/Spanish to French to Arabic and back. A group of Palestinian women took to Trini, not just because she looked Arab, but because she intelligently addressed revolutionary concepts they were interested in. The next day they invited Trini—not me, mind you—to tour the center and talk to more women.

Also while in Paris, my East L.A. friend Rubén Guevara—former front man for Rubén and the Jets, founder of the Con Safos band, and performance personality Funkahuatl—happened upon a poster for my reading at Shakespeare and Company. Rubén couldn't believe his eyes: Here was one of his homies in Paris at the same time he was there. I practically jumped when I saw Rubén among the audience. It turned out he was part of a Chicano art and performance show that featured painters, performers, and rappers, including a few I knew from the old days.

Trini and I ended up at a party for the East L.A. people, hosted by the sponsors of this tour. A DJ spun Chicano oldies and rock LPs while we danced, East L.A. style, to the tunes. A number of the Parisians took photos of us as we partied like we were back in the barrio, with our *gritos*, fancy dance moves, and hearty laughter.

My son Rubén was a happy and rambunctious baby. As soon as he walked, he ran. As soon as he talked, he rambled. He seemed to love being alive, eager to try anything, to touch everything, to climb every railing. Trini had a hard time. She wanted to be a good mother but often felt lost. She was a good mother, of course, but Rubén knew how to tax her patience. Against my advice, Trini put a child leash on the boy whenever they went out on the street or shopping. I appreciated why—he'd run into the street quicker than a head could turn or feet could catch up to him.

With me, however, Rubén paid attention, listened, obeyed. I set strong parameters, mostly by being consistent. And I used the bass in my voice to place an invisible gate around him if I had to. I refused to leash him.

I also never hit Rubén. I eventually stopped hitting Ramiro and Andrea. Almost every adult who lived with my oldest kids smacked them. This ended for me when one day those in a community gathering questioned why I struck then ten-year-old Ramiro for no good reason. I had no answer other than that's what my mother used to do to me. My kids deserved discipline, guidance, teachings, modeling, clear and loving parenting. They didn't need to be hit.

When Rubén was two years old, I'd walk him around our rough Humboldt Park neighborhood. Modified cars drove past with their radios or tape decks blasting house music, hip-hop, or salsa. Ghetto mechanics worked on cars in the street. Roosters and chickens roamed the hallways of three-story brick apartments.

Our neighbors loved to come out of their cramped apartments or down from the stoops and hold Rubén, talk to him, kiss him, call out *benditos*. At almost every gate and fence, Rubén stopped to climb. I let him, keeping my arms close in case he slipped. But he managed to put his small feet into the right spaces, holding his balance, and keep climbing. He never fell.

Next door to us lived a thirteen-year-old Puerto Rican girl. A stray bullet had shot off her foot when she was three. She took care of Rubén from time to time. She treated him like a baby doll, pushing him around in his stroller, gently placing a bottle of Mama's milk into his tiny mouth, pretending he was hers.

Yet, at age fifteen she got shot again when a bullet meant for her boyfriend claimed her instead. This time she didn't survive.

My oldest son, Ramiro, entered this environment headfirst. He craved the excitement, the violence, the edge. By 1991, Ramiro was in worse trouble—he joined a gang at Roberto Clemente High School. Fights were constant. I once had to watch a doctor put eleven stitches in my son's brow following an altercation.

Sure enough, Ramiro and I clashed over his gang involvement. I yelled, told him he wasn't going to be in no gang, that he had to obey my rules. He decided to run off into the cold Chicago night without a jacket. I chased him from street to street, alley to alley. I couldn't catch up — by then I had gained weight. When Trini was pregnant, I formed a belly as she got bigger. Only she delivered the baby and got back into shape. I didn't.

For two weeks, Ramiro eluded me. I went to the school. I visited the homes of his friends. I put the word out that I wanted to talk to my son. Once I drove around in a police car trying to find him. This ended when a friend of his, one of the local gang youths, came to my door to tell me that Ramiro needed to talk to me, even if he acted like he didn't.

Ramiro was in a gang of about thirty young men, all Puerto Ricans except for a few Mexicans, a couple of African-Americans, and a white dude. They were called the Insane Campbell Boys, named after a street. They had enemies everywhere. So while this gang was small, they were tough, taking on all comers, even the larger gangs and gang alliances that permeated Humboldt Park. Shootings were constant and Ramiro became one of the shooters.

He was now fifteen.

Trini and I moved the family to West Evergreen Street on the boundary of West Town and Wicker Park. This was the same stretch of street where Nelson Algren once lived, that Chicago writer of the downtrodden with books like *Never Come Morning*, *The Man with the Golden Arm*, and *A Walk on the Wild Side*.

We moved into a basement apartment a few doors from rattling, screeching El train tracks several feet above a cobblestone alley. Rubén had his own room. Trini and I had ours. Ramiro slept on the living room sofa. Ramiro actually had to run through lawns, climb fences, and sneak around a back alley to get home since he had many enemies there.

One day I almost got my head bashed in. I had a Bronco then, with no spare tire on the back door and the metal studs sticking out. As I removed groceries, I looked around and saw half a dozen young gangsters with tire irons, bats, chains. They were looking for rival gang members and came upon me. I was in my late thirties, but for them I looked gangster enough.

"What you be about?" one of the youths demanded.

I didn't have time to say anything—one dude pulled out a metal bar from his jacket. The others were readying their weapons. In my mind I quickly played out what I had to do—grab the guy closest to me by his coat, pulling him into the metal studs. If that didn't stun the others, I'd punch somebody else, perhaps take away a weapon. I wasn't going to survive this attack. But I was going to take one or two down with me.

Just then an older Puerto Rican dude yelled from up the street, running as fast as he could toward us.

"Don't hurt him—he's our neighbor. He's new here. He's not in a gang."

The toughies stopped. Apparently they trusted this guy. Without skipping a beat, they put their weapons away and dispersed. One guy put out his hand and apologized. I shook it. I would have to be on their good side if I was going to last in this neighborhood.

One morning I met Tony Prince in a leather booth of an old-time diner. We talked about how many of our friends were having problems with their kids. Some turned to drugs, bad crowds, running away, even suicide. This was the lot of many young people in the early 1990s. Tony himself had two daughters who were doing well but were always susceptible to what the streets harbored for any searching, unhinged youth.

Tony was also godfather to Ramiro—"Nino Tony." I was also "nino" to his girls.

As I grabbed for my coffee, I expressed how discouraged I was in my dealings with Ramiro. Tony and I often shared our doubts and fears about the family issues we went through.

With Ramiro deep into rabble-rousing, I saw my life all over again. I saw myself at fifteen running the streets, yelling out the gang name, shooting at rivals. My son ended up like me, perhaps idealizing my gang life although I never talked about my past with my kids. But they knew: the tattoos, the way I walked, perhaps stories shared with other family members. One thing was for sure—if I barely survived that life, the chances that my son would weren't good.

"I don't want to drive Ramiro away anymore," I told Tony. "I have to stand by him through these problems. If I push him out, I know he'll die. But I also can't let him get stuck in the madness. I have to find a way to remove him from this life."

"Well, Ramiro is the only one who can do that," Tony said. "You have to find a way so that this becomes his decision."

"You're right, Tony, but he can't seem to grasp that he's worth fighting for, that he should want to live, that he's smart and should have a decent life. In his mind he's a fuckup and now he wants to be the biggest fuckup of all."

"Just remember he's had a lifetime of brainwashing, of being told he's no good, of being stomped on at every turn. You can show him the other side of his story."

"I know, I just don't want to fail—I can't. My son is precious to me. Yet I know it's on me now to find a way."

Not long after that talk, I received a phone call. The police were holding Ramiro for assault after some dudes were jumped near the high school. When I went to pick him up, the police had prepared to ship him to the Audy Home, the Cook County Juvenile Detention Center, which at the time was the largest youth lockup in the world. I didn't want him there, knowing how L.A.'s juvenile hall and surrounding jails drove me in my teens to do worse.

One officer offered an alternative—if I could get Ramiro into a psychiatric treatment hospital on the city's West Side, they would turn him over to me. I agreed, but I knew Ramiro wouldn't go for this. So I tricked him into going, which I hated doing. I didn't see any other way.

I told Ramiro we were going to see a counselor. Ramiro went along but didn't know I had packed his toothbrush and other essentials. Once through the hospital doors, the staff and I explained he was going to stay for as long as needed. Ramiro felt betrayed. He tried to get away, but the staff held him and pushed him into a locked area. The staff told me to leave as Ramiro yelled and kicked while staff members tried to get him into the resident section of the hospital. I left him there, second-guessing myself all the way home. I didn't know if this would work, if this was the right thing for him. But I had to try. I had to save my son.

I saw Sandy Taylor at a Book Expo in late 1991 in New York City. I was there to promote *The Concrete River* and meet other writers, publishers, and agents.

Earlier that day I had been trying to autograph copies of my book at an author's signing area. I sat next to Mickey Mantle, which was cool, except he had a line that curled around the large hall and into the street. I had nobody. I eventually signed two books for people who were leaving Mantle's line and wanted to know who I was. I think they felt sorry for me.

I had lunch with Sandy and made a proposal—would he be willing to publish a memoir about gang life that I was writing? I was putting together bits and pieces of my life from my early days, through the gang and drug years to my late teens, when I walked out of my barrio, surprisingly intact. That old manuscript I called *Mi Vida Loca* served as the main source material. I wanted this for my son and others like him.

There were no major books about Chicano gangs from the viewpoint of someone who actually survived them, although there were a number of studies and social research. The older gangs in East L.A. were close to a hundred years old. There were mothers who had lost two or three sons. But as far as memoirs or real-life accounts of them were concerned, there was nothing. I thought I finally had the literary dexterity to make this happen. I felt a book like this had to effectively put together the stories, the details, the suffering as well as the successes, in a manner that didn't glorify *or* demonize this life—and could point the way out.

Sandy didn't hesitate. He accepted my proposal, offered me some *feria*, and gave me eight months to pull it together. They were stressful months, with work, family concerns, and community commitments to consider. I managed to quit LTP so that I could concentrate on the writing, at great risk, although I stayed on with WMAQ-AM.

In the middle of my writing—it was April 1992—Los Angeles exploded in violence after four police officers were acquitted in the beating of Rodney King. I saw the mayhem on television—the burning buildings, people shot, the looting, the beating of the white truck driver, and the uprising of gangs, African-American as well as the more varied and larger Chicano and Central American gangs.

I decided to fly into L.A. and visit my old haunts in South Central, where much of the burning was going on, and in East L.A., which had only sporadic incidents but could erupt at any time (eight months before the 1992 rebellion, violent disturbances had flared up at the Ramona Gardens housing projects in Boyle Heights when sheriff's deputies shot and killed a Big Hazard homeboy).

I visited with old friends. I talked to police officers and families. I also met with Bloods and Crips, some of whom were having unity meetings to bring peace and justice to their neighborhoods. And I encountered members of the mostly Chicano gangs, including Eighteenth Street, then considered the largest gang in the country, as well as Mara Salvatrucha, the Salvadoran gang.

Two men from the Crip-Blood unity efforts, Kershaun "Li'l Monster" Scott of the Eight Tray Gangster Crips and Cle "Bone" Sloan of the Athens Park Bloods, electrified TV audiences when, in a number of interviews, they eloquently expressed the political and economic nature of the rebellion. They called for badly needed resources to pour into these streets that had been left to their own devices since the disappearance of jobs from major industries had destroyed most meaningful work while the drug trade became *the* economic life of the most neglected areas.

I met with Li'l Monster and Bone and we wrote a *Los Angeles Times* editorial on the violence with solutions to eradicate the root causes. This piece was later reprinted in other books and publications. I also interacted with other gang-intervention workers in Amer-I-Can, Mothers ROC, Hands Across Watts, and, later, the Community Self-Determination Institute. And I sat in on the founding meeting of Rock-A-Mole (rhymes with "guacamole") Productions, which created free cultural festivals for years in Pico-Union and South and East L.A., as well as underground hip-hop CDs and films, including a documentary about music and the fight against poverty called *The Ultimate Song*.

All this figured prominently in the memoir I was writing. When I turned the manuscript over to Sandy at Curbstone Press, I had incorporated what happened in L.A. and how we needed a new imagination in working with troubled youth, particularly in gangs. This book became *Always Running: La Vida Loca; Gang Days in L.A.*

Things at the psychiatric treatment hospital didn't fare well. The staff had my son constantly strapped to a bed or drugged. I fought this. I wanted them to address his issues, to help him cope, to provide a therapeutic basis for wellness. But they insisted they had to contain his anger, which seemed wrong to me. It was precisely when he was angry that he needed to express what he was dealing with. With the constraints and drugs, he no longer wanted to say or do anything. While this kept Ramiro out of the Audy Home, I was troubled by how the hospital staff handled him.

On top of this, the insurance from WMAQ-AM refused to keep providing for his care. Ramiro had been in the hospital for three months and a psychologist and a psychiatrist agreed he needed more time. The insurance company wouldn't yield—the costs were already exceeding $35,000.

Before Ramiro's release from the psychiatric treatment hospital, the staff did one last thing with my son. On the day he was going home, they told him to go to the basement, where they supposedly had arranged a going-away party. Ramiro went downstairs only to confront a number of burly staff guys. They beat up my son, something he failed to tell me until years later (a big problem with my kids).

By then Ramiro had also been knocked around on the streets by police officers on at least two occasions. One time he ended up with a fat lip, swollen eyes, and bruises on his body. The police released him and he called me from a phone booth a block from the station. The officers didn't want me to lose it at the station when I came to pick him up.

I got so angry—the same thing had happened to me in my youth. I wrote. I ran. But I didn't react by dealing with the police directly. I didn't want to screw up everything for Ramiro, the family, or myself.

We did get a lawyer to look into suing the police, but without Ramiro being hospitalized, near dead perhaps, the police claimed he did the damage himself by resisting arrest. It was their word against his, the disadvantage I had from my own last arrest as a youth.

There were other things to deal with as well.

Ramiro didn't let us know that his girlfriend at Roberto Clemente, a good-natured and smart eighteen-year-old Puerto Rican, was pregnant. We had to find out in an incensed phone call from the girl's mother. Not cool.

The young lady was not in gangs and tried to be a positive influence on Ramiro, although he wouldn't leave the gang for her. Despite our concerns about her having a baby so young, in late 1992 she had a beautiful boy named Ricardo.

I was now a granddaddy at age thirty-eight.

The girl's family at the time didn't want anything to do with us. Her mother convinced the young woman to take the baby to another state, where they've lived ever since. I went to see Ricardo when he was a year and a half old. Ramiro and Camila visited a couple of years later. It wasn't until Ricardo was fifteen, in 2008, however, that I got to see him again. He was doing well with his mother and her husband, a decent man who adopted Ricardo when he was a child.

I drifted alone into bars on poetry nights, my face inside bottles, enjoying the amber waves of beer. For years, I visited two to three bars a night—clubs like Estelle's, the Borderline, Decima Musa, Red Dog. Poetry was the excuse, as good as any. *Be true to my art.* But this was not what kept me there.

It was the way tequila germinated inside me. How the rum, whiskey, and beer deluged the mind, replacing the sunken spirit with "spirits." How I longed to clamber over onto a stool, far away from hurt, stress, kids, into nothing but a fermented existence. The drinking coated the membranes, the capillaries, the iron taste in the back of my throat. It aligned the nerves, the unstable cells, the disjointed emotions, pulling everything together again, even as my eyes blurred and inspiration drowned, anything bright fading. Only then could I face the tearless nights. Only then could I sleep, without dreams, descending into a cavernous mouth.

When things got dicey at home this was where I ended up—the bars, the clubs, listening to poetry, reading poetry, not giving a hoot about poetry. After last call, I often maneuvered myself over to the Old Town Ale House, an after-hours joint. There was a crusty old mural painted years before of local poets, comedians, other personalities. I wasn't one of them, but I still painted myself onto the wall. I might as well have been imbibing with the characters. Sometime between two A.M. and dawn, consciousness petered out. I drove home like this often and never knew how I got there.

I loved my family, but I wanted to be in the bars more. When drinking, I was exultant, transmuted, no responsibilities, flirting with strange women, or even women I knew, like fellow poets. A couple of times I woke up in the beds of such women, not my wife, after a night of heavy binging.

I was destroying myself but also the writing—and for the most part I didn't care. That is, until I managed to envision Trini's face, as well as the faces of Rubén and Andrea, while drinking, reading poems, searching for the next bar.

Until I remembered Ramiro needed a dad.

My son's drowning forced me to rethink my own drowning. I had been a cowardly father, a scared father, a drunk father, and even when I was okay, when I was just a dad who hugged and played with his kids, it was with the backdrop of absence, being too busy, unavailable.

In a weird way I became my dad.

I also knew I was losing Trini, who was supposed to be the lasting love, who tolerated so much, who often didn't know what I was doing or where I was going. I sensed a door in her heart closing.

And, of course, my "Rubénski." Once he tried to hug me and I didn't pay attention. I was working on papers at my desk, distracted. He went over to his mother in tears and said, "Dad doesn't love me." He was four.

———

It was my Native American friend from Kansas City, Katrina Coker, who found a recovery path I might consider. She visited Chicago once and asked me to join her for a talk at the Blackstone Hotel. I had no idea what this was about. I went anyway.

It turned out to be an extensive presentation about a Chicago-based recovery program. Their strategies emphasized your rational mind, self-recovery, tapping into your own capability to fight the urge to drink or take drugs, strategies you could muster from within yourself, to defeat the addictive voice that appeared to hold you helpless and hopeless against drugs or drink or self-destruction.

The change was within the damaged psyche, not somewhere outside oneself. Just as your mind rationalized drinking or drugging, it could be reoriented and trained to rationalize not drinking, not drugging, not destroying. Whatever caused the damage wasn't as important as the individual responsibility to change this.

I was ready for this kind of program. I had tried other recovery programs and failed. But after finishing the memoir, most of which I wrote after drinking all night, I tapped into a healing energy I didn't know I had. The stories I thought I'd forgotten poured out of me, at times like a flood. After I was done, I felt restored, having finished a journey of sorts, through my personal inferno as well as waters of reconciliation. After this process, sobriety spoke to me in a way it hadn't at any other time.

This allowed me to make the conscious decision at the start of 1993 to stop drinking altogether, although like with heroin, I had relapses, anxieties, fevers, and dire moments when I wanted to sprint down the street to the nearest bar. By then I recognized these as part of the healing process, not just falling back.

I also had to renew all my relationships, many of which were begun, and in some cases destroyed, during my drinking years. I could no longer have my father, my mother, the barrio realities, the impoverished environment as the basis for my continued annihilation. Having material poverty is one thing, but I had to stop being poor in spirit. I now needed to tap into the abundance we all carry in our internal creative reservoirs, in our imaginations. Just like the earth has its regenerative powers, despite internal and external abuse and turmoil, we need to tap into our own mother capacity to revive and start over. I felt like I was shedding old skin, embroidering a new soul, becoming a man of variety and colors, not a black-and-gray phantom among the furnishings and paintings in the bars and clubs—or the living room and porch of my home.

This was, as Trini would say many years later, "a delicate artful challenge."

Chapter Nineteen

My daughter, Andrea, now fourteen, was having her own troubles with Camila.

Camila and Andrea lived here and there in L.A., wherever they could, often with family or friends. After Ramiro got dispatched to Chicago, Camila worked hard to get Andrea into a private school for well-off students, mostly white and Asian. A scholarship for Latinos helped with the extremely high costs.

This was one of the best things Camila ever did.

Camila and Andrea were by then living in a shack in the Maravilla district of East L.A. Residents often tapped into public power poles for electricity. Andrea rode several buses from the poorest sections of the barrio for miles (and through starkly different neighborhoods) to get to the school, which catered to families in mansion-laden sections of Pasadena and San Marino. Friends invited her to their expensive homes with swimming pools and tennis courts.

Andrea never brought any of them to her "home."

Then, after somebody reported the makeshift housing, county officials brought in bulldozers to remove the shacks where Camila and Andrea had been living. The officials didn't care about forcing people out—all Mexicans, most citizens or with papers—or about destroying the meager property they had.

After that Camila and Andrea had to live in their car under a freeway overpass until they could locate other living arrangements. Meanwhile, Andrea continued to take public transportation to the private school and participated as much as possible, as if everything was just fine.

Going to the private school was worth it: The challenges helped Andrea stand out.

But she also began to stand up to her mother, and like with Ramiro, I got another call from Camila about needing to be a father. So late in 1992, in the middle of the school year, Andrea came to live with us in Chicago. I enrolled her at Whitney Young Community Academy, known by then as one of the best public high schools in the city.

Like Ramiro, Andrea was also strong in her school subjects. But her behavior was a hundred times better.

Andrea lasted half a year at our place until Camila decided, after several long talks, to transplant herself to the Windy City. With Ramiro getting in more trouble, we agreed the kids needed both biological parents in their lives. This was a tremendous sacrifice for Camila, and to her credit, she committed to it. Now Camila and I—with Trini's essential role as stepmom—had to work together for the benefit of these children.

Andrea again moved in with her mother in a cockroach-infested apartment on North Avenue near Rockwell. Trini and I found a second-floor apartment on North and Leavitt. Ramiro continued to live with us. At one point we had his best friend, a Puerto Rican youth named Pedro, on house arrest there after the courts determined he had nowhere else to go.

This was another rough section of town. Two dudes almost jumped Pedro when a couple of girls set him up, but I chased them away. And I once admonished Ramiro for sticking his head out of the apartment window after a dude had just gotten shot in the head at the corner liquor store. Stray bullets from such shootings struck more than a few onlookers sneaking a peek out of windows.

Camila had a string of boyfriends in Chicago. Most were okay, but at least one of them was married. I felt Camila's estimation of her worth as a woman and person was deeply marred. She was still good-looking, but, like me, she had put on some weight. Nonetheless, she knew how to charm the male species—these guys included a mechanic for her car, a post mail carrier, a dude she met at a shopping center.

One of these men moved in. We thought he really cared for Camila. But damn if the asshole didn't try to molest my daughter. Andrea fought him off and ran out of the house before anything happened. He tried to make this go away by leaving notes in her books and her school bag that said she shouldn't tell. Andrea responded by confronting her mom, telling her to get rid of the guy or she'd leave. Camila, for some reason, found this difficult to accept.

This time, however, Andrea told me.

I rushed to Camila's apartment. Camila was there. Calmly yet firmly, I told the guy to gather his stuff and get out of the house.

"You have two choices," I said. "You leave now and get help, or I contact the police."

Actually getting the police involved in this ghetto/barrio wasn't an option. They often didn't investigate or give credence to such charges unless real physical damage had been done. I used this anyway. The guy stammered, didn't know what to say. He tried to beg, even claimed he didn't do anything, but I wasn't buying it.

Then he seized a butcher knife from the kitchen. *Damn, here we go again with one of Camila's men.* Like before with Ernesto I didn't back down. I glared at him while his eyes darted all over the room, to Camila, to the ceiling, to the floor. When he didn't scare me away, he turned the knife on himself and threatened suicide. But I saw through the bullshit and told him to stop fucking around.

Like the punk he was, he put the knife down and started packing.

I did talks, readings, and workshops from Brooklyn to Boston, San Antonio to Albuquerque, Tucson to Tacoma. Largely trained through the Chicago Teachers Center and their Writing from the Source program (its director, Anne Schultz, became another mentor of mine), I facilitated writing workshops in elementary, middle, and high schools for the most neglected students, lasting six weeks or more. Also, besides the homeless shelters, I managed workshops in several Illinois prisons. I also entered the Audy Home. I went there for several years to draw out the writing, poetry, and stories inside incarcerated youths, even when a few staff and teachers didn't believe the wards had this in them.

One time I took Ramiro to a talk I did at Jacksonville Correctional Center in the western portion of the state. I wanted to show him how messed up a place like this could be, but also how we can help prisoners discover their own expressive powers. Ramiro was writing poems and read a couple.

At the facility, we saw one of the founders of the main gang Ramiro's homies were partners with—an older dude in his forties—who seemed to appreciate why I was helping my son get out of a gang. He told me why—he had lost two sons to gang violence but was behind bars and couldn't even go to their funerals.

Always Running came out in January of 1993 in hardcover. A painting by Mexican master artist Rufino Tamayo graced the cover. Curbstone Press received a couple of large grants to do marketing and publicity. This included paying a top-notch book publicist to map out a promotional campaign, unheard of for small presses at the time. This publicist was a godsend—she schooled me on how to conduct myself in the mass media, such as broadcast interviews. I then got sent out on a three-month, thirty-city book tour.

Finally, Trini and I agreed it was time for me to quit work, which consisted of the night shift at WMAQ-AM. We committed to my life as a full-time independent writer, a gamble since beyond the tour we had no way of knowing whether I'd garner enough speaking and writing gigs to keep me busy and paid.

Trini at the time worked as a court interpreter. This was a job with benefits. It required high-level Spanish- and English-language skills. Tests and trainings were periodically done to keep the interpreters at the top of their game. Law concepts and jargon had to be understood and properly translated. People's lives, in particular those of poor Mexicans and Puerto Ricans, were at stake. This job helped us while I tried to develop my writing into a financially stable profession.

By then Ramiro had been kicked out of Clemente High School. I got him into another school on the North Side, but Ramiro didn't last a week. He berated a teacher who yelled at him. This school, unfortunately, had a zero-tolerance policy. Even with my urgings about giving Ramiro in-school discipline so I could keep him off the streets, the principal refused.

I then hit on an idea: Why not take Ramiro with me on part of my book tour? We could talk, interact with others, and hopefully stave off pressures for Ramiro to be active in the gang. We figured we could do this only the first ten days. Those were mostly devoted to major TV and radio shows—*Good Morning America*, CNN's *Sonya Live* and *Talk Live*, National Public Radio's *Fresh Air* with Terry Gross—as well as publications like *Entertainment Weekly* and *The Face*.

This combination made for effective commentary. I had left gangs and drugs twenty years before. But Ramiro was living this now. I had hindsight. He had the immediacy of the issue. Ramiro was also extremely articulate.

Gangs flourished in the 1980s and 1990s more than at any other time in U.S. history. Drugs and firepower, which had been at the periphery of most street gangs, were now at the heart of them. And after the L.A. Rebellion of the year before—and the rise of so-called gangster rap—most Americans and media were interested in U.S. gang life.

ABC's Charles Gibson was the first to interview us. All the interviewers were friendly. Ramiro spoke about neglected youth, about lack of jobs and training, about how suppression—more police and prisons—only made the problems worse.

Yet a couple of the interviewers put Ramiro against the wall—*Why are you in a gang when your dad is working hard to get you out?* But he made valid points: He said his gang was the only group of people he trusted, that everyone else at one time or another lied to him and couldn't be counted on, how he'd die for his "nation," which interestingly gave him a reason to live. Contradictory words, but insightful.

We ended up in key cities—New York; Washington, D.C.; Chicago; Los Angeles; San Francisco. Back in L.A., we stayed in a Beverly Hills suite, several floors up, overlooking the city, with numerous rooms and doorways. I invited L.A. friends to hang with us, including Kershaun Scott from the Crips-Bloods unity efforts.

In Chicago, we were on various media outlets, such as *The Oprah Winfrey Show*. Oprah was taping a show on gangs. At first she had booked only African-American guests. But with the publication of my book and the proliferation of Latino gangs in the country—they were more numerous than African-American gangs, and in some cases older—Ramiro and I were asked to appear. Yet it took a while for things to get started. In the greenroom, I had a dialogue with peace advocates from L.A. and Chicago.

Finally, when it was time for us to get onstage (Ramiro and I actually talked from the audience), I felt pressured to get to my next media interview. The shows were overlapping. Oprah gave Ramiro and me a good five minutes to speak and she showed a copy of my book on the air.

In the middle of the program I walked out with my son so we could be on time to the next interview. Producers were baffled. They gave us coffee mugs and let us go.

When I told the publicist about this, she replied: "You don't walk out on Oprah Winfrey!"

I didn't know. I just wanted to come through on my schedule. Later I found out Oprah's producers told my publicist I'd never be invited on her show again. Really, it was a mistake, an amateur move, from a first-time major book writer.

One kick we got out of this was driving through our 'hood in a limousine. Oprah had the limo pick us up and take us back home. Ramiro, like he was a big shot or something, poked his head out and yelled to his homies and the pretty girls strolling along the sidewalks.

The tour continued after Ramiro went home and Rubén joined me for about twenty days. He was four years old when I went through Connecticut and Massachusetts. Again, the boy climbed statues, trees, mailboxes.

A snowstorm also hit the East Coast, with snowdrifts up to the knees. We kept going until we found out that Rubén had chicken pox—his symptoms weren't evident at first. We quarantined Rubén at a hotel for more than a week and also found a babysitter who was immune to chicken pox. I continued to speak in the community and schools as well as media outlets, although a few events got canceled due to the snow.

After returning home with Rubén, I went on to midwestern cities—in Minneapolis I brought Andrea along. She was quiet and didn't cause any problems. It was just her nature. When Andrea had to go back home, I moved on to cities like Denver, Louisville, Nashville, Miami, Philadelphia, Tulsa, El Paso, Albuquerque, Madison, and San Diego, among others. Trini accompanied me on a couple of these trips. Rubén came with me to L.A. for two weeks.

During all this a bidding war escalated among eight major paperback publishers for my book. One of Curbstone Press's board members negotiated the deal. At one point he wanted to know what we should ask for.

"I don't know, but whatever you do," I declared, recalling how bigtime publishers had rejected my first manuscript out of hand some ten years before, "make those people pay."

We finally agreed to go with Touchstone Books/Simon & Schuster, which obtained the rights for six figures plus a marketing plan—that book came out in 1994, accompanied by another, albeit smaller, publicity tour.

Unfortunately, with my absence, Ramiro got into more trouble. One weekend, he got involved in an incident where shots were fired, but nobody was hit. As it turned out, the shooter, one of Ramiro's boys, didn't see the police officer witnessing the whole thing from inside a patrol car down the street. Ramiro was now seventeen, which meant he'd be tried as an adult.

"You guys are the dumbest smart people I know," I told them.

One good thing was that Patricia Zamora, Michael Warr's wife, was a youth worker at Casa Aztlan Community Center in the Mexican Pilsen barrio. Pilsen was known for many gangs—La Raza, Ambrose, Latin Counts, Bishops, Satan Disciples, and Gangster Party People, among others. She invited me to work with young people from a couple of these gangs.

I'd already had a few of Ramiro's homies gather in the basements or backyards of the apartments we lived in—to talk and to help them find work, positive outlets, and mentoring. Besides Pedro, a few of his other homies lived with my family, mostly on house arrest. So combining our efforts was a grand idea, unprecedented since this would involve two different barrios—Pilsen and Humboldt Park—with two different nationalities, Mexican and Puerto Rican.

Ramiro and his friend got jail time and probation for their brainless action. I thought this would get Ramiro motivated to stop his gang activities. And with Patricia Zamora and her group working with his friends, I figured we might curb their most destructive acts.

Camila also got active. The combined group soon consisted of the most troubled youths and some of their parents. Even Andrea participated—she was no gang member, but she brought her smarts to the table.

With Patricia's experience in youth development, we created a new kind of youth work with strong youth-adult collaborations and intensive real-life mentoring.

One day I stepped out of the El train and climbed down the stairs of the Damen Avenue station in Wicker Park. I noticed a teenage girl in a hoodie making out with a dude with cropped hair. When I turned around, I got a good look at them and realized—*híjole*—that girl was Andrea.

I stood next to them. Andrea looked up—her eyes went wide and she tried to push the guy away. He looked at her like "What?" She whispered, "My dad's standing right behind you."

The dude turned around, embarrassed. I shook his hand, asked his name and what was going on. Andrea introduced this guy as her boyfriend. I told him to come to the house so I could get to know him better. Then I excused myself and kept on walking.

Andrea didn't get into big trouble, so I didn't lose it about the boyfriend. He came around and was respectful. Unlike Ramiro, the squeaky wheel, Andrea turned quietly around her issues, inside her solitude. But this could often be more troublesome than dealing with someone like Ramiro, who needed attention and usually got it.

Andrea tried to come through, get good grades, not complain or make noise. She wanted to be invisible, unnoticed, left alone. She also harbored low self-esteem and a bad self-image. She had her grievances, most of them internalized, unexpressed, numbed.

It wasn't that Andrea was a "good" person and Ramiro was "bad." She learned to survive by pleasing others, getting good grades, going along with the program. But she didn't follow her passions, she had no big dreams, she didn't really know who she was. Both of my oldest kids had real gripes against their mom and me, the schools, and the social system. One lashed out, overturned the tables, wouldn't adapt. The other found a way to hide, get by, but in the process sacrificed purpose and meaning.

As Andrea once expressed to me years later, people like her often got "rewarded" for their compliance. People like Ramiro were usually punished for their defiance.

After the incident with Camila's boyfriend, Andrea moved back in with Trini and me. This time Andrea had her own room, although she often closed herself inside. Trini tried to talk to her. Get her out of the room. Invite her to help with dinner, or even just to eat. Andrea rarely let herself out.

One day when Andrea wasn't home, I walked into her room— strewn about the floor were books, games, clothes, stuffed animals, papers. Camila was not like this. She constantly kept a clean home, even if it was in a bad neighborhood. Something was happening to Andrea, but she wouldn't talk about it.

Andrea's grades suffered during this time, and I didn't want her to get lost. So we enrolled Andrea at Josephinum Catholic High School in Humboldt Park, an all-girls school with some three hundred students. The nuns were nontraditional and wore no habits, but I could tell they were still nuns: stern, protective, demanding.

Andrea went through her junior and senior year at Josephinum. Although she didn't graduate with top grades and had to go to night classes and summer school to finish on time, she had high test scores, and she managed to get her diploma.

At Andrea's graduation ceremony, held at the church next to the school, I videotaped my daughter and her friends. At one point, in the background, I saw a boy through the camera lens, about seven, climbing the stone-inlaid walls at the back of the church.

"Man, some parents just don't know how to control their kids," I remarked.

Then I realized that kid was Rubén.

Rubén in those years was all over the place. In preschool, one counselor declared he was "psychotic," which really distressed Trini and was totally uncalled for. In kindergarten, a public school official recommended giving Ritalin to Rubén. This drug was for children with attention-deficit disorder.

"No, we won't have him on drugs," I said. "There's nothing wrong with Rubén—what's wrong is the environment."

Trini agreed. She spent a long time trying to figure out what made up this environment. Rubén's class had forty kids. They were stuffed into hot aging bungalows and played on cement that was cracked and upended. Spiders and other bugs were biting many of the children.

With other concerned parents, Trini started a newsletter called *High Expectations.* They fought the terrible conditions these kids were forced to be in. TV crews were brought in to document the terrible facilities. In time this group got the school district to build a computer center and a decent play area where kids could run around and not get hurt.

Meanwhile, we transferred Rubén to a Native American focus school. They accepted him as Native American through my Rarámuri roots. Also he looked as native or more so than the other kids in the program, which included Lakota, Ojibwa, Menominee, and children of mixed ancestry.

We were grateful—Rubén had fifteen kids in his class. His teacher paid attention to him, focusing on Rubén's needs and also directing him to do better, to act properly, but with a caring hand. In time Rubén found his balance, becoming active in theater and other school events. His grades improved.

Rubén didn't need Ritalin, which was meant to change him. He needed his caregivers to adjust to his genius, his way of expression, to consistently provide the right parameters so he wouldn't be all over the place. He needed a dynamic setting so that he'd become the poised, intelligent, confident, and artistic young man he'd eventually grow up to be.

I learned something about myself—I loved to travel. I had this prevailing wanderlust and was particularly drawn to places far removed from the concrete world I lived and worked in. During the early years of my writing life, I managed trips to London, Rome, Milan, Puerto Rico, and Groningen and other visits to Paris, once with Chicago poets.

Then, only a month after the *Always Running* book tour, San Francisco poet/writer/editor Alan Kaufman invited me on a tour of Germany, Austria, and the Netherlands. It was labeled a slam poetry tour, the first of its kind in Europe, and included such luminaries in the performance poetry world as Paul Beatty, a poet and novelist who won the Nuyorican Club's poetry slam a few times; Dominique Lowell, powerful Bay Area spoken word artist; Neeli Cherkovski, a poet and writer best known for his book on Charles Bukowski; and my good friend Patricia Smith.

Although we were labeled slam poets, we didn't slam—we just performed. We hit nightclubs, libraries, theaters, universities, and literature houses in Berlin, Nuremburg, Erlangen, Cologne, Frankfurt, Salzburg, and Amsterdam. I was taken aback by the audiences in East Berlin, now united with West Berlin. We had hundreds of people inside and outside the venues, many standing on top of cars, to hear us. Despite not understanding English and relying on translated copies of our poems, they mostly fell in with the rhythms of our words.

We rode on trains and also drove through some of these cities in a rented minivan. I asked to drive when we jumped on the Autobahn so I could hit high speeds.

Although I had stopped drinking by the beginning of the book tour, I felt that in Europe I could make an exception. This was a monster lapse. I began to down those dark German beers in large bottles. Man, could people drink in Germany. And I was right behind them.

The problem was my body had been craving the alcohol for some time. Feelers appeared to be reaching out from my skin, anticipating the drink. When an alcoholic lets go of drinking for a while and then gets back, the effect is often more potent—and potentially lethal.

At one point, in Salzburg, Austria, I drank about a dozen black beers. One person in our party kept count, worried about me. But I acted fairly normal, having conversations, laughing. This person didn't know I had already blacked out. Soon after I stepped away from where my friends were sitting and kept walking. I didn't look plastered, so nobody was worried.

I was plastered out of my mind.

An Austrian wall held my shadow, my body stretched out on the ground along an ancient walkway. I had a hard time opening my eyes. Where was I? People maneuvered around me, talking in fugues I didn't recognize, one stepping over my legs. I felt as if I were dying. I hadn't felt this since I last ODed on heroin so many sidewalk slumbers ago.

I managed to rise up from this spot to face the somber street, to glimpse my mortality reclining against a lamppost. My friends were long gone. Sometime the night before I had wandered off from where we had gathered at an outdoor drinking joint.

This strange place, alien enough to break my hard-fought sobriety, pulled me into its steely grasp, harsh violin music between my ears, fooling the fool into believing again. I numbly went through my pants pockets. I found a card with the name and address of the Salzburg hotel I was staying at. I noticed a lone taxi parked up the street and showed the driver the card. I didn't say anything, but whatever expression he saw on me told him what he needed to know. He opened the door to the cab, made sure I didn't hurt myself getting in. Drove me to the hotel.

I paid the cab driver, and he pushed off as if all his nights were spent picking up shadows.

The next day, I found my friends. We packed and left to take a train to Berlin. On the way out of the hotel, I briefly excused myself from the others, walked to the public restroom in the lobby, and threw up as soon as I opened the door.

When I returned from Europe, I went back to the recovery program, detailing my experiences to men and women who readily understood my predicament, readily embraced my fears. But I also began to look at other ways to stay clean. Going to meetings all the time, although cathartic, didn't entirely work for me.

Yet for a long time to come, I still felt the painful pull to stop by the bars. For now the meetings were necessary. A few times I called a rehabilitation hospital that catered to struggling addicts. In my most torn-up states, I conversed with one of the staff, sometimes for almost an hour. She calmly listened and emphasized that she was there for me if I needed her. She asked me to come to the hospital a few times, which I planned to do but never did. I didn't know her name, but without her it would have been harder to make it. She provided a voice to strengthen my own "stop drinking" voice, the one I had to learn to use twenty-four hours a day.

Then, finally, I told Trini about my recovery—she didn't know about this. I went to meetings and was afraid to tell her. Afraid she'd see a weak person. Afraid she'd want to leave. When I told her, my tears flowed. I related how I snuck around to meetings like I snuck into bars. I didn't want her to see me desperate and then have her walk out. By rights, she should have.

But Trini didn't leave. She cried when I cried, not saying much, letting my outpouring tell the tale. Letting this say more than I could have in letters I wished I had written to all the mentors, to the former wives, to my kids, to confused lovers. Letters I wanted to compose every night of my life until I expired, letters about the brutal awakening this sobriety thrust on me.

Trini cried when I cried, as I sat on my office chair in front of my computer in our home that I could have destroyed, like other households, unless I opened up, tasted the salt of Trini's torment, and appreciated she would still be there, as she was then, sliding up to me and placing her arms around my shoulders, and me feeling so ashamed, so bone hungry, so liquefied soul, so blood-red sorry and damn near death-tired.

New York City–based photojournalist Donna DeCesare covered the civil war in El Salvador for four years. Soon after the peace accords of 1992—ending twelve years of fighting with seventy-five thousand people killed and more than a million refugees—Donna came across a heavily marked Salvadoran youth at a hospital. The young man was a recent deportee from Los Angeles and a member of an L.A.-based street gang.

The tattoos on his body were extensive, something Donna had not seen in El Salvador before. He had a large EIGHTEEN STREET on his back. He was also HIV-positive from sharing dirty tattoo needles. This dude didn't survive, but before he passed on he talked to Donna about the L.A. gang members who were now flooding El Salvador. Although there were different gangs, the main ones were La Mara Salvatrucha and La Eighteenth Street.

Donna contacted me in the middle of the book tour. She'd read my memoir and wanted the two of us to apply for a grant to document this phenomenon. The Center for Documentary Studies out of Duke University in North Carolina offered the Dorothea Lange-Paul Taylor Prize, one of the best collaborative project grants in the country.

Making phone calls to go back and forth on the narrative, as well as sending faxes from different cities, Donna and I patched together what we had and submitted our proposal. Sometime during my travels, Donna called to inform me we had won that year's prize against some formidable competition.

Later in the summer of 1993, Donna and I went to Los Angeles, to the Pico-Union barrio, where by then Central Americans had been arriving as war and economic refugees for at least a dozen years. This is where Mara Salvatrucha (MS) and Eighteenth Street were born.

We also visited Central American neighborhoods in Westlake, MacArthur Park, Koreatown, South Central, and Hollywood. And we entered two prisons, including the Youth Training School in Chino, to speak with more Salvadoran gang youth.

Mara is a Central American term for any grouping of street corner youths, taken from the word for soldier ants. At first I misunderstood, thinking this word was tied to the Maravilla district of East L.A., with more than two dozen gangs since the 1920s that placed the word *mara* after their barrio name—such as El Hoyo Mara, La Rock Mara, Lopez Mara, and Marianna Mara. I was wrong. I had to be instructed about life and culture from El Salvador that at the time I had no clue about.

On the other hand, one thing that impacted me was how Chicano these young people had become. Although Salvadoran gang members are proud of being Guanacos (and Guatemalans of being Chapines), they were now part of the growing fraternity of La Vida Loca. Their stance, their style of clothing, and their tattoos were derived from the older and larger Chicano gangs. They even incorporated Chicano slang (*mara* notwithstanding), with words like *ese, vato, trucha, morro,* and *carnal* entering their vocabulary.

Levels of trauma from war-torn and impoverished Central American countries met another level of trauma on L.A.'s streets.

Unfortunately, Salvadoran gangsters also adopted one of the terrible outcomes of Chicano-style gangs: highly organized and violent barrio warfare. Now enemies, MS and Eighteenth Street brought that warfare to El Salvador—and eventually to Guatemala, Honduras, and parts of Mexico.

This happened when federal authorities created a gang task force after the L.A. uprising that included the deportation of thousands of gang members. And by 1996, immigration law changed so that any undocumented person convicted of a felony or serving more than a year in jail would be targeted for deportation. Since then over seven hundred thousand have been repatriated, the vast majority to Mexico and Central America.

Despite large numbers of forgotten youths, with their own long history of conflicts, these countries had never seen the intensity of organization and gang violence that came with L.A.-based gangs. They simply had no resources or even the slightest experience in how to stop these highly stylized gangs from overrunning their countries.

As Donna and I came to find out, such large numbers of criminal and other street-raised deportees are enough to change a culture.

In December and early January of 1994, Donna and I flew to El Salvador to interview gang members, their families, police, government officials, and others about the growing gang problem there. We traveled to the departments of Usulutan, Sonsonate, Santa Ana, San Vicente, La Libertad, and San Salvador. You could see the presence of MS and Eighteenth Street—their graffiti on walls, and on occasion dudes sporting baggy pants, bald heads, bandannas, and extravagant tattoos.

In San Salvador, Donna and I entered many densely populated slum communities of makeshift houses with corrugated tin roofs. In the rural communities, people lived without flooring, with shoeless children standing in swirls of dust. There were no jobs or schooling for the large numbers of deportees. And the police were completely overwhelmed and outnumbered.

In addition, few U.S. deportees had family in El Salvador—many of them hardly spoke Spanish. For protection, they recruited from tens of thousands of homeless children and teens, orphaned by the war but also by abject poverty. Many of these kids—I saw children from age six to fourteen—were glue sniffers, sleeping on sidewalks, and often killed by vigilantes hired by local businesses. MS and Eighteenth Street had a fertile ground to build up their armies among these children.

We visited two prisons in El Salvador—San Vicente and the largest, Mariona. These were medieval-type institutions with little protection from guards, who carried ancient rusty rifles that appeared to be nonworking. Families brought the prisoners food and clothing. Many inmates had machetes and other weapons in their *chambitas* (makeshift huts built on the yard). Battles between L.A.-based gangs and other homegrown groups, but also between MS and Eighteenth Street, led to several prison riots, with many deaths.

We talked to kids tied to smaller local *maras* that existed before the L.A.-based gangs arrived. They banded together, committed crimes, but not like the L.A. homies. Soon many of the smaller *maras* were joining MS or Eighteenth Street to survive. At the same time criminal *bandas* existed in El Salvador that committed high-level crimes. Some resisted the new gangs, others joined them.

After overcoming their initial mistrust, the gang youths eventually warmed up to Donna and me. They seemed to respect that I was Chicano and still sported some of the old-style tattoos. One dude talked to me in the Chicano slang he had picked up in California prisons, just to see if I was the real thing.

I tried to convince some of them to let go of the barrio warfare from thousands of miles away and unite, all L.A. deportees, to help build their country. It didn't go over, however, in a country that at the time had no way to incorporate these young people into its threadbare social, political, and economic fabric.

Interestingly, even though these gangs were embroiled in deadly wars, outlawed, hunted down, they were primarily native youths who for centuries had the same roots, the same history, the same cosmology, but were now enemies, insanely hating one another, willing to die for neither wealth, land, family, legacy, nor fame. They seemed to kill and die for something unfathomable, something I understood— and tried to overcome. Yet they still carried a measure of nobility, "at odds with circumstance," as the poet Theodore Roethke once put it, at odds with a hypocritical, superficially limiting, unimaginative, and soul-dismissive reality.

Over time the phenomenon of L.A.-based gangs in Mexico and Central America became big news, although I was confounded by how misinformed most of the media was about MS and Eighteenth Street (later called MS-13 and Mara 18). Law enforcement, in particular, targeted these gangs, setting up task forces, roundups, and conspiracy cases that most media ate up. Both the media and law enforcement tended to present these associations as singular and self-contained, as if they had no history, no influences, no roots.

Nor any remedies.

Many of the people I interviewed in 1993 and 1996 from MS and Eighteenth Street were killed, youths with names like Scoobie, Negro, and Topo. Over the years both gangs had been hit hard in Central America, and many of their members had become unusually destructive.

Still, a few made something of their lives—one *vato* I knew ended up in Europe as a painter. Others became founders and leaders of Homies Unidos, the gang intervention/prevention nonprofit organization that helped many young people get out of the gangs. Some started families and "matured out" like thousands of gangsters had done for generations. Some are now gang intervention experts and peace advocates.

Donna and I also participated in a peace gathering in San Salvador called Salvadoran Youth Confronting Violence. It was 1996 and nongovernmental agencies, churches, community-based groups, members of the new national police, and others—including members of MS and Eighteenth Street—came together to create the first viable peace plan. In the end, police officers and gang members, priests and evangelicals (who had their own rivalries), and even deadly enemies among gangs embraced one another. But the right-wing government in El Salvador at the time sabotaged these efforts. They instead brought in LAPD members as consultants and embarked on *"mano dura"* ("firm hand") antigang policies.

Soon law enforcement and the media went to extremes in dogging Central American gangs. These gangs weren't angels or lightweights— I knew better. But like all street gangs, and most criminals, all they needed was a chance to live, to mature, to study, to better themselves, to be properly initiated into society and allowed to restore their communities through their own interests, talents, and capacities.

While recent government efforts have included a *"mano amigo"* ("friendly hand") and some rehabilitation, the repression more than anything contributed to the *maras'* growth and entrenchment. It seemed the social system through war and poverty created these gangs, pushed them underground and forced them to become better organized by suppressing them, and then established a profitable industry of prison and law enforcement to deal with them, but with no lasting solutions.

This was never more evident to me than in my work with Chicago gangs.

Chapter Twenty

Ramiro, behind the wheel of his mother's car, raced through the Humboldt Park neighborhood one warm Chicago day, through one-ways and main drags. His passengers included two of his friends and two gang girls they'd picked up earlier that day. Street mixes—Chi-town-style house music—blasted from the cassette player.

Behind them, a carload of gang rivals gave chase.

Ramiro turned toward the park, but the vehicle behind him rammed his car, forcing him to crash into the National Guard armory there. One of his homies, apparently unhurt, ran off. The other homie took off through the park to get help but ended up being chased and bricked by two different gang rivals—he barely made it out of there. Ramiro and the two girls were still in the car, but one girl had her face busted up and a broken arm. Ramiro, with minor cuts and bruises, carefully pulled the moaning girl out of the vehicle. With help from the other girl, they made it to a nearby apartment complex.

Meantime, the dudes who had chased them threw gasoline on Camila's car and set it on fire.

Ramiro opened the entrance to the building and placed the injured girl in the alcove. People from the first-floor apartment peered out from behind a slightly opened door. Ramiro requested they call for help. He then told the girl she'd be okay, not to worry. Ramiro looked outside through glass in the front entrance. He spied the enemy car, haphazardly parked in front of the building. Its occupants strode toward the building. One dude held a handgun.

Leaving the girls near the stairway, Ramiro stepped out. The gunman walked menacingly toward him with the weapon pointed at Ramiro's head. My son stared back with a hardened expression.

"You can kill me now, dawg."

Just then the arrival of police forced his rivals to scramble back to their car and split before they could shoot Ramiro. The cops ended up taking Ramiro to jail. His mom, pissed as hell, got him out that night. The girl with the broken arm was placed in an ambulance and driven to a hospital.

In late 1993, Trini and I bought our first house together on Central Park Avenue in Logan Square. This was a community with a large Puerto Rican population that nonetheless had huge swathes carved out by high-end developers and yuppies.

Our neighborhood was still barrio at the time. Nearby multistory apartment complexes held hundreds of families, drug dealers, gang members, the poor. The Imperial Gangsters were the main gang here. An offshoot of the Latin Kings, the two gangs were now bitter enemies.

The house we lived in was more than a hundred years old, with a staircase, hardwood floors, high wood moldings, and a full basement with a bedroom. A rat-infested garage lay in the back, which we tore down to build a carport.

We had youths from Ramiro's gang as well as from Patricia Zamora's youth group meet in the backyard a few times. Others not in gangs, but affected by their presence, also took part. A few Imperial Gangsters came around.

Patricia organized what she called "peace retreats," weekend camping trips to forest preserves outside Chicago. Many of these young people had never been to a forest preserve. The first time, we took about twenty-five young people and a handful of adults.

That first night a fifteen-year-old girl sold herself for $5 in one of the tents. Others went around to camping sites stealing wallets and other valuables. Another brought crack cocaine. One of the kids began heroin withdrawals. At one point, rangers on horseback threatened to close us down. We insisted we'd pull everybody in line.

The next morning, we gathered everyone together and had a serious heart-to-heart. I told them that we'd have fun, but it would be healthy. We'd have talks, and everyone would respect one another. Adults were there to help, not babysit. But we all had to abide by mutual agreements. I also offered to drive anyone who wanted to go back to Pilsen or Humboldt Park/Logan Square if they couldn't make such agreements. After a couple of hours, many of the young people felt bad about the night before. Only two of them accepted my offer. I drove them to the city, dropped them off, and drove back, an hour or so each way.

Sure enough, in the next two days those who stayed paid attention, talked about their issues, told spooky stories and jokes, and behaved admirably. This served as the basis of the kind of work we'd do from then on—guide, offer resources, and help prepare hard-core gang members and other troubled youths to live decent and meaningful lives. It wasn't going to be easy. There was hardly any precedent to follow.

In the fall of 1993, I spent two weeks in Seattle at the Centro de la Raza teaching poetry for eight hours a day with about thirty inner-city kids, ages six to sixteen. This ended with a collaborative reading at the world-famous Bumbershoot music and arts festival. Composer and saxophonist Amy Denio created original music to the poems—a project she called *Tempesta—an Urban Rhapsody*.

I invited Andrea to take part. She was already composing compelling poetry. She was sixteen then. The kids were fantastic, despite initial mishaps, problems, tantrums, and holding back. Close to five hundred people showed up for our final performance, where I also read my own work after the youngsters opened up their hearts to the community.

One day at the bed-and-breakfast Andrea and I were staying at, I had a visitor. Michael Meade was a respected storyteller and mythologist who for at least two decades by then had been teaching in men's conferences with such healer/teachers as Robert Bly, James Hillman, Jack Kornfield, William Stafford, and Malidoma Somé.

Michael's cross-cultural events included ancient stories from around the world, drumming, songs, poetry, dance, and emerging rituals—all under the auspices of his nonprofit organization, the Mosaic Multicultural Foundation.

Michael had apparently received *Always Running* from one of his sons, who recommended that he read it. That day Michael came to invite me to be a teacher at an event in January 1994, held in the Santa Monica Mountains near L.A. I didn't know what to expect. I had never been to a men's conference. Just the same, I accepted. Michael's way of explaining this work intrigued me. I was open to new study, new beginnings, new relationships.

For one thing I needed help with Ramiro. I was at a loss on what to do. Ramiro's mother's car was ruined after the car chase with his enemies. He could have been killed, perhaps his friends as well. Ramiro's run-ins with enemies became more frequent. Soon after that he was arrested for another shooting while on probation for the first shooting. This time we managed to prevent a long prison term: Ramiro was sentenced to four months of boot camp instead.

There were days I wanted to give up on my son, to throw him out of the house as my parents had done with me. But I felt an even stronger pull to stand by him, to steer him, reprimand him, too, but always with the love of a father I had not always shown. Not "tough love," but the patient and heartbreaking love of someone who must weather every storm, every spiraling descent, while still maintaining his presence and integrity.

I flew into L.A. to take part in my first Mosaic Men's Conference with these worries on my shoulders. One of the other teachers told me I looked like Atlas with a misshapen world on my back. Still, something broke through inside me that week, through my seemingly impenetrable exterior and rock-hard interior, through my defenses, excuses, and masks.

The men didn't stir, didn't stop me, didn't get bored or upset. At one point during my first Mosaic conference, I spoke for forty-five minutes, nonstop. I talked about the gang life, the people I stabbed and shot, the funerals I attended. I talked about the heroin, the way it seemed to glow from the center of my being, how it melted through my body. And, of course, the drinking.

I talked about the women I hurt—Camila, Leti, Aileen, Deborah, Yolanda, Sarita, Maydé, and even now, my Trini. About the detached heart, the wounded heart, the stone heart. How my heart had gone mad with dope, drink, sex, living on the brink, and how now I had to face it all, wrestling with whatever courage and character I might yet forge out of the betrayals and long stream of inadequacies.

I related how my father's lunacies seemed to reflect off the mirrors and glass of every dwelling. How now I had to fill the gaps in my own fatherhood, often with no direction or model. How my children would live fully or get wrecked by what I did, what I said, and how I had to properly address their issues and reproaches.

Some of the men sat there; some stood; all listened, holding my words. It was unlike anything I'd ever experienced. I didn't know why I trusted that they would contain this. I never trusted this with others before.

The men opened up a space where instead of bullets I'd bring poems. And when I was through, I was no longer Luis Rodríguez. No longer clay in unsteady hands. No longer perennial son of a conquered race. I had a deeper name, an indigenous name, unknown but as old as the stones, crevices, and trees of this land. This name was in my bones, in the marrow, in the salt of my regrets.

When I finished speaking, I hung my head and didn't care that I cried. I drew from unmined psychic caves, mountains of failures, a vast tsunami of grief. That day I belonged to all men, all lands, borderless, always exiled, always welcomed.

I returned to Chicago and couldn't explain to Trini what I had experienced. But she saw another face below the fallen one, another voice rising up my throat, the beginning stages of a broken person coming together.

I dedicated myself more seriously to the youth work. Patricia and I, along with the young people, held working meetings to establish a new organization. In August of 1994, we launched a youth conference at the University of Illinois, Chicago (UIC), a large campus in between the Mexican Pilsen barrio and Greektown, and next to housing projects filled with generations of African-American families. The youths called this gathering Youth Struggling for Survival '94. Around two hundred young people and adults showed up.

The founders included Patricia, Camila, and Andrea. Ramiro read a poem to open our proceedings. I did the keynote address, asking the group to imagine something that had never been done before but had roots in ancient stories, cultures, traditions.

Over the years, YSS would have the involvement of hundreds of young people from at least twelve Chicago communities as well as Aurora and DeKalb (including African-Americans from Uptown, where Patricia later worked as director of Alternatives/Youth Net). Whole families took part. Besides mine, there were the Arrellanos, the Restrepos, the Arguellos, the Venturas, the Vasquezes, more than one Hernandez, and Frank and Louise Blazquez and their children.

At one point we had a rough time obtaining a meeting space outside our homes. With zero-tolerance policies in community centers, settlement houses, and schools, YSS was getting turned down by most everyone.

Finally, the Agape Center, a Christian-based group with a building in Little Italy, opened up their basement for weekly meetings. This was a great space, but for the first few weeks the mostly Mexican, Puerto Rican, and African-American members of the group had to endure stare-downs by the Italian-American neighbors whenever they walked in the area.

YSS people remained cool. After more meetings and a few visits to the pizza joint across the street, the neighbors realized these youths came to do positive arts-based and healing work, not to rob them, and lightened up. We were then treated with smiles, light ribbing, extra servings of fries.

Camila and I had twenty years of loving, hating, raising kids, abandoning kids, manipulations, treachery, and, finally, trying to help young people. Twenty years to the day before the YSS founding conference, we had gotten married in a barrio church in East L.A.—full of illusions, naïve perhaps, yet with eyes that had already seen too much.

After our ruined union, we pushed through different lovers, twisted roads, crossed purposes. But with Ramiro in so much trouble and

Andrea in need of loving attention, we cut across our nonsense and deprived egos and regrouped as partners in parenting as well as for positive community change. The terrible things we did to each other as immature young adults had to be pushed aside—our kids warranted a cohesive loving family.

I began to see Camila as a sister. I relied on Camila more than anyone else in this youth work. She was the person I called on for ideas and strategies. She was the one I talked to about the inner workings of the group, of the kids, of the other adults. Patricia was my other sister. These were two women—my *compañeras* on this embattled front—who sacrificed, labored, and also put me in my place when needed.

Ramiro had two other babies, a year apart, by two different women. Again, we found out about them after the babies were born. I tried to talk to him about safe sex, about unwanted pregnancies, about seeing babies for their own value, not like trophies on a mantel. After Ricardo was born I thought Ramiro had learned this lesson.

Apparently not.

The babies were two girls. We loved them as our new grandchildren: Anastasia was born in April 1994 and Amanda in late May 1995. Because the mothers didn't talk to each other, and rarely with us (and soon had nothing to do with my son), Trini, Camila, and I made sure to involve ourselves as grandparents as much as possible.

As difficult as this was during the first years, in time our granddaughters got to know us, came to expect presents and cards on birthdays and holidays, and became integrated into the family. The circumstances of their births were not their doing. Once the girls arrived into this world they belonged. They had their innate proclivities, their own special contributions to make. They needed nurturing and support like all children.

The other baby born in 1994, in late June, belonged to Trini and me.

When I was still drinking, Trini once said she didn't want any more babies if I had anything to do with it. This was excruciatingly hurtful to hear. But it was my fault. I wasn't around. I was emotionally not present, never mind physically gone, during the last years in the bars. Trini's words, among other things, impelled me to finally quit. Trini, who wanted one more child, relented when she saw how committed I was to staying clean. The new baby, a boy, became my sobriety child.

I was supposed to return to Germany with other Chicago poets, but I canceled since the trip was going to be around the time of the baby's due date. Trini's job as a court interpreter provided the insurance. We went to a hospital in Humboldt Park that was known for years as the "Puerto Rican Factory."

As Trini went into labor, I drove her to the hospital. Again, Trini was calm, prepared. This time Camila came around. At first we thought she was going to hang out in the waiting room. But she kept wandering into the labor room, even as Trini got close to giving birth. With Camila standing nearby, Trini whispered a request into my ear: "Please don't have Camila in here. I only want you with me when the baby is born."

I talked to Camila and told her we appreciated her being there, but we didn't want her in the labor room. She was disappointed, but respected our wishes.

The boy's birth was without worries. He came out headfirst like he was supposed to, with a full head of Indian hair, similar to Andrea when she was born. I wanted to name him Jacinto. But as soon as the baby was cleaned and wrapped in a blanket and cap, the nurses placed him on Trini's stomach and she insisted he be named Luis. I didn't think he should have my name, which I wasn't too fond of to begin with. I thought he needed his own name. But who was I to argue? Trini said she saw a Luis as soon as she glimpsed his face, a name she apparently liked.

That night he became Luis Jacinto.

I left the hospital early that morning, soon after I saw that Mama and son were doing fine. I planned to return later that night to take them home. I was slated to film a video of one of my poems for the *United States of Poetry* series on PBS-TV. I drove to Milwaukee, endured about eight hours of filming for three minutes of video (the video, unfortunately, got dropped from the lineup and never aired), then jumped on the expressway back to Chicago. With traffic, I kept Trini and little Luis waiting.

When I arrived at the hospital, the nurses and Trini were stressed. She'd been sitting in a wheelchair with baby in the waiting area for half the day (the hospital needed the room for another mother-to-be). Man, did I blow this. Anyway, we got home and all this vanished in the eyes of this little guy who looked so native, so naturally Mexika, so much like a son of this vast, old, and breathing land.

Angel was one of Ramiro's best friends, also an Insane Campbell Boy, who attended one of the best Chicago schools, an honor student. He showed respect whenever he came to the house.

Ramiro's gang was in the middle of a war between the Insane section of the Latin Folks alliance, led by the Insane Spanish Cobras, and the Maniac section, led by the Maniac Latin Disciples. This intra-Folks conflict had already taken many lives.

One morning, Angel, then fifteen, was riding to school with his aunt when a car pulled up at a red light and opened fire, killing Angel instantly. The same shooters got to one of the Campbell Boys' main dudes, our friend Pedro. Pedro was shot while sitting on the stoop of his building. He got hit in the back, leg, and hand but survived.

Ramiro was stunned. I went with him to check in on Pedro, who was in a large dormitory building with other gunshot victims in Cook County Hospital. This was in the mid-1990s and wars were popping up all over the city. Pedro was talking revenge, payback, mobilizing the other Campbell Boys with their guns.

Ramiro agreed. I did not.

"Look, Pedro, I know you're hurting and that Ramiro and you, along with your boys, are sad about Angel's death," I argued. "I say don't retaliate. Deal with your grief, help Angel's family, deal with your own recovery. Don't send these guys out like blind soldiers—this will only bring on more shootings, and whether you're aware of this or not, you're endangering your homies as well as my son. People will listen to you. Don't sacrifice any more of your friends. Angel was a big enough loss."

"But we can't let this stand," Pedro tried to say, although in pain. "We have to get back at them fools. They killed my best friend. Angel's gone, man. We have to or they'll think they can hit us anytime."

I continued, "I know about this. Remember where I came from. Remember why I'm working with kids to help pull them out of the fire. It's in your hands to make this different, to make this right. What you're saying, anyone can do. But this only brings more death. I don't want Ramiro caught up in this. What you say carries weight. I'm asking you to choose peace, to choose life. Not death."

It took a while, but, finally, with tears of rage streaming from his eyes, Pedro promised to stop his boys from attacking.

"Nah, dawg, we can't do that—we have to go to war," Ramiro said, trying to convince Pedro. "We're ready. Just give the word. We can't let Angel's death go unanswered."

Pedro hesitated for a moment, his mind rolling about what to do.

"Your dad's right," Pedro finally responded. "We have to chill. We don't want any more of our boys killed. I'm calling this off."

I believed in Pedro. He was a real leader, a thinker, whom I had given books about Puerto Rican liberation, about conscious fighters in groups like the Young Lords Party. Ramiro didn't like this, but I told him this decision was the best one for all of them. I'd been through this before. The war had to stop.

To help decrease gang warfare in the North Side and South Side neighborhoods, I met with several leaders and organizations to consider a meeting of people involved in violence prevention and gang intervention. Initially this involved organizers from BUILD, the Street Intervention Program at the YMCA, Latino Youth, Mothers Against Gang Violence, the Illinois Violence Prevention Project, and the Community Renewal Society, among others, Christians and non-Christians alike. Our goal was to obtain a level of gang peace among Latinos in at least two communities—Logan Square and Little Village.

We called this the Increase the Peace Network.

The Little Village barrio was a mostly Mexican enclave with two major gangs, the Latin Kings and Two-Six Nation, which had been carrying on a devastating war for decades. One church had a wall with an ever-increasing number of names of youths killed. We began peace-making efforts—truces, cease-fires, talks, and whatever else was likely to help reduce the deaths.

In Logan Square, "peace zones" were created where gang leaders, businesses, schools, churches, and presumably police would cooperate to keep away drug sales and violence—while providing jobs, schooling, and services. This worked well, with rival gang leaders ceasing all hostilities as they met in *tablas* (boards) to quell rumors, work out differences, address beefs.

Although gang leaders were willing to take part, and most held up their end, it was the rest of the community that fell down. Police were the first to refuse assistance. Then the schools with zero-tolerance policies pulled away. Businesses followed suit. We had peace. But as many have said for a long time, there can be no peace without justice, economic means, community engagement, ongoing and comprehensive programs.

Through the Community Renewal Society, we attempted to establish "sanctuaries" where troubled youths, including gang members, even those who had committed serious crimes, could get help: social services, therapy, drug treatment, job referrals, legal counsel, and spiritual guidance. A sanctuary protected the young people as well as those providing services from legal and other interferences.

No crimes or gang activities were ever sanctioned. What was sanctioned was a process of healing, education, and positive contribution. Those who had arrest warrants were encouraged to turn themselves in, but with proper legal counsel. In Logan Square we found a church and began to build a framework for this work.

But, again, we had no money, no paid staff, and, despite our efforts, few resources to obtain sustainable backing. By then most federal and other funding was going to "antigang" proposals, law enforcement, jails. The conservatives in government, even some Democrats, were driving social policy toward punishment, not rehabilitation.

The end result: more gangs, more violence, and the squeezing of so-called gang communities, where now Chicago gangs spread to other parts of the country as well as Latin America and even Europe—similar to what happened with gangs from L.A.

Finally, we convinced a pastor at San Lucas Church across from Humboldt Park to allow us to create what we called the Humboldt Park Teen Reach. The program included computers, tutoring, books, creative activities, and more. YSS took part, as did YMCA's Street Intervention Program and BUILD. The first year we came together to plan, write, and eventually obtain an initial state grant of $180,000.

Another thing we introduced to the Increase the Peace Network was Native American/Native Mexican healing traditions, such as the sweat lodge (known as the *inipi* in Lakota or *temazcalli* in Nahuatl). This came about through our interactions with Nane Alejandrez and Barrios Unidos of Santa Cruz, California.

For two decades prior, Barrios Unidos, under Nane's leadership, had stopped many gang wars and helped transform young men and women into peacemakers in some of the most violent barrios of California. In the mid-1990s, they sponsored national peace summits in which Increase the Peace took an active role.

From there we attended other urban peace gatherings in Chicago; Kansas City; Washington, D.C., El Paso; and California, in which gang members, including Ramiro's boys and various other Chicago gangs, many bitter enemies, took part. Barrios Unidos helped with the creation of Homies Unidos, which dealt with Salvadoran and other Central American gang youths in Los Angeles and in El Salvador.

Barrios Unidos also had strong ties to Native American and Native Mexican/Central American elders, teachers, dance groups, drummers, singers, practitioners. In 1995 I went to my first sweat lodge in California. I landed on a most welcoming ground.

From the time I was a teenager, I had tried to connect with indigenous ideas and traditions. I again circled back to a spiritually engaged life, not through "religion" or church, but through the recognition of the divine in everyone, that even with our general brokenness, we stand with the sacred in all of nature, all relationships, in the mix and flow of all life.

In this quest, I found ties to all spiritual practices, knowing in their essence they were the same, though in their features they were complicated. Jesus, Buddha, Muhammad, Black Elk . . . all were great teachers if one sought their truths through a metaphorical and poetic process, and not by the literal, stagnant, or doctrinaire. Now I felt compelled to find out more.

One weekend, with the help of Mayan elder (and sundancer with the Lakota) Julio Revolorio, the Increase the Peace Network held ceremonies with about seventy-five gang youths, males and females, in a large campground outside Chicago.

As we gathered, Latin Kings and Two-Sixers began to square off— apparently one dude in attendance had been shot recently by another dude who showed up. This didn't bode well. We separated the two groups into different sections of the camp.

The next day, Julio placed us all in a circle and for hours held us spellbound with teachings and stories of his native Guatemala and the civil war there, in which his wife was killed. Afterward, he had the males and females create their own sweat lodges and prayer ties.

Others already steeped in this tradition assisted both groups, but it was obvious the women were better able to cooperate and work well: Their lodge, made with flexible river willows, was perfectly round and symmetrical. The guys' lodge was off center and leaning to one side.

When everything was ready, we prepared to enter the lodges (men in swimming trunks or shorts, women in cotton tops and long skirts). I saw these gang enemies standing behind one another, with tattoos and bullet holes on their bodies, quietly and solemnly enter the blanket-covered lodges.

Inside was total darkness, with no way to distinguish among gangs, races, nationalities. We were one people with commonalities in hurt, prayers, seeking wellness.

Songs in Lakota, but also Nahuatl and K'iché, were offered. Many earnest words were uttered. Julio had earlier heated rocks for hours. These represented the Stone People, the grandfathers and grandmothers, our ancestors, holders of the world's stories. These in turn were placed into the center of the lodge during each of four rounds. The steam rose when Julio poured water over the red-hot Stone People and, due to the blankets draped over the willow frames, stayed within the lodges to remove the toxins from our bodies and spirits.

As a cleansing ceremony we endured the heat, however uncomfortable. We were in the womb of mother earth. Each round represented each of the four directions, the cardinal points, but also the cycles of life. The young people as well as the adults crawled out of their lodges renewed.

Later that night, without any prompting from the organizers, a group of Latin Kings walked over to where the Two-Sixers were sitting around in their section of camp. It looked as if they were going to start trouble. Instead these dudes stretched out their hands and offered apologies, and soon deadly enemies sat down at a fire to share, to have a dialogue, to live peace, to revel, even for an instant, in community.

Chapter Twenty-one

Shadowed by Monument Valley's eerie rock formations, I spoke to Navajo youths in Kayenta, Arizona. A few were in L.A.-style or Chicago-style gangs—the two most influential street gang styles in the country—or gangs of their own making.

Alcoholism and suicide rates, like in most native reservations, were extremely high. I also visited the towns of Shonto, Dennehotso, Chilchinbito, Chinle—I recall kids coming up to me so I could sign their T-shirts, book bags, arms.

I returned a few more times, including as a facilitator of a deeply felt youth conference with Navajo teachers, counselors, judges, poets, police, and others. We also took part in sweat lodge ceremonies in the snow. At the end of the conference, the participants were in tears, hugging each other, focusing on young people who were largely neglected and then punished when they dared to "get in trouble" just to be seen.

Through my interactions with Luis Ruan, a Chicano with Purepecha roots from Michoacan, Mexico, whom I met on my speaking circuits, I hooked up with a medicine man named Anthony Lee and his wife, Delores, both in their late fifties at the time. The Lees lived in the Lukachukai community, adjacent to the Chuska Mountains. They became friends and teachers.

At Luis's request, I participated in my first peyote ceremony there. At first I thought this violated my oath against drugs and alcohol. But it turned out that peyote in its natural state, and used with the guidance of roadmen, was medicine, not a drug, not addictive, and healing for all ailments, spiritual and physical. On the rez, it was the leading way to overcome drug and alcohol addictions.

The peyote, with deep ties to Mexico, called to me.

Finally, I opened up to Trini about native spirituality. She listened and wanted to learn more. I invited Trini to take part in a medicine ceremony with Anthony and Delores on the Navajo rez. This all-night ceremony—with medicine songs, water drums, prayers, and peyote in cut pieces as well as a powder and a tea—brought Trini and me even closer, even though we had difficulty staying awake. Finally we greeted the dawn in a state of joy.

Sometime during that trip, Trini asked Anthony if he was part Mexican, saying he looked like her dad. It turned out that Anthony's family/tribal clans included the Nakai, "the wanderers," a Navajo term for someone from Mexico. Trini then told Anthony and Delores the story about how her father had disowned her twenty years before when she left home to attend college. They must have seen the hole in her heart from that experience. On that trip the Lees decided to "adopt" Trini.

In ceremony, we finalized this spiritual adoption, which traditional Navajo elders and their families often do, tying the tribe to other indigenous people. Anthony recognized the indigenous in Trini, whose roots in Jalisco were with the Huichol, also known as the Wixáritari. In adopting Trini, this couple essentially adopted the whole family. At age twelve, Rubén underwent a Navajo rite-of-passage ceremony with a sweat bath inside a lodge made of earth and a prayer meeting inside a teepee, which he had to learn how to set up. One of his cousins and several "uncles" (friends and family members) stood with him.

Aside from this, I made several trips to the Pine Ridge reservation, including participating in ceremonies and events with YSS. Eventually this sparked a crucial contact with Chicago gang youth and Lakota native young people.

Many youths on the rez were turning away from their elders and traditions. The Mexican and Puerto Rican youngsters (and a few blacks and whites who joined us) told them they wished they knew their own native traditions. They pleaded for the Lakota youths not to join gangs like they did—losing friends, siblings, even parents. They suggested these young people get closer to their Lakota customs and rituals.

"If I could live my life over again," remarked one Pilsen teen, who a year before had held his dying brother in his arms, "I would learn my Mexican indigenous ways and never join a gang."

At one point, we were supposed to speak for a half hour at the KILI community radio station on the rez. We ended up there for three hours, with many on-air calls and people walking long distances to the station to meet YSS members.

Back home, we had to make major changes. With the new baby, and Rubén still a handful, Trini and I decided she'd quit the court interpreter position and be home full-time. She also helped me organize the many lecture and reading events that were coming my way from around the country.

Trini was also tired of the injustices she saw in the courts. As a court interpreter she could not intervene or provide legal counsel to defendants, many of whom were poor Spanish-speaking men and women. This was too much to bear day in and day out.

I told Trini to let this job go. We'd try to make my writing/speaking business get off the ground. We had to—I was now part of an ongoing national debate on youth, gangs, and inner work. It was important that we be better organized to help impact institutions and policies.

Andrea and I had the biggest fight of our lives. She was working on going to college. I was proud of my daughter and what she had to do, against great odds, to get there.

Then she threw us a bombshell. Andrea had a boyfriend named Ben, a tech-savvy young man, who asked her to move in with him.

I took this to mean my daughter was giving up on college, her plans, her life. I feared she'd live with this guy and her life would get reshaped into a domestic existence that I knew she didn't want. But she seemed to have no strength at the time to oppose it.

She was eighteen.

"M'ija, I can't let you do this," I said at Camila's house, where Andrea and Ben decided to tell us. "You've done so well in school. You have many goals, and you need to get a good start on these before you settle down. You'll have time to make a household when you're ready. It's too soon now."

This all sounded familiar. It was similar to what Miss Daniels, Camila's high school teacher, told me when I talked about marrying Camila, who was also eighteen at the time. Those many years ago, I had argued with Miss Daniels. But now—like Miss Daniels did with me—I asked Andrea to wait on a home life until she obtained the work and aims she valued for herself.

As a father, as someone who has seen too many lives wasted, stalled, or empty, I didn't want Andrea to fall into the same traps. I became like Miss Daniels.

Andrea cried. Ben tried to convince me it was going to be okay, and I saw he was taking my old role. I insisted that Andrea was going to ruin what chances she had to better herself if she left with this impulsive and impatient young man (wasn't *that* familiar).

My words were smoke in the wind. Like Camila and me in the early days of our relationship, my daughter and Ben were going to go ahead with their romance, move in together, and possibly derail Andrea's education.

I had no more ability to broker the world with my daughter than I had with my son. Ben and Andrea found an apartment above Camila, who was now living in the mostly Mexican barrio near Chicago and Grand streets.

Like me, Andrea was going to make her own mistakes. Of course, this also meant she was going to live her own life.

My granddaughter Catalina was born in June 1996. Andrea was the same age that Camila was when she had Ramiro. Obviously, I couldn't now oppose the union between Andrea and Ben. They now had this incredible child, named after my grandmother, and whatever wrong or right was done to bring her into being, it was right that Catalina was born, that she was healthy and would eventually launch a purposeful life, one in which her choices and our loving guidance could combine so she'd eventually bring her own kind of beauty and goodness to the world.

I didn't think Ramiro would make it, but he endured four months of an intensive boot camp—with lots of yelling, consequences, structure. The instructors were former marines. The inmates of color worked without pay cleaning and fixing roads, medians, and railroad tracks in a mostly white rural community, although this didn't look right to me.

Still, Ramiro graduated with flying colors. I attended the graduation ceremony. Ramiro marched up to the stage in uniform. "Yes, sir," he shouted when addressed. It looked great, but I could see the seeds of failure in the whole process.

Ramiro also had to spend three months under house arrest after his release and two years on parole. At first he was okay—built, handsome, bronze-skinned. He organized a number of political discussions with YSS and other youths. We now had young people from all over the city and a few suburbs. We were getting great word of mouth for our approach to youth engagement and mentoring.

Yet, in a matter of weeks, Ramiro got tired of being home, unable to leave except for school or work assignments approved by his parole agent. By then he had already been in Joliet State Prison, the Vienna Correctional Center, and even the Jacksonville Correctional Center, where he once went with me to read poetry.

In prison and boot camp, everything was enforcement. But home was loose, unstructured, binding but in another way where more was tolerated. Ramiro either needed strict all-out control, which was good only for the short term, if that, or he needed time and a process to learn self-discipline, some skills, an art, having a cause, a meaningful spiritual path, and eventually full possession of his life. This would take longer but could lead to a long-range, life-affirming result. Hardly anyone wanted to do the latter. However, neither prison nor boot camp dealt with real intervention for the long run.

I was also high-strung and stressed during that period. Not drinking, for the first few years, was agony. I raged often. I had anxious moments that I didn't know how to deal with. And I was getting kidney stones, intense headaches, borderline diabetes, gall bladder stones, high blood pressure, high cholesterol, chest pains.

More than a few times Trini took me to the emergency room.

By then, PBS-TV had a documentary series called *Making Peace*, produced by Moira Productions of the Bay Area. This show featured leaders who worked actively for peace in violent, poor, mostly black and brown communities. I became one of those they decided to high-light.

The director of my segment was John Valadez, a young Chicano filmmaker, working with his Asian-American wife, Ling Hsu. I got to do video diaries, a new way of documenting lives at the time. The producers gave me a small Sony video camera that I took on trips and to meetings. Alone in a hotel room, my office, or the backyard of my home, I set up the camera in front of my face and put forward my thoughts, my apprehensions, my take on things.

A film crew also came around several times one year, during some of our most active YSS meetings and events, and even on a few of my trips. They captured the original plays, the baseball games, the intense dialogues, the ceremonies we did with the young people, adults, and mentors.

They also documented the death of three young leaders in YSS, killed on different occasions. These were young men heavily involved in gangs who changed their lives, who had gained trust and aspirations. Whose families were breathing easier after years of arrests, drug use, loud living room arguments.

Then we got those phone calls—they'd just been shot.

Police in ski masks were rumored to have killed one of these guys after the young man exposed the drug-and-gun-running scheme a police officer conducted in the Pilsen barrio. Rival gang members shot and killed another Pilsen kid, who in his spare time played with a mariachi group. And the third young man had just gotten out of the Insane Campbell Boys, was thinking of leaving gang life altogether, but got convinced by friends to join the Insane Spanish Cobras. A week later, rivals spotted him inside a car in the parking lot of a hamburger stand and shot him.

The film crew went to the funerals, documenting the grieving families and friends (the final film, however, showed only one of the funerals). They witnessed how my heart broke frequently in this work with all the deaths, hospital visits, strained dialogues.

One dude, who also appeared in the film, was shot three times a block away from my house after leaving one of the meetings. I saw him later in the emergency room. He sat up from the gurney, bleeding. He smiled and waved at me.

I shook my head (he eventually made it).

Others were getting arrested. A few ended up doing hard time.

A focus of the film became the relationship between Ramiro and me. The film ended when my family took Ramiro to court to serve a short prison term for one of the shootings he was involved in. We were doing all this great work, saving many lives, but also inundated with so much violence—and a glaring failure: My son was *not* making a suitable turn to a peaceful and healthy life.

The TV series finally came out in 1997. The segment I worked on was called "Youth Struggling for Survival: Like Father, Like Son." It aired for about a half hour on numerous public TV stations. On top of that, the producers made sure the film was shown to around two hundred community gatherings throughout the country.

Pedro recuperated well from the shooting that sent him to the county hospital. Afterward, he laid low for a while. But one day, as Pedro walked his pit bull down the street, he spotted one of the leaders of the gang that had killed his homie Angel and had also shot Pedro. The dude was dropping off his young daughter at school.

Pedro, who held back the gang from revenge, who cried so much at Angel's funeral, who later bottled up his pain, somehow figured the time had arrived for payback. He wouldn't let his boys do this, but Pedro felt he had to. He rushed back to his house, grabbed a gun, and as his enemy began to drive away from the school Pedro ran up to the dude and pumped him full of bullets.

The manhunt for Pedro was extensive. People were rousted, houses raided. Pedro had killed a major player in the intra-Folk conflicts. After the killing, others died like I knew they would—all-out war. Pedro left the state.

Yet, for some reason the police thought Pedro was hiding out at our Logan Square house. One day they raided my home. Seven Chicago police officers took part. Ramiro was the only one inside. He had the cordless phone in his grasp, calling for help.

If the police managed to break down the door like they wanted to do, I'm sure they would have shot Ramiro, perhaps using the cordless phone for the "we thought he had a weapon" excuse. Ramiro told me later he looked out the window to see who was banging on the door and yelling, "Police—open up!" He recognized two of the officers from a recent court appearance he had on behalf of a friend beaten by police. He figured this was their way of getting back at him. He turned off the lights, reached for the phone, and hurried to my home office.

Whatever the police were planning, I foiled it.

Like years before, when I arrived in time to save Ramiro from a bunk bed that had fallen on top of him, I stepped out of a taxi just prior to officers busting through. I was returning from one of my trips. I saw the armed officers and walked up to my porch with luggage in hand, saying, "What's going on here?"

"Who the hell are you?" one officer asked, gun drawn.

"I live here. You don't need to knock the door down—I'll open it."

I thought they would tackle me and pull me out of the way, but I got the key, put it in the lock, and swung the door open. In the darkness I saw Ramiro with phone in hand.

The police were irate. They searched the house—they didn't find guns, drugs, or Pedro.

Two more times, a total of fifteen police officers raided my home in a matter of weeks. Again, they had nothing to use against us. I felt they were targeting me for the street peace and gang intervention work I was doing. I figured part of this had to do with my public statements about police sabotaging the peace-zone efforts. It was possible their entryway to get to me, without his knowledge, might be my son.

Pedro was finally arrested in Florida after a year on the run. Officials extradited him back to Illinois. I visited Pedro in jail and tried to help any way I could. But Pedro faced extremely serious charges.

What Pedro did was wrong. But I also knew what Pedro was made of. He was a natural organizer, someone who in other circumstances, perhaps in another skin, in another social class, might run corporations, schools, institutions.

But like too many of our best young people, he got caught in the lifeless and soulless gang world he grew up in and after a fairly quick trial was found guilty and sentenced to forty years in the state's correctional system.

Jeff Biggers, former director of the Flagstaff Literary Festival, and his Italian-born wife, Carla Paciotto, were now living in the Sierra Madre Occidental of southern Chihuahua, Mexico. This was the section of the range known as the Sierra Tarahumara, including the Copper Canyon, where some eighty thousand Rarámuri natives lived in and around half a dozen canyons, a canyon system deeper than the Grand Canyon.

Carla was studying the bilingual education programs of Rarámuri natives for her dissertation at Northern Arizona University. Jeff and Carla invited me to visit the Copper Canyon—also known as *La Barranca del Cobre*—for ten days in June 1999. They had already been there almost a year. I brought with me Erik Bitsui, a twenty-four-year-old Navajo who once worked with Jeff on the literary festival. Erik and his mother had taken part in ceremonies with Trini and me on the rez. A tall, long-haired, imposing young man, he was making his first visit to indigenous Mexico.

We flew into Ciudad Juarez, on the border of Chihuahua and Texas. Our plan was to take a bus to Creel, the main town in the Sierra Tarahumara, with stops that included Chihuahua City, where my mother was born.

At Creel, Erik and I exited the bus and a dozen Rarámuri children surrounded us with outstretched hands. Due to the intense poverty (people were literally starving) and the growth of tourism, begging had become part of the culture. Some children learned to do this as soon as they walked. We were told not to give them anything or else we'd be approached all day.

Jeff was there next to a dusty and mud-caked four-wheel-drive vehicle.

Creel had less than four thousand people and only a few hours of electricity during the day. The rest of the surrounding area had no electricity or running water. The Chihuahua al Pacifico train—one of the most spectacular train rides in the world, which went from Los Mochis on the Pacific coast to Chihuahua City—stopped at Creel. Hotels and stores lined up along the one main street that ended at a square and church. Many native people walked around in tire-soled sandals and what is considered traditional Rarámuri attire: men in breechcloths and plumed-sleeved shirts, women in long print dresses and colorful scarves.

Storefronts sold souvenirs of Tarahumara drums, violins, dolls, baskets, pots, masks, and walking canes adorned with corn husks. "Kwira va," the native greeting that means "How are things?," was written on a wall.

The Rarámuri were a large indigenous group that pushed themselves deeper into the Copper Canyon with the arrival of the Spanish in the 1500s. In search of gold and other minerals, the Spanish forced the natives into slave labor and a number of native rebellions were brutally put down. Over generations, many natives were killed or starved out.

Jeff drove us for a long time along one paved road and then veered off onto dirt pathways, bumping across natural potholes, including a large mud pit, on our way to Cusarare (Place of Eagles), a vibrant Rarámuri village. Cusarare had a mission, built in the mid-1700s. It had been long abandoned, but some natives took it upon themselves to open the doors and periodically clean the floors, where the faithful could pray (there were no pews). Some walked for up to six hours every Sunday morning to attend.

Dirt roads curved around the mission and led to the wood or stone huts the people lived in. As we entered the village, we saw people everywhere with dark brown skin, thick hair, and exquisite native faces.

We stopped at the wood-and-stone residence of an older native man and his wife. They also owned a small plot of land for corn, a horse, and other animals. Jeff and Carla were living behind the cabin in a former storage unit, heated by a wood-burning stove called a *calentón*. They put up a small solar panel that provided power for lights, heating the shower, and laptop use for around three hours a day.

Down a long wooden fence, Erik and I were given two separate rooms in the only "hotel" available at the time—it had no water, no electricity, and no toilets (there was an outhouse that one got to by walking across several yards of horse manure).

Jeff took us to communities, schools, health clinics, and the most remote living areas. We even visited preconquest ruins and caves with prehistoric wall drawings.

The Rarámuri were for the most part reserved and quiet. Every stranger, including me, was called *chabochi*, a word originally used for the Spanish, but now meaning anyone outside the tribe. According to Jeff the word originally meant "face covered in spiderwebs."

The people insisted on calling Erik "the Apache." Although Apaches and Navajos are related (they're both Athabaskan and both call themselves Diné), they are not the same people. Erik didn't like being an "Apache." But the people there knew about Apaches, not Navajos— more than a hundred years before, Apaches had traveled as far as the Sierra Tarahumara in hunting and raiding parties.

The natives were so wary of strangers that if you came across a woman by herself, or a group of women and children, they might turn their backs to you. When they did greet you, they wouldn't shake your hand. If they managed to reach a hand forward, it was to barely touch palms and fingers. Some of this reluctance to make contact, I was told, may have come from centuries before, when smallpox ravaged whole villages after the Spanish arrived.

Things opened up when I let people know I was part Rarámuri and was searching for my roots. Without knowing exactly where to look, I sought the ancestral birthplace of my great-grandmother and grandmother, who, according to stories my mother told me, left the Copper Canyon during the Mexican Revolution to keep from starving and ended up in Chihuahua City, where they were promptly renamed Manuela and Ana. We never knew their indigenous names.

For some of the natives, this was an endearing gesture on my part. As one man told me through an interpreter, "We're glad you've come to seek your family. Usually when Rarámuri leave, they don't come back."

A few of the people invited me into their homes, something they normally wouldn't do. I spoke to families in their skimpy shacks. While a few of them had animals, the traditional natives used them only to fertilize their fields. They lived on corn-derived foods, in particular the bland-tasting corn powder called *pinole*, often mixed with water as a drink. This staved off hunger and provided energy for work.

Most people still used the ancient *metate* and *mano*, the corn-grinding stone and handheld stone grinder. Women often spent hours pushing the *mano* back and forth against kernels of corn to make the powder used in their drinks, their tortillas, and their ceremonies.

One time I noticed a perspiring young woman grinding corn inside a stone hut wearing a Chicago Bulls T-shirt. I lived in Chicago and asked Jeff how she may have obtained that shirt.

"They get clothes from a local charity where people from the United States donate," he explained. Imagine that—Da Bulls in Tarahumaraland.

Jeff, Erik, and I went deep into the sierra, surrounded by immense pine forests and plants of all kinds. We stepped out of the four-by-four and continued climbing and descending on foot.

Our guide was a native man named Tomás, who also brought along his wife and two children. They were kind to me—I had to stop every fifteen minutes or so to catch my breath, that's how out of shape I was. At times, the family made a small clearing beneath a bush and lay down as they waited for me to continue. Jeff asked if I wanted to stop and go back. I said, no. I was determined to hike as far as we needed to.

Finally we stood on a ledge, several thousand feet above one of the canyons. At the very bottom was the fast-moving river known as Río Urique. The whole scene was peaceful, serene, lush. Then out of nowhere, I saw a couple of native children peeking through the shrubbery.

"How'd they get here?" I wondered out loud.

"They are people of the caves," Jeff explained. "These are one of the few cave-dwelling peoples of the world."

The closer we got to the mountainsides the better we spotted caves and cliffs filled with families. They often had mortared doors to blend into the surroundings. From a distance I was hard-pressed to see any openings—but there were hundreds. The caves were created when air bubbles formed after lava inundated the area millions of years ago. Some caves were massive, holding many families, like a small commune. Other caves were smaller, for one or two families, or for storage.

One night Jeff, Erik, and I slept in a cave in the area of Vitorachi. It was more like a rocky overhang. I wrapped myself up in my sleeping bag, concerned with scorpions, snakes, and other creatures that roamed the ground. It felt good, however, to wake up there in the morning, hearing birdsongs and the sound of rushing water.

Near the end of our stay, and after I had darkened from hiking in the sun, one of the natives said he figured out where my family may have originated—I looked like some people he knew. We then drove for miles to find them, finally arriving at a log cabin in the middle of nowhere.

An old couple emerged: The woman was thin and gray-haired, the man weather-beaten with a goatee. Tomás talked to them in their language and they soon invited us to come inside for *pinole*. In their small dark living room, Tomás told them I was looking for my roots, my connections to the tribe, for family. I think the couple thought I was homeless. The woman looked at me and in a kind voice told Tomás that they'd be my family, they'd take care of me.

My eyes watered.

I returned from Chihuahua to sad news. With Catalina still in diapers, Ben and Andrea had broken up. In the short time they were together, things became confused, chaotic. Andrea said Ben was abusive, manipulative, a liar. He had a veneer of being decent and hardworking. But much of his two-sided personality came from having maneuvered through eighteen foster homes in his young life. Ben was raised by the system. Even though he was finally adopted, he'd learned by then that survival meant knowing how to slick and trick his way through relationships.

Trini and I asked Ben to stay with us. Catalina deserved a father. If he was under our roof, we could work closely with him. I felt this might help Ben fulfill his role. Ben appeared to do well the first week or two. He painted our porch. Worked on the yard. Was polite. But things began to go awry. We caught Ben in a number of lies. He gave little Rubén a video game system and then took it back, which I didn't appreciate. We stopped trusting him.

One day, after about two months, Ben asked to leave the house. He apologized to Trini and me, saying he was using us, lying to us, and he just couldn't keep doing it anymore. Of course, we knew this and said, "Then don't do it."

For Ben, it was easier for him to move out than to stop the games he played. That was the last time we ever saw Ben. He left Andrea and Catalina's life after that and never returned.

Despite the setback of living with Ben, being on welfare and food stamps, and trying to make ends meet, Andrea rebalanced herself, with nothing but determination to pull her through. She finished college as a single mom. And even worked full-time during some of this period.

Camila and I helped as much as we could, taking care of little Catita when possible, providing financial help when necessary. We also helped to get her work—Andrea once served as YSS director.

The day Andrea went up to receive her diploma, with a BA in behavioral science, I stood up to make my way toward the back, away from family and her friends who all sat together with graduation balloons in a cluster of seats halfway into a packed auditorium. I needed my privacy so that I could shed tears of joy, of love, for my special daughter, my only daughter, my Andrea.

Andrea also came through in raising Catalina, moving against the overpowering influence of Ben and others like him. She knew from experience how to get relationships wrong, experiences, unfortunately, her parents often modeled for her. But if she got our bad examples and made some good out of them, then she had a leg up in determining the best ways to go when it came to men—and to guiding her own child.

Of course, my daughter had her issues: She could be inflexible at times and she closed down far too often. For years she kept to herself, and in the process hid her true personhood.

I admire Andrea for finally pulling things together out of this obscurity and achieving what few thought was possible. When my father died, he had eight children and more than thirty grandchildren—Andrea was the first of all of them to finish college.

Not long after her graduation, I asked Andrea if she'd let me be her father again. She exploded—where was I when she was a baby or when she needed me as a little girl and later as a confused teenager? I thought about the few times I held her as a child, the wonderful way she used to kiss my cheek, caress my morning stubble. But also how I missed her school events, open houses, dance lessons in *folklórico*, more than a few birthdays. What Andrea said was true—I neglected her far too often. And I'd have a lifetime of regrets because of this. But I couldn't make up for it. I could only commit to being a better father now.

I knew these words might be perceived as hollow. That perhaps they were too hobbled to traverse the extensive distance I created over the years, the extra pain of the move to Chicago that my kids had no say in—I didn't even consider how they felt. But this was all I had . . . pathetic pleas from whatever place of fatherhood I still stood on.

Andrea probably should have told me to drop dead. Instead she said fine, she'd let me be her dad again.

Chapter Twenty-two

The night was warm. I prepared myself for bed. My thoughts were on Ramiro and the myriad of problems he kept getting into. I also worried about Rubén and Luis, my other boys, still growing. I considered as well the back-and-forth dealings with Andrea, her baby, and concerns around Ben. And I went round and round in my head about my other grandkids from different mothers, each with their own uncertainties.

I loved them all—these were my family. But that night all this seemed to collapse around me. Family, writing, working with the young people—most of whom did well, but more than a few were in deep trouble. I did all this voluntarily. Also the poetry scene: Tía Chucha Press, the Guild Complex, workshops in prisons, homeless shelters, schools. Most of this was voluntary.

For income I hustled. I was now self-employed—speaking, reading, and writing. Over time this worked out well. But in the early years it was a strain. Trini was astounding at organizing my public events, which were becoming more frequent. But we still managed to get into shouting matches. I learned how difficult I could be for Trini as a business partner. Much of this irritability, again, was linked to my new-found sobriety.

That night I lay down in the second-floor bedroom, unable to sleep. I had insomnia for some time, mulling over work and home predicaments as well as how to make ends meet. Later, as I dozed off, I heard Ramiro and the mother of his oldest daughter shouting. I got terribly annoyed. They were outside, just below my window. I got up, put on my pants and shirt, and stormed down the stairs. I confronted Ramiro. I then heard him say, "Fuck you."

Fuck me?

That's when I lost it. The thing was, he didn't say this to me. He was still arguing with the mother of his child. But I didn't get that part. Everything in front of me turned red—my head erupted in lights. I couldn't see straight. I rushed up to the bedroom. Trini was there, nervous, confused, not knowing what to do. I wanted her to stop me, but she couldn't. It wasn't her fault. She knew how I could get. And she had no strategies, no way to soothe the monster I'd become. I rushed back down two more flights to the basement bedroom where Ramiro had gone after my initial outburst.

I got into my son's face, pushed him. I called him out. Ramiro tried to reason with me, to calm me down. But he also had difficulties with rage. Soon we were both yelling.

I dared Ramiro to fight me. I wanted an excuse to kick his ass. Ramiro wasn't much of a fighter (eventually he would be, especially behind bars). We took our arguing farther into the basement, away from his room. Trini was behind me, trying to get me back upstairs. Ramiro's "baby mama" was trying to talk him into walking away. His daughter, not even three, looked scared. I blocked all this out, locked inside a frenzied state. Then Ramiro picked up a hedge trimmer from the garden tools in the basement. He threatened me with it.

"Go ahead . . . use it!" I said, provoking him.

Ramiro came at me. I moved, part of the hedge trimmer scraping the side of my big belly, drawing a little blood. But I also sensed something else—my son was trying hard *not* to hurt me. I'd have known if he was going at me with all his strength. He wasn't. Ramiro just wanted to keep me off him. That's when I realized what a stupid ass I was.

At this point my granddaughter's mother, who was small in stature and relatively thin, tackled Ramiro. I saw her fly at him from another section of the basement. They both landed on boxes and plastic bags filled with clothing, the hedge trimmer falling to the ground.

Aware now that Ramiro was making sure I didn't get hurt, seeing his daughter distressed and then her mom risking herself to pull my son away, I stopped. I had no more words. No more rage. No more energy. I walked away and back up the stairs, pushing past Trini, who looked hurt and unsure.

The last thing I recall was Ramiro cursing me out as he left with his child and the kid's mother, taking a few items, threatening never to return.

Things between Ramiro and me were now in pieces.

I didn't know how to mend the damage I'd done. We had accomplished much with Ramiro—helping his friends, creating Youth Struggling for Survival, staying in touch in boot camp and when he was in prison. That night, it all fell apart.

Camila, I have to say, seemed sympathetic. I called her the next day and she listened while I explained how wrong I was, how I shouldn't have blown up. She wanted me to know it was bad what happened, but she understood my frustration. I was thankful for that.

Ramiro refused to talk to me for weeks. Trini attempted to convince both of us—she stayed in communication with Ramiro—to listen to each other. She brought his younger brothers to see him. She especially wanted Ramiro to know she didn't want us stuck in a hurting relationship similar to what she had with her father.

A couple of times, Ramiro showed up to YSS meetings. I had to muster the courage to break the silence. This whole thing was my doing. I had to make it right. Finally that's what it took, me breaking down and talking to Ramiro. We finally did. There were explanations. Apologies. Not everything was well, but it was a start.

I still believed Ramiro could remove himself from the criminal and gang culture. My hope was that he'd let go of the madness at around the same age I did. He was now twenty-one. Ramiro had three children. It was time for him to grow up, be a decent father as well as a creative and self-driven person.

Like all young people, my son had incredible strengths. He had a talent for speaking. He also wrote poems in a small notepad that he kept in his back pocket, even in the streets. Yes, he raged, but he was trustworthy, perhaps to a fault, hanging in with the Insane Campbell

Boys even as most of his friends left the gang or joined larger multi-sectioned street associations. Eventually there would be no more Insane Campbell Boys.

But Ramiro had trouble letting go. I called him "the last of the Mohicans."

My son then tried to live by himself, attend college, and get a job. But work was a problem for someone with felonies and on parole. The stigma of an ex-con closed many doors to a half-decent working life. It appeared that the system was setting it up so many of these guys ended up back in the joint.

Ramiro—with the United States. attaining the highest incarceration rate in the world—was being directed toward one option, like increasing numbers of poor and working-class men and women: prison. Unfortunately, too many young people got funneled in, and most of them believed this was *their* idea.

I began to lose weight, close to thirty pounds near the end of the 1990s. I worked out at the local YMCA. I still had a long way to go, but I felt better than I had in years. My writing life had also reached new heights. I published more books of poetry as well as two children's books and had plans for a novel, a short-story collection, and a nonfiction book on creating community in violent times.

Always Running, the book I had carried inside me and in papers and computer files for more than two decades, the book that almost wasn't published, had become a best seller—and one of the one hundred most censored books in the United States. Battles to ban the book swept through cities like Rockford, Illinois; San Jose, California; and Kalamazoo, Michigan. In the Los Angeles Public Library system, it eventually became the most frequently checked out—and apparently the most frequently stolen—book. This was when teachers, booksellers, and librarians became my biggest supporters, ensuring—in some cases with a fight—that my books were accessible to students, parents, administrators, the public.

I also had gigs throughout the United States, at conferences, universities, colleges, public and private schools, migrant camps, homeless shelters, urban war zones, neglected rural communities, Native American reservations, and more. I wore a cap and gown for the first time, in my early forties, when I did the commencement speech at a Chicago-area college.

I often frequented prisons and juvenile lockups around the country, mostly maximum-security joints in states like Illinois, Texas, Arizona, Nevada, Pennsylvania, Connecticut, Indiana, Michigan, Oregon, Nebraska, New Mexico, Washington, and North Carolina. Included in these were the most well-known correctional institutions of California, such as San Quentin, Folsom, and Soledad—where my old friend Manazar had spent time. And I helped in peace efforts between the country's main street gang alliances—Norteño and Sureño, Bloods and Crips, Folks and People—as well as with local gangs in both urban and rural communities.

In 1998, I recorded a spoken-word piece called "Civilization" with music on the hip-hop CD of Italian rapper Flycat, who at the time I called "the Cholo of Milan" because he was the first to take aspects of Chicano culture to Italy. Magazines about everything from tattoos to lowriders carried my story.

My community work, especially with YSS, the Increase the Peace Network, and the Guild Complex, also received recognition. We obtained grants to keep this work alive, and new people emerged to continue what we started.

All of this was beyond my wildest dreams. My writing and my community activism were coming together. I didn't have to work for anyone else anymore. I was my own boss, exactly the way I wanted it.

I also took part, with Nelson Peery and others, in the founding of the League of Revolutionaries for a New America, which brought together revolutionary thinkers and activists of all stripes, in particular those emerging organically from within unions, churches, PTAs, the arts, youth organizations, the dispossessed—anyone affected adversely by the continuing crises in the global capitalist economy, particularly in the United States.

The world was changing. Community leaders had to change as well. To sweep aside all political systems based on archaic industrial models and conceptualize ones born of our developed brains and heart—imagination as well as science. Social activism needed vision, direction, and new forms of organization, not just for the short term, but for a truly equitable and just conclusion for all—in the daily struggles for the immediate needs of the poor and working-class, we also had to represent and fight for their future.

The country needed leadership that Nelson said could "see farther and feel deeper."

In addition, by the late 1990s Tía Chucha Press was a viable small press for poetry. Our authors included some of the best of Chicago's poetry scene, but also nationally important writers such as A. Van Jordan, Kyoko Mori, Diane Glancy, Ricardo Sanchez, Terrance Hayes, Nick Carbo, Melvin Dixon, and Virgil Suarez. We were truly cross-cultural, and the main thing we looked for was compelling, socially engaged poetry, which most publishers weren't publishing.

Finally by then, guided by the Blazquez family and their teachers, I'd received an indigenous name in a circle of the Kalpulli Yetlanezi Tolteka Trece, derived from the several-thousand-years-old Mexika calendar called the Tonalamatl. We used the year in the Tonalamatl that corresponded to the year I was born in the Gregorian calendar. This new name, Xikome Tochtli, or Seven Rabbit, I've used in ceremonies and key observances.

Ramiro as well appeared to be doing better—recruiting youth for mentoring, arts development, and indigenous spiritual practices. We now linked closer to the Mosaic Multicultural Foundation by bringing participants, such as gang members, to various national youth conferences.

So it was a good day in early 1997 when Mosaic's Michael Meade and healer/organizer Orland Bishop came to facilitate a weekend sleepover event at a community center of the Jane Addams Hull House Association on Chicago's North Side. In attendance were leaders and young people from various community organizations, including YSS. Ramiro was slated to come on the Saturday of that weekend to speak. We waited for him in anticipation of a heartfelt presentation.

It was a good day, the culmination of years of hard work. We had the sense that we were on the verge of a breakthrough. We developed meaningful ties between youth and their parents, mentors, and elders. We articulated new concepts that were arts-driven and spiritually grounded. And we addressed the essential covenants needed to keep communities relevant and vigorous.

It was a good day.

Ramiro never made it to the Hull House center. We waited and waited. Calls were made to the house, to his friends. We didn't hear anything about him until later that evening, when we received a phone call from my friend Michael Warr, whom Ramiro had reached—my son was being held in a city police precinct.

I contacted Ramiro's lawyer, Julie Aimen, one of the state's leading defense attorneys, who had represented my son in his last case. She took a liking to him back then. Ms. Aimen made calls to various police stations to find out where Ramiro was exactly.

The next day, Camila and I attended an arraignment. Ms. Aimen was already there. We had no idea why Ramiro had been arrested. Finally, when his name came up, the judge read the charges—three counts of attempted murder, including against two police officers. One person, a truck driver, was in the hospital. Bail was set at $2.5 million. Ramiro was looking at forty years to life.

Ramiro had also been badly beaten—even the judge drew back when he saw my son's battered face.

Although I continued to write, to speak, to carry on with my community and literary work, things changed radically after Ramiro's arrest.

I now devoted much of my time and funds to trying to keep Ramiro from serving a life sentence. I wasn't going to get him released—my son was going to be held accountable for what he did. But I fought so that the state wouldn't lock him up and forget about him, as they've done to thousands of others before and since then.

Julie Aimen, in a case whose cost should have gone into six figures, agreed to take on this effort for a fraction of what she normally charged. What I wanted to do seemed impossible. Even Ms. Aimen, whose knowledge of the Illinois court system made her an impressive choice, was skeptical that any judge would back off a life sentence for Ramiro. Even though the truck driver survived, the police officers were adamant—they wanted Ramiro put away for good.

To counter this, the complexities of Ramiro's life, the circumstances of the shootings, and other social, psychological, and familial factors had to be taken into account. Many in the community rallied to his side. There were consequences for Ramiro's actions—we accepted that. But not all of this had to be punishment.

Ramiro also needed personal awareness, to work with the dark aspects of his life as well as his numerous assets, to consider another possibility—that this ordeal could be truly transformative.

Too many people were rotting away in prisons, their lives fixed and determined by their worst acts. Too many were being written off and devalued. A price had to be paid for one's wanton and criminal improprieties, but a major aspect of this price needed to be healing and a coming back to community for its enhancement, not debilitation.

So as part of our strategy, we held off on an actual pleading of guilt. We agreed to have a bench trial instead of a jury trial, with a judge whom Ms. Aimen felt was stern but open to something different and consequential in a case like Ramiro's.

We hired the Midwest Center on Correctional Justice to do a thorough study of Ramiro's psychological assessments and personal history, including the terrible situations Camila and I put him through—we had to be honest and admit our own complicity. All of this was to establish a root cause for what Ramiro did.

This organization conducted extensive interviews with family members, psychologists who had treated him, and others. Eventually, they summarized their findings in a bound sentencing report for the judge. Included were letters from people across the country, most from those who had attended Mosaic men's conferences, lobbying against a life sentence for my son and for a serious consideration of all mitigating factors. This was largely unheard of.

At every hearing, we had family, YSS members, and other community people, all respectful, show up in court in support of my son. At a couple of hearings we counted thirty people or more. Chicago police officers also made their way down the courtroom pews. Sometimes they made fun of our group. One officer called us a "circus."

Ramiro was held in an electronically controlled maximum-security building in the complex of jails that Cook County maintained on the outskirts of the Little Village barrio. Called Division XI, these cell blocks supposedly held the "worst of the worst" in a stark and sterile environment.

When I first visited Ramiro, he was behind thick glass with only a phone to converse through. He looked upset, anxious. As we talked, at one point Ramiro had a tear in his eye—I had not seen my son show this kind of emotion since he was a kid. As Ramiro glanced away, I envisioned the infant whose finger I held after he was born; the seven-year-old who loved to play with sticks, pretending they were swords; the battered boy who ran away at nine from L.A. to find me in Chicago. I never wanted to see my son like this. Everything I had done the past few years, including *Always Running*, was to avoid such a moment.

"*M'ijo*, you will have to go through this," I responded. "You did what you did and nobody can change that. But I will make you a promise— we'll be there, the whole family and many from the community, every step of the way. My hope is to prevent the life sentence. So please, son, hang in there for as long as it takes. I can't say what a lesser sentence will be. I'll let you know as soon as I do. Meantime, you have to stay here, as messed up as it is. Your life is on the line, and there won't be any easy way to make sure you don't spend the rest of your years behind bars. But that's what we're here for—to convince the judge not to throw you away."

Ramiro agreed that day to work with us. But every time I returned, week after week, month after month, he was more restless, more desperate.

"When will we know about the judge?" he'd ask.

"I don't know," I answered each time. "I hear from Ms. Aimen that the longer this takes the better it looks for you."

But Ramiro hated the intense security, the lockdowns, the threats, the fights. At one point he yelled, "I gotta get out of here, Pops. I don't care what I have to do. I'll plead guilty. I'll take the life sentence. I just have to leave this shithole."

"No, you can't. This is a decision you don't want to make in haste," I warned him. "Believe me, whatever we are able to work out is going to be far better than forty years to life. But be patient. Trust me, son. For once, stand by what I'm saying."

Reluctantly, Ramiro accepted this, despite the risks he confronted in Division XI, which he wouldn't talk about, although he hinted that rival gangs were staking him out.

Months became a year. We brought Ramiro's daughters to visit, only toddlers then, sometimes with their moms. Many friends came — one of my best friends visited him almost every Thursday. Of course, so did Camila, Andrea, Catita, Trini, the younger boys.

Ramiro became everyone's son. Letters arrived from all over the United States. I addressed his predicament in various interviews and during public talks. People fondly remembered Ramiro from the radio and TV interviews we gave some four years before, from the various publications that covered our story, from the poems he read when I first embarked on the book tour.

However, I wasn't making Ramiro into a "political prisoner" or cause célèbre. Ramiro committed harmful acts. He was not being railroaded or picked on. He was not like the thousands of conscientious fighters around the world, agents of social change, who were imprisoned, tortured, or even killed for their ideas, for their activism.

There was nothing heroic in what Ramiro did on the day he was arrested.

My son simply went nuts in an overblown, overdrawn incidence of road rage. That's what the shootings were about. Not even gang warfare or robbery. This time it was a reaction to something a truck driver said to Ramiro at a downtown intersection as he was trying to get home and prepare to take part in our presentations at the Jane Addams Hull House center.

Ramiro told me he had a gun in the glove compartment for protection — he still had enemies in the streets. I responded that guns and him, like guns and me, were not good partners. He'd reach for a gun first before trying out more sensible, and far less bloody, options. I knew I had. I never replaced my guns after they were given away, sold, or stolen some years before—and I've been fine without them.

With Ramiro was another young man, who was driving. This dude apparently cut a truck driver off in traffic. The truck driver shouted something to the two of them. Whatever humiliating curse words he directed at them were enough to set my son off. Like mine at my worst moments, Ramiro's mind went red, lights blazing beneath his eyelids, steeped in a seering whirlwind of sensations. He reached for that gun, stepped out of the car, went up to the truck's cab, apparently put a foot on the steps to the cab, and shot the guy through his arm and chest. Ramiro stepped away as he watched the dude fall to his side.

Ramiro returned to the car, and that's when it hit him—what had he done? He thought the truck driver was dead. Ramiro's life and work, the bad and good times, his mistakes, his aspirations and hard work, time with his kids . . . these all vanished in that instant.

As soon as Ramiro entered the car he told his friend to drive off. But an unmarked police unit with two officers was nearby. They gave chase. Ramiro's world began to unravel, and his thoughts dove deeper and deeper into the void.

Ramiro directed the driver to turn the car around, going the wrong direction on a one-way street. The driver pleaded for Ramiro to let this go. But Ramiro felt there was no way out. He fired toward the police officers from the passenger-side window. He said he aimed above their heads. He didn't want to strike them—he wanted to find an opening to get away. The officers, under fire, panicked. They shot through their own windshield glass. Bullets flew back and forth but nobody was getting hit.

Then in the middle of the Wild West shootout, Ramiro's gun jammed.

The driver turned the car down several streets and pulled over. Ramiro told him to run. It was my son's impulses that brought this on and he didn't feel his friend should have to pay for this. Hesitant at first, the dude finally took off in the direction of ice-roofed homes and frozen streets. Ramiro never turned in this guy, again demonstrating the level of loyalty he upheld, even during what seemed to be the end.

For just then Ramiro had this thought: *It's time for me to die.* As sirens closed in on him, and with a nonworking firearm, Ramiro figured he'd point the gun toward the police and get blasted—suicide by cop.

But evidently a spark of choosing life rushed back. Ramiro threw the gun beneath another car and sprinted toward a liquor store. He made his way inside and into a back storage area. He took off his hoodie sweatshirt and stuffed it into an icebox. Soon, with helicopters overhead and police car units surrounding the building, Ramiro walked around the store as if he were buying something. Suddenly officers grabbed him. The store owner pointed him out as the guy who had just run in wearing a hoodie.

For some inexplicable reason, police officers took off Ramiro's pants and underwear after they handcuffed him. They dragged him outside into the cold winter air half-naked. In the back of a police van, still restrained, my son was beat on by several officers. A couple of them slipped on his blood.

"You can sue me!" an officer declared as he struck Ramiro in the face.

At the precinct, detectives interrogated Ramiro, now with clothes on, wanting him to give up the driver. My son remembered what I've always told him—don't say anything and ask for a lawyer. This riled up the detectives, one of whom began kicking Ramiro in his chest and body. At one point, somebody rammed his head into a pillar.

The police now indicated they knew who he was. One officer even made threats they'd come after *me* if Ramiro didn't provide them a name. But Ramiro insisted he would talk only to a lawyer. A detective supposedly made a call to other officers to go to my house and have me arrested. Ramiro correctly perceived this to be a ruse.

Finally Julie Aimen located my son and stopped any more interrogations.

It was a warm September day in 1998, a year and a half after Ramiro's arrest.

That's when Ramiro had his last day in court. For months, Ramiro was ready to move on to state prison. He was done with county jail. He was prepared to get a prison cell, do his time. The issue was how much time Ramiro would get.

If he accepted the court's plea agreement, he'd be sentenced that same day. On the other hand, if Ramiro turned down the proposed sentence and pled not guilty, he'd be given a trial date. All negotiations would be off. If found guilty, the most likely conclusion to such a trial, he'd get the maximum sentence possible.

We had a full house in court that day. The truck driver who had been shot was there, as were police officers. By then our families in Southern California—both Camila's and mine—had come together to support my son despite living more than two thousand miles away. As with my family, some of Camila's siblings had become evangelical Christians. Yet they weren't judgmental. They rallied in support of Ramiro, providing money and letters and accepting his phone calls. I was most grateful.

Also standing by us were the activists, our native elders, and some men from the Mosaic conferences as well as the young people. They realized that anybody could move beyond their most contemptible acts and that redemption must be built into the heart of any judgment.

That day, outside the courtroom, friends and family gathered in a circle to pray. In an unexpected move, the truck driver who Ramiro shot walked up to me and tapped my shoulder.

"I'm sorry about the time your son will have to do for this," the man remarked after I turned around. "What he did was wrong. I had to see my daughters cry as they saw me with tubes in my body, not knowing if I'd make it. But I feel for your family."

I stretched out my hand to shake his.

"I'm truly grateful for your courage," I responded. "And on behalf of my family, we apologize for the pain and suffering you've gone through because of my son."

The police officers didn't bother to talk to us. I'm sure they didn't like the agreements being worked out with the court.

Everyone in the circle got to say a few words for Ramiro.

"This whole situation is devastating," I said when it was my turn. "But it also has blessings. I thank the Creator for allowing Ramiro an opportunity to receive a far lesser sentence than most people would get under the circumstances. I'm also thankful he's still with us. At any time during the shootings he could have been killed. Others could have been killed. It's a blessing no lives were lost that day. I'm thankful also we met the guy who did get shot, who felt compelled to offer apologies to us. He didn't deserve what happened to him. I also thank the Creator for allowing this community to mature, to learn vital lessons from the difficult journey our son and family must endure. Such journeys can be fonts of grace and hope. None of what's happened should be in vain. With every adversity, we must get stronger as parents, as family, as community. I will hold to my promise—I will stand by Ramiro. Camila and I brought him into this world. We'll be there every step of the way. A'ho."

Inside the courtroom, we heard from Julie Aimen that the judge wanted to give Ramiro twenty-eight years. For shooting at the police officers, Ramiro could have received twenty years to life per officer. The judge put both of these together into one twenty-year sentence. Then he imposed another eight years for shooting the truck driver. Two gun-related charges, with six years each attached to them, were dropped.

"I want to thank you all for the report I received from your lawyers," the judge declared from the bench. "Also the letters—they were quite enlightening. I wish all my cases were as prepared as this."

But a hitch developed in the bullpen, where Ramiro had been waiting after being removed from his cell in Division XI. Ms. Aimen came up to me and said that Ramiro was reneging on the plea bargain. He told Ms. Aimen he wanted a trial. That he'd take his chances, that as far as he was concerned forty years to life and twenty-eight years were the same.

"You have to talk to your son," Ms. Aimen said, frustrated. "The judge is close to pulling the deal off the table. The judge will only give you fifteen minutes with Ramiro. You have to convince him to take the twenty-eight years—or that's it. If Ramiro wants a trial, the judge will accept a not-guilty plea and set a trial date. This will be costly, lengthy, and the end result will be Ramiro's conviction and a life sentence."

Let me say now—no parent should ever have to convince their child to take twenty-eight years instead of going to trial and ending up with forty years to life. This was one of the hardest things I'd ever done. I was convincing my son to take a sentence that for him, in his world, was not just.

A problem was that a part of me felt I should be doing some of Ramiro's sentence. I couldn't take full responsibility for what Ramiro did—he had to own this. But a major reason why my son was in bad shape, why he raged so much and felt lost, was due to my own neglectful parenting, my drinking, my focusing on work instead of family—always something else over Ramiro.

And I thought of his mother, who also made terrible mistakes. Then there were the drunken husbands and abusive boyfriends. And schools that pushed him away. And the police officers and psychiatric hospital staff who beat on him. And rival gang members who tried to kill him. Ramiro was in a constant state of high alert, a reaction to previous trauma and neglect. I also thought of the deteriorating economic and political realities we all lived in, enacting daily tragedies of this caliber or worse, creating many Ramiros. Yes, my son pulled the trigger. Yes, he almost killed people. He almost had himself killed. He had to feel the weight of what he'd done. I couldn't take that away from him.

But it wasn't just Ramiro's hand holding that gun that day.

A uniformed bailiff escorted me into the bullpen. We went through thick metal doors. It was dark in there, steel bars surrounding us. I hadn't been in a bullpen in twenty-five years. Ramiro was the only one sitting inside. I sat down next to Ramiro, the bailiff over our shoulders.

"Son, we only have fifteen minutes," I told him. "You need to take the twenty-eight years. We worked hard for this. I heard you'd figured what the judge offered and what you could get after a trial were about the same. Well let me tell you—there's a hell of a difference between twenty-eight years and forty years to life. You may not think so right now, but someday, in your cell, when you least expect it, you'll know what I mean. This is the shortest time the judge will allow. I'm sure you'd like less, we all would, but this is what's in our ball court. You have to decide, and you have to decide now."

Ramiro argued with me, trying to take a stand against reason. But I told him how the family, YSS, and members of the community were all there for him. Finally, with little time to spare, Ramiro remarked, "Okay, Dad, I'll take the twenty-eight years. But so you know, I'm not doing this for me. I'm doing this for all of you."

"Well, *m'ijo*, that's too bad, because this is your life, not mine or anyone else's. But, for now, that's fine. We don't have time to keep hashing this over. You needed to decide so we can move forward. We'll have plenty of time later to go over why this was the best decision."

I walked out and reentered the court. I told Ms. Aimen that Ramiro had agreed to take the deal. After Ms. Aimen talked to the judge, it was time for Ramiro to be brought in. The bailiff accompanied Ramiro into the courtroom. My son was chained at his wrists and ankles. Ramiro glanced briefly at the large group in court. Without saying a word, he sat down next to Ms. Aimen in front of the judge.

Camila and I, as his parents, were allowed to step up to a wooden pedestal just behind our son. As we approached the stand, I felt Camila shake. I knew she was doing her best not to break down. I held her. Even though I also wanted to fall apart, we both tried to stay firm.

The judge had Ramiro declare his plea. Ramiro said, "Guilty," and the judge reminded him this had to be his decision, uncoerced, with clear mind. Ramiro said it was. The judge then allowed Ramiro to say a few words.

"I want to apologize to my family and to the community, and to all those who stood by me, for all the suffering I've caused them," Ramiro stated in a robust voice. "I also apologize to the person I shot. I'm truly sorry for my actions."

The judge nodded, then he announced to the courtroom that Ramiro would be remanded to the Illinois Department of Corrections for a term of twenty-eight years. A few gasped. After Ramiro left the room and we stepped out into the hallway, Camila let her tears fall.

Even though this was the best we could get, even though the judge was helping us, it still hurt to hear my boy be given so much time—the slow-death time, the stopped-destiny time, the kind of time that has no seed, no healing, no return-to-life policy. Yet, if properly aligned, with family and community's long embrace across steel bars and razor wire, in the tanglement of his gifts and intellect, Ramiro might yet blossom and find light in the encroaching darkness. We might yet continue the father-son heartbeat between us. And drawing from the well of his latent powers, Ramiro might yet find his way home.

Epilogue

Thirteen and a half years.

Ramiro was finally released from the Illinois Department of Corrections on July 16, 2010, after serving thirteen and a half years. He was thirty-five. Although a Cook County circuit court judge sentenced him to twenty-eight years for three counts of attempted murder—rolling in the year and a half spent in the county jail—Ramiro was let go with less than half the time served due to good behavior on his part and to relieve overcrowding.

One development in my son's favor: Just before his conviction, the state's highest court declared unconstitutional the legislature's "truth in sentencing" law, where a convict had to do 85 to 100 percent of his sentence. Ramiro became one of several thousand prisoners who had "good time" built into their sentences (another truth-in-sentencing law was later enacted that evidently passed constitutional muster).

In those years, Ramiro was locked up in Joliet, Menard, Centralia, Logan, the Pontiac Farm, and Danville. The first three years were his roughest. A few times he was put in "the hole." He had fights. Guards harassed him.

By the seventh year Ramiro gave up gangs and drugs—an extremely hard thing to do behind bars, especially in the general population. He wrote me a letter saying he finally understood what I was trying to do with *Always Running*, with Youth Struggling for Survival, with the family. Ramiro dedicated himself to Mexika and other indigenous traditions, letting his hair grow long, attempting prayers and small ceremonies in his cell. He read books. Watched TV. Wrote and illustrated greeting cards—he remembered everyone's birthdays and anniversaries. He became good at handball.

Ramiro also did something I never did: He earned two associate of arts degrees, in horticulture and culinary arts, when colleges were allowed to provide courses to prisoners (because of "tough on crime" policies, many classes in prisons have been cut or drastically reduced since then). After that Ramiro served briefly as a teacher's aide, helping other prisoners, and even managed a correspondence course in auto mechanics.

Upon his release, Ramiro moved into one of the city's best transitional housing centers for parolees, where he was to spend a year and a half with an ankle monitor. He was able to enjoy open-air visits, work and weekend passes, a room with unbarred windows, and reentry programming (including Alcoholics Anonymous, life skills, anger management, counseling). The *Chicago Sun-Times* even interviewed him when he took part in a jogging program directed at the homeless and parolees.

Camila stayed in Chicago and did all she could to help Ramiro while he was incarcerated but also upon his release. His two daughters in the state—his three kids were now teenagers—resumed relating with him, as well as former YSS members and other longtime community leaders.

Thirteen and a half years.

These were difficult, especially for Camila and me, wondering every day how our son was doing, praying he'd be safe. Ramiro actually finished a total of fiften years behind bars since the age of seventeen—fifteen Christmases away from home. As long as he was in the hands of the state, I never had a good night's rest.

In the first years after his conviction, Ramiro often phoned angry, depressed, on an emotional roller coaster. I had to listen, remain even-keeled, yet provide love, guidance, solid ground. As the years passed, however, these conversations involved more laughter, shared memories, good thoughts.

Ramiro became considerate and generous, giving what he could to his kids, his younger brothers, up-and-coming gangsters seeking help, talking about seeking enriching options instead of dead ends, about how to live a truly inspired existence.

He even helped me a couple of times.

During his incarceration, I wrote Ramiro a letter every month, whether he wrote me back or not. I visited my son at least once a year. A few of the years I was able to visit him up to three times. I received phone calls from him whenever possible, even though phone companies overcharged for these collect calls.

Camila made her home in a South Side Chicago suburb and visited Ramiro often, although with work-related injuries (she had back problems and knee surgeries) this became physically complicated. Years before she had married a retired Cook County sheriff's deputy—with thirty years in the department—who was decent to my son and a welcome member of the family.

However, ten years prior to Ramiro's parole, Trini and I made a fateful decision—to return to Los Angeles with our boys. We both still had family members there, including, at the time, our mothers. Trini's family—now blessed with many nephews and nieces from her remaining nine siblings—was active, hardworking, for the most part college graduates or college bound.

This departure was hard for Ramiro, yet he said he understood the value of reuniting with family, in particular for my other sons. Andrea and Catalina later joined us, living with us for a few years (my youngest son, Luis, only two years older, became like a brother to Catita). With her credentials, Andrea taught elementary and high school students, until she became a teacher, then the director, of a cooperative preschool program. My daughter and granddaughter have since lived in other places in and around L.A., although never far away.

I kept my promise not to abandon Ramiro. None of us did. He was still our blood, our hope. Ramiro and I learned, stage by stage, to grow this once-uneven father-son thing into something that was indispensable, despite the distance, despite the razor wire. When we signed off from calls or visits, Ramiro and I always said, "I love you."

Ramiro once pointed out how fortunate he was to have family stand by him, especially during the most desperate years. He told me that many prisoners he knew had no one there for them after about two or three years.

———

When we first moved back to L.A. in June of 2000, Trini, the younger boys, and I resided in the same house in the Pacoima barrio where Trini spent most of her childhood and adolescence. Within a year we bought a modest 1950s home in the city of San Fernando with guesthouse and office in the back—exactly what I needed.

Yet we didn't just settle down. We stayed active—in making peace, community, and new institutions. With my son in prison, I refused to be stagnant. My life became a whirlwind of work, speaking, mentoring, organizing.

I'd passed the most critical stages in sobriety. My focus now became family. I wanted home to be stable, a place for solace and warmth. This took some doing, often undermined by my own blowouts, but in the long run (drawing on Trini and the boys' own stable natures) we created a loving household.

For one thing, I never put down my younger sons. They're normal boys, Rubén and Luis. Without such wounding interactions, they developed into rational and deep-thinking young men. As a teen, Rubén took up the guitar, but also reading, writing, video games, movies. Luis started art classes on the weekends with a mentor who taught him painting, sculpting, and cartooning. Writing, however, became a growing interest (unfortunately, Luis became hearing impaired from an ear infection during a bout of pneumonia, although he'd learned to adjust over the years).

The most wonderful thing about the boys was how they got along. They loved each other, sought each other's counsel. Rubén became a positive influence on his younger brother. I thought siblings were meant to bite each other's heads off. But they never hurt or exploited each other, as brothers often do. In a poem, I wrote they'd become close "like hummingbird to flower, breath to poems, moonlight to water."

One good thing was that Trini and I had a touchstone, a renewing space, a spiritual practice that allowed us a constant state of healing. Trini and I helped create sweat lodges in the Lakota style (intertwined with Navajo and Mexika teachings) behind the Pacoima house and another in the large backyard of a San Fernando sober living home. Aided by Luis Ruan and the Yaqui/Rarámuri Hector Herrera, our brother-in-law, as well as community residents and their families, we eventually helped hundreds of people, including gang and other troubled youths from Homeboy Industries, Youth Mentoring Connection, Homies Unidos, ShadeTree Mentoring, Unity Bridges, and Street Poets. Battered women, rape victims, addicts, gang members, and just regular folk found cleansing and community there.

The sweats were the oldest earth-based ceremony among the first peoples of the continent. They were a means, not an end, toward clearing up the mind, heart, and soul in exploring one's particular centering, purpose, destination.

Then in late 2001, Trini and I founded Tía Chucha's Café Cultural in Sylmar, California, along with our brother-in-law Enrique Sanchez. With assistance from a social entrepreneurial fund of the Liberty Foundation, and eventually two mortgages on the house, we established a multiarts, multimedia community gathering place—a bookstore, coffee bar, performance space, art gallery, and workshop center for the visual arts, music, dance, theater, film, and writing.

In many ways Tía Chucha's Café Cultural embodied the spirit of the work I did in Chicago with the Guild Complex, the slams, the café/gallery world, the homeless, and prison workshops. In 2003, we set up a sister nonprofit called Tía Chucha's Centro Cultural (with the assistance of singer/musicologist Angelica Loa Perez and Chicano hip-hop artist and organizer Victor Mendoza) to deal with the workshops and performance events. This included the creation of an annual outdoor literacy and performance festival called Celebrating Words: Written, Performed and Sung, with bands, poets, spoken-word performers, dancers, theater, local vendors, author panels, books for sale, and free-book giveaways.

In time we had our own resident Mexika *danza* group, with the name of Temachtia Quetzalcoatl, led by one of the few women heads of such groups, Monique Orozco. They blessed our openings, festivals, and the benefit events we did for four years at the Ford Amphitheatre in

Hollywood. The *danza* group trained new participants, complementing our indigenous cosmology and language classes at the center. And we helped two young leaders, Brian Dessaint and Mayra Zaragoza, teenagers then, establish the Young Warriors youth empowerment group at Tía Chucha's.

At first people wouldn't enter our doors. We saw mothers stop with babies in strollers, look through the tall windows cupping a hand over their eyes, and then keep strolling. Perhaps they were intimidated—the place, with its warm earth colors, looked nice, artistic, *Chicanote*. Little by little they began to check us out. To peruse our books. To have coffee. Because there were no art galleries until we arrived, a few thought we were selling the picture frames. Slowly they got it, they got us. Artists, poets, singers, and sculptors found us when they noticed the café lights. A lady who sold tamales door-to-door in Pacoima sang at our open mic; a Guatemalan carpenter became our emcee. Hip-hop heads, punk and ska bands, *son jarocho* performers, Mexika cosmologists, and actors showed up to perform and teach. Then gang members trickled in, tentative artists. Whole families made their way, sometimes to listen to speakers on roots, literature, culture, and healthy living.

During a time when Tía Chucha's most needed it, people like John Densmore of The Doors came through with financial assistance. Remarkably, so did Bruce Springsteen—he remembered me from the steelworkers' food pantry and writing/theater workshops back in 1984. Bruce invited Trini and me to visit backstage at a couple of his concerts. And once he allowed Tía Chucha's to set up a table and donation buckets during a performance at the Sports Arena. This was all a testament to Bruce's big heart and long memory.

Still, Tía Chucha's had a few setbacks in its first years. The worst was when our landlords pushed us out of our original space when they drastically raised our rent to make room for a high-end Laundromat. The thousands of dollars we put into the coffee bar, Mayan motifs, and painted walls were relinquished when we had to tear everything down. Later our equipment, shelving, refrigerators, ice machine, roasting machines, books, neon sign, and more were stolen or destroyed in two break-ins at the private warehouse where everything had been stored.

But we persevered, leasing another space in Lakeview Terrace, then moving a third time back to a Sylmar strip mall that soon became our long-term home.

In 2005 I brought Tía Chucha Press over to Los Angeles. I had continued to run it, although until then it was based in Chicago as part of the Guild Complex. Since then Patricia Spears Jones, Richard Vargas, Luivette Resto, Susan D. Anderson, Linda Rodriguez, Chiwon Choi, and others have been published. For over twenty years, TCP cranked out beautifully designed poetry collections and chapbooks. We were proud when one of the poets we published sixteen years before, Elizabeth Alexander, was chosen to read one of her poems at President Barack Obama's inauguration in 2009.

By 2007 Trini and I disbanded the privately owned café and donated everything to the nonprofit. Now grants and the community pay for the space through donations, benefits, book sales, and lots of love. Trini and I do all this without compensation—we never wanted Tía Chucha's to feed our family or to benefit us monetarily. Trini, as manager of the café and the cultural center for most of that time, worked long hours making everything happen, with mostly part-time staff and great volunteers.

There were many fascinating stories tied to Tía Chucha's. One involved a maintenance mechanic who never read a book before he began going there—then in one year he read thirty. Another was of a fourteen-year-old Chicana walking the Sylmar streets, thinking of suicide. She came upon the drums—the *huehuetl*, the "old ones"—of the Mexika *danza* group practicing in front of our place. She had never heard this before, even though it was in her heritage. She stopped to listen. She came every Monday, sitting on the sidelines, watching the dancers perform. Finally she joined the group, learned the rituals, the songs, the dances, the Nahuatl words. About a year later, in a circle of *danzantes* relating their experiences, she told this story, with tears in her eyes, and announced to the group, "I don't think about dying anymore."

Even with Ramiro behind bars and Tía Chucha's Centro gaining momentum, I traveled throughout the United States. I spent ten weeks in North Carolina in their largest writers' residency in history—I did twenty-one events a week, including at schools, prisons, juvenile detention centers, churches, turkey farms, migrant camps, universities, and the Cherokee reservation. I walked the Ninth Ward streets of New Orleans, still devastated, houses torn apart, families uprooted, about a year after the levees busted during Hurricane Katrina. I spoke in public and private schools throughout the land, including high schools such as Garfield in East L.A. (featured in the movie *Stand and Deliver*) and Eastside High in Paterson, New Jersey (from *Lean on Me*). I did more media talks, interviews, appeared in various documentaries, and was a recurring honorary cohost with Dominique DiPrima on the talk show *Front Page*, KJLH-FM, Los Angeles. A couple of times I appeared on Stevie Wonder's radio show at the station, and once sang "What's Going On?" by Marvin Gaye with Mr. Wonder on keyboards—this was a dream come true.

But I also took my messages and verses around the world.

I once sat among tattoo-faced gang members in Guatemala with two staff members from L.A.'s Homeboy Industries, the jobs-based gang intervention program started by Father Greg Boyle in Boyle Heights. We had come to this poor and violent Central American country in 2007 to speak in communities, in churches, on the radio, and at universities about inventive and redemptive ways to work with gangs. When we entered the cell block of one of the big *maras*, the guards locked the steel doors behind us, leaving us there for around three hours. Although some news outlets, as well as U.S. and Central American law enforcement agencies, claimed these gangs were unlikely to be rehabilitated. The young men inside were respectful, wary, of course, but in the end listening intently, full of prospects for change.

In early 2010 I also addressed audiences in the most violent city in the world at the time, the border town of Ciudad Juarez, region of my birth. I visited a prison outside of Chihuahua city and a juvenile hall in Juaritos (what the locals affectionately call Ciudad Juarez) as well as plank-and-chicken-wire slums, libraries, community centers, human rights groups—*charleando* with social justice leaders, poets, activist youths, graffiti artists, comic book illustrators, and others.

My other trips in the early 2000s included the multilayered metropolis of Tokyo; the invigorating countries of Venezuela and Argentina, including the poorest slums of Caracas and Buenos Aires; and cultural centers in Germany like Stuttgart and southern German universities such as Tübingen.

I also took in the chaotic beauty of Mexico City (where a version of Tía Chucha's Centro was re-created in the Zocalo during their 2006 book fair) and the vibrant city of Guadalajara (where in 2009 Tía Chucha's helped organize the first lowrider car and bike show for the largest book festival on the continent). And in the summer of 2010, I spent two weeks in Manchester and London speaking at universities, in social centers, in Afro-Caribbean communities, at a nightclub, at the country's Home Office, and at Her Majesty's Young Offenders Institution on England's southern coast.

In ten years I'd also stood at the heights of Machu Picchu and Cuzco with teachers in the Quechua traditions; taken part in ayahuasca rites in the Amazon rain forest; visited a medieval castle in Heidelberg, Germany; prayed in a Buddhist temple in Tokyo's Asakusa district; sung songs near the lava flows of Hawai'i; read poetry accompanied by Italian jazz musicians in Sarajevo, Bosnia-Herzegovina; and tight-fistedly climbed rickety wooden stairs to the top of Mayan temples in Tikal.

Most of these trips addressed the growing gang violence in the United States and elsewhere. To assist an urban peace process, I helped create the *Guide for Understanding Effective Community-Based Gang Intervention*, the first publication of its kind in the country. I did this with forty other gang intervention specialists, urban peace advocates, and researchers in close to two years through the office of L.A. city councilman Tony Cardenas (Trini's brother), working hours upon hours, without pay. In February 2008, the L.A. city council approved this guide, which has since been introduced to various municipalities, counties, states, and urban peace organizations, as well as Congress.

And, finally, my story as a youth offender who had been given a break from serving a long prison term in my late teens was included in the amicus curiae brief to a legal argument heard by the U.S. Supreme

Court in November 2009. The issue: ending the life sentences of juveniles for noncapital crimes. This case involved two young people given such sentences in *Graham v. Florida* and *Sullivan v. Florida*. The brief also included the stories of accomplished writers, actors, lawyers, and politicians—such as Charles S. Dutton and former U.S. senator Alan K. Simpson—who in their youth also committed serious offenses but were kept from serving the long prison terms that had now become the norm for youth offenders. In May 2010, the highest court in the land declared such sentences unconstitutional, opening the door to ending all life terms for young people and other injustices.

About a year prior to Ramiro's release, I decided to do a vision quest—*hanblechya*—on the Lakota reservation of Pine Ridge, South Dakota, under the guidance of an elder/headsman, whom I met through my friend Frank "Tekpaltzin" Blazquez. Trini also joined me along with Hector Herrera, fire keeper and water pourer for our San Fernando sweat lodge circle.

We stood, sat, or danced the "four days" outside (mind you, the Lakota count a day and a night as two days, so we were on the hill for two days and two nights according to the standard calendar). We were separate from one another—with no food—under a canopy of stars or blazing sun, on a green and brush-laden land, with electrical storms and high-velocity winds, and then rain and more rain.

Cold, wet, hungry, I used this time to think about the past, my son's ordeals, and where we were going as a family, community, country, world. I recalled the young man I used to be, lost to drugs, homeless at fifteen in the streets of L.A., seeing the world through the barrel of a gun. These experiences made for a deep initiatory passage that separated me from family, community, myself. These passages continued through the heat and noise of the mills, construction sites, and refineries. They included my ventures into revolutionary activity and study, marked by fights against police abuse and workplace battles in the United States as well as experiencing uprisings/wars in Mexico and Central America. I may as well add my reporting and poetry work. And I can't forget my years in the bars—even the collapses of my loves and marriages.

In the end these all involved access to new knowledge and encounters, returns, countless welcomes, and then the imparting of my own medicine in the form of words, talks, ideas. This meant acknowledging and living out the primary agreement to follow our destiny, our calling.

I've also handed myself a key obligation: to teach, to give back, to consider what I leave to the world and not what I may gain.

Then about three weeks prior to Ramiro's release, I had a health scare, a hypertensive crisis. I had an extremely high blood pressure reading. I then checked into the local county health clinic for indigent people. Like millions of Americans, I had no health insurance.

However, in the next few months I'd be declared diabetic with more emergency visits for gallstones, a throat infection, and a partially detached retina in my right eye that required emergency laser surgery. Tests indicated that I had a battered liver. I also had slipped discs in my back, which I attribute to my industry days, along with pain that at times doesn't allow me out of bed. Today I'm committed to doing what I must to maintain a healthy lifestyle for whatever time I have left. Although death is inevitable—part of life, requiring its own orientation— I plan to be around for some time.

When Ramiro was paroled he entered a world of 3G networks, iPods, Twitter, and hybrid cars that didn't exist when he was sentenced. At the same time the country was undergoing one of its worst financial downturns. Ramiro became part of a growing number of "unemploy-ables"—even college graduates who did everything "right" were unable to find jobs. Yet in such times, in such declines, when darkness and uncertainty reign, the best of us can still emerge.

Like others, Ramiro has to forge a new beginning, become part of a new economy, one based on the imagination as well as the powers and energies we all possess. It's aligning professions with passions, oriented toward a proper relationship to spirit, nature, the earth. For the time being, it's important that Ramiro follow his own pace, that he not get pressured to do more than meet the essentials: to seek his own balance; to be a patient and guiding father to his children; and to slowly, but surely, discover his unique gifts and the best means to deliver them to a battered and hungry world.

When I first saw Ramiro at the transitional housing center a month after his release, outside of his prison blues, he almost looked the same as when he was first sentenced. He was dark-faced, with large dark eyes, barrel chested, although now he had curly long hair in a long braid, a few strands now gray. He appeared healthy, happy.

Whatever we'd done to hurt each other was long dealt with. This was a time to forgive and to learn. The message Ramiro got most of his life was that he didn't matter. I wanted my son to know he did matter, that what he does matters, that even his anger was righteous but needed strategies, tact, finesse. He needed to know there were many ways to go, many cures, and to draw from his mind and heart while regaining authority and clarity at every turn.

Ramiro finally made his appointment with freedom, which is only free if he learns the limitations, the natural laws governing all processes, and the required measures to deal with them. Freedom is the appreciation of what you can't do so you can do what you must do. Despite the hard road getting there, Ramiro seemed to understand how liberating it was to be fully responsible for his actions, inactions, choices, life.

One of the most moving moments was when Andrea and Catita arrived from L.A. to see Ramiro. We waited for them at a Logan Square park in a reunion with some of the original YSS members, now married, divorced, with kids, a couple running their own businesses. As soon as Andrea saw her brother, she embraced him tightly, tears in her eyes. I thought about what they'd suffered together, in households that held more terror than safety, in various states of abandonment, but also how despite all this, despite the distances and a world that pushed them to its edges, they still knew how to share, to grow, to hold on to the healthy ties that bind.

Regardless of what happened, I'd be stuck to them. Although they were grown up. I'd still be inside their moon-eyed hopes as well as their dejections. If Ramiro returned to prison for any reason, I'd be right with him. If he married, had more children, made a decent living, I'd rejoice with him. I couldn't hold his or Andrea's hand through the next phases of their lives, but somehow, in the shadows, not far, welling with father-love, I'd be standing there.

Ramiro was also given a weekend pass to another part of the state, where his fifteen-year-old daughter Amanda was celebrating a young woman's ceremony in the indigenous tradition. His other daughter, Anastasia, participated (she'd had a similar celebration a year before, but without her father there), as well as Catalina, Trini, and Camila. In attendance were other family and friends: Mexican, Puerto Rican, Native American, black, white. Beautiful words and tears of joy abounded. A sense of completion, of circles connected, of dangling threads pulled together, and the relief of having come this far, permeated my thoughts.

Here's an excerpt from the first thing Ramiro wrote after his parole:

I've had over thirteen years of psychological warfare. My mind has been a battlefield with many casualties. Disconnections. Reconnections. Everything's new. It feels good to see my kids, my family, and everyone who has supported me. It feels good to know that on this next journey of my life I don't have to do it alone. This is a new journey for everybody. All the hardships, the struggles, were not just my own. While I did time, everyone else did life . . .

As I stepped out the prison door, and saw my family and friends standing in front of me, I didn't want to look behind me. Behind me was desolation. In front of me was absolution. Now I'm going forward. Taking advantage of all my support. Not afraid to ask for help when needed. For too long I was trying to do everything alone. I was selfish and weak. Full of pain and full of pride. Holding on to so much anger. Never knowing what I was truly angry at. That's all over with.

All that sadness and hurt, I want it to be gone. I look into my children's eyes and all I can do is smile. I wake up with a smile. I walk everywhere with a smile. I smile because I finally made it home.

A familial and community crisis erupted with Ramiro's imprisonment. But instead of letting this destroy us, split us up, tear us down, we gathered ourselves—this interesting family, this necessary community, with all its diversity and antagonisms—into dignity and closeness, into an uneasy steadiness bound by love.

About the Author

Luis J. Rodríguez was named an "Unsung Hero of Compassion," presented in 2001 by His Holiness, the Dalai Lama. He's been a recipient of a Lila Wallace-*Reader's Digest* Writer's Award, a Lannan Poetry Fellowship, Paterson Poetry Prize, Carl Sandburg Book Award, *Chicago Sun-Times* Book Award, a Sundance Institute Arts Writing Fellowship, and other recognition. Luis has recently been interviewed on NBC's *Nightly News with Brian Williams*, CNN's *What Matters*, Head Line News's *Leaders with Heart*, BBC London Radio, PBS's *The NewsHour with Jim Lehrer*, Discovery Channel's *Life Force*, and ESPN's *30 for 30*.